M000218248

Instructions for using AR

LET AUGMENTED REALITY CHANGE HOW YOU READ A BOOK

With your smartphone, iPad or tablet you can use the **Hasmark AR** app to invoke the augmented reality experience to literally read outside the book.

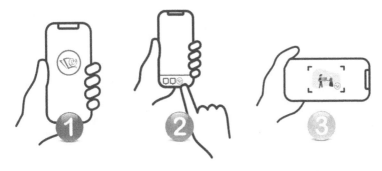

1. Download the **Hasmark app** from the **Apple App Store** or **Google Play**

2. Open and select the ⬡ (vue) option

3. Point your lens at the full image with the ⬡ and enjoy the augmented reality experience.

Go ahead and try it right now with the Hasmark Publishing International logo.

ENDORSEMENTS

If you have the foresight to plan for retirement, you must read *Your Retirement: Dream or Nightmare?*. Author Rajiv Nagaich, a preeminent elder law attorney, has given you a retirement roadmap. With passion and candor, he shares the story of a loved one's personal retirement nightmare which drove him to law school for the sole purpose of helping others avoid the pitfalls and achieve a healthy and successful retirement. This book tells a moving story while informing you of the steps needed to create your own retirement plan. It addresses the issues and warns you of the unexpected pitfalls. If you or a loved one are planning to retire, read this book!

—**Richard Tizzano,** Esq., author of *Accidental Safari*

Rajiv Nagaich stands out as a fierce advocate for those who wish to age in place on their own terms.

—**Stephanie Haslam**, Elder Law Attorney, Seattle, WA

Finally! Rajiv Nagaich makes all the pieces of the overwhelming retirement puzzle fit together.

—**Randy Foley**, client via Facebook

Now we can "age on" with confidence that we won't outlive our finances or be a burden to our children.

—**Jean Kuhlmann,** client via Google

Rajiv shows you how the system really works and what you need to pull everything together for a safe and happy retirement.

—**Chandra Lewnau,** Elder Law Attorney, Seattle, Washington

MUST READ!!!! This book is superb. Rajiv has an understanding of Life Planning unlike any other. For anyone aging, with aging parents, or aging loved ones, in other words EVERYONE, this resource is one of a kind and more useful than any I have previously read. I wish I had this knowledge when I was in my younger years as it could have been shared with so many beloved friends. As a Reverse Mortgage professional working exclusively with an older population......... this book has VALUE BEYOND MEASURE.

—**Laura J Kiel,** Certified Reverse Mortgage Professional MLO 54755

Mark Twain famously said, "everyone complains about the weather, but no one ever does anything about it." It is a pity Mr. Twain never met Rajiv Nagaich! In this must-read eye-opener, Rajiv begins by delivering the rare accurate weather report on aging in America today--a 70% chance of misery. Then he boldly proposes to change the weather. Can we really radically change the odds in our favor? Rajiv emphatically and convincingly answers yes! In this practical, first-of-its-kind, step-by-step guide, Rajiv expertly and entertainingly explains how to turn your forecast for tomorrow from storms to clear blue skies. *Your Retirement: Dream or Disaster?* is a game-changer.

—**Scott Schill,** Attorney

I highly recommend this book. Rajiv has the ability to take complex legal issues and break them down into common sense options for families. His use of personal and professional true-life experiences makes this book a compelling read...not an easy task for a book about the law. I plan on sharing it with my family, friends, and clients as a starting place for their future planning. I also look forward to watching how Rajiv continues to change the way we think about planning for retirement!

—**Patricia E. Kefalas Dudek,** Attorney

As a Palliative Care physician, I have had the privilege of attending to grieving families as they face the loss of their loved ones. Very often, the most devastating events are the legal and financial aspects that surround the loss. Rajiv as a tireless advocate for patients and families has put together this must read book on how to navigate the barriers to plan for retirement and stand a chance to live with dignity and protect your loved ones

—**Juan C. Iregui,** M.D., Palliative Care Physician

Rajiv's passion for serving older adults - which is really everyone, eventually, we hope - emanates through this great book. He helps us face a gut-wrenching dysfunction in our society, and hands us the secret map to its solution. As we all grapple with the harsh realities that come with an aging population, Rajiv's message shines as a beacon of hope - that with the proper plan, we may all live a long life filled with dignity and love.

—**Ben Harvill,** Certified Financial Planner

Rajiv Nagaich's book, and for that matter his whole career, aims to burst the false bubble of the golden retirement with the reality that too often occurs when aging is accompanied by physical or cognitive decline. But, fortunately, he then provides the tools seniors, their families and their advisors can use to create the fulfilling old age they deserve.

—**Harry S. Margolis,** Attorney

This book opened my eyes to what retirement planning really should be. The gaping holes of boilerplate wills and advanced directives are literally useless if you don't assemble the day-to-day instructions for your loved ones to follow. It's time to sit down with my kids, talk about my plan, and cover the steps from A-Z. There's so much practical advice here; I feel like I now have a detailed map from which I can navigate this rocky road called retirement.

—**Jill Choi,** Director, Health Information Management, CDI, & UR at Nationwide Children's Hospital, Columbus, OH

YOUR
RETIREMENT:
DREAM OR DISASTER?

How to avoid the
HIDDEN TRAPS IN RETIREMENT PLANNING ADVICE
that turn old age into a living nightmare for 70% of Americans

RAJIV NAGAICH, J.D., L.L.M.
WITH GAYLA ZOZ

Hasmark
PUBLISHING
INTERNATIONAL

Published by
Hasmark Publishing International
www.hasmarkpublishing.com

Copyright © 2023 Rajiv Nagaich
First Edition

No part of this book may be reproduced or transmitted in any form or by any means, electronic or mechanical, including photocopying, recording or by any information storage and retrieval system, without written permission from the author, except for the inclusion of brief quotations in a review.

Disclaimer

This book is designed to provide information and motivation to our readers. It is sold with the understanding that the publisher is not engaged to render any type of psychological, legal, or any other kind of professional advice. The content of each article is the sole expression and opinion of its author, and not necessarily that of the publisher. No warranties or guarantees are expressed or implied by the publisher's choice to include any of the content in this volume. Neither the publisher nor the individual author(s) shall be liable for any physical, psychological, emotional, financial, or commercial damages, including, but not limited to, special, incidental, consequential or other damages. Our views and rights are the same: You are responsible for your own choices, actions, and results.

Permission should be addressed in writing to Rajiv Nagaich at info@rajivnagaich.com

Editor: Brad Green brad@hasmarkpublishing.com
Cover Design: Anne Karklins anne@hasmarkpublishing.com
Interior Layout: Amit Dey amit@hasmarkpublishing.com

ISBN 13: 978-1-77482-251-7
ISBN 10: 1774822512

TABLE OF CONTENTS

DEDICATION

Dedicated to the loving memory
of Bill and Vivian Wallace.

"And to the love and dedication of Dr. Bankey B.
and Sharda D. Nagaich."

FOREWORD

For about as long as I can remember, working for networks like ABC, FOX, and NBC, I have been telling the stories of amazing people doing amazing things in amazing places all around the world. Add to that my 13 years as one of the hosts of Access Hollywood, working alongside incredibly talented game-changers, it is not a stretch to say that it takes something truly exceptional to elicit a "wow!" from me. Author Rajiv Nagaich has done just that with his game-changing book *Your Retirement: Dream or Disaster?*

I was introduced to Rajiv through a mutual friend and sensed his deep passion straight away. With his expertise in elder law and retirement planning, Rajiv has helped thousands of clients plan their retirement journeys over the years. I could clearly see that it is his life's mission to help as many people as possible avoid disaster in their retirement years.

Rajiv's mission comes from a personal and tragic experience in his own life, having witnessed his wife's parents go through a retirement disaster that simply could have been avoided. This personal story is recounted in the book, painting a clear picture of how and why Rajiv changed his life and his career focus to that of elder law.

What I love about this book is that it's not just another dry and boring retirement planning guide. We've all read a few of those! By contrast, this book is filled with practical advice, real-life stories, and a healthy dose of humor. Rajiv's writing style is engaging, and he excels at simplifying complex topics, making them accessible to someone who has never given retirement planning a second thought.

Through the pages of this book, I came across many eye-opening stories, statistics, and revelations about the common system of retirement planning that left me shaking my head in disbelief. For instance, Rajiv points out that nearly 70% of us will not take our final breath in our own home or in a place of our choosing. Take a moment to let that sobering thought sink in.

The good news is that Rajiv has given readers an incredible blueprint for their retirement planning process. Another aspect of the book that I appreciate is that Rajiv doesn't only focus on the financial aspects of retirement planning, but takes a truly holistic approach. The book emphasizes the importance of staying active and engaged in retirement, while guiding readers on how to create a fulfilling and enjoyable retirement lifestyle.

Your Retirement: Dream or Disaster? has become one of those rare books that I always keep close so I can easily refer to it at any moment. Its value extends far beyond the first read, and that speaks volumes about what Rajiv has accomplished.

I have no doubt that this book will become a go-to resource for anyone seeking to ensure that their retirement is a dream and not a disaster. So, dive into this book, take notes, and be confident that you are setting the stage for a retirement lived to the fullest!

Enjoy!
Tony Potts

ACKNOWLEDGMENTS

It would take at least a dozen pages to name all the people who have played a role in bringing my approach to retirement—and by extension, this book—to life. As I look back at the process, I want to acknowledge those whose paths have tracked closest to mine on this incredible journey.

The word "thanks" seems like too small a container to hold the gratitude I feel, especially to the United States of America, the nation that welcomed me with open arms more than three decades ago. If I hadn't made the decision to come to the U.S., I wouldn't have met the people who were the catalyst for this journey: my late in-laws, Bill and Vivian Wallace. I owe a deep debt of gratitude to Bill and Vivian, as well as the entire Wallace family, for allowing me to use their experience as the basis for the system of retirement planning covered in this book. My own parents were also instrumental in the process, and my success would not have been possible without their support. My late mother, Sharda Devi Nagaich, taught me compassion and love, and my father, Dr. B.B. Nagaich, taught me discipline and perseverance. All those skills have been crucial along my journey, and I am grateful to both of my parents for instilling them in me.

This book would not have been possible had I not encountered the National Academy of Elder Law Attorneys when I did. A collection of talented attorneys who dream, work, and share, NAELA was instrumental in my development as an attorney. You will see them mentioned repeatedly in the pages of this book.

I am grateful for the thousands of clients I've had over the years who trusted me to help them create better plans for retirement. These were the early adopters of the *LifePlanning* approach to retirement planning, and they helped me refine the system over time. Without them, the ideas that led to the creation of *LifePlanning* would have never been conceptualized.

My office staff has also played a major role in the fulfillment of this lifelong dream to document my approach in a book. Many staff members have come and gone over the years, and I am especially grateful to those who have stuck it out with me. You know who you are!

Finally, this book wouldn't have happened without the support of my family. They have put up with my being gone every Saturday for 22 years and counting. I am especially grateful for the patient and loving support of my wife, Jamie. To her, I say "+1." She'll know what I mean.

PREFACE

I took a deep breath as the production assistant attached the lavalier microphone to my lapel. Technicians were scurrying around in a last-minute frenzy, making final adjustments to the set of *Master Your Future with Rajiv Nagaich*, my first public television special.

Five minutes to showtime.

The lights were blinding, but I managed to make out familiar faces in the studio audience, more than a few of whom were my clients. One caught my eye, giving me a thumbs up. "Good luck, Rajiv!" she said with a smile.

One minute to showtime.

I was ready.

Everything in my life had led to this moment. I could see the entire journey in fast motion in my mind's eye: the triumphs, the tragedies, the missteps, and the victories on the road to changing the way Americans plan for and navigate their retirement years. Memories were swirling in my head, all converging at this moment.

The most important memory of all in this pre-shoot reverie was of the two people who started it all: my in-laws, Bill and Vivian Wallace. Who could have guessed that my path would have intersected with theirs? What were the odds?

Meeting Bill and Vivian changed my life forever. I loved them both more than words could say. Their lives ended very differently. Bill took his last breath alone in a nursing home room, his head on an institutional pillow; the whole of his being reduced to a name on a chart. Despite my family's best efforts to give Bill a different ending, we were swimming upstream against a current we couldn't see, caught in a dysfunctional long-term care system that warehouses frail older adults and calls it progress.

The injustice enraged me. The rage motivated me. I was determined to understand why Bill's life had ended the way it did. I had to do something to prevent other older adults from suffering the same fate. It was the least I could do for Bill.

By the time Vivian's time had come, I had learned a great deal about this invisible system and how to navigate it. Thanks to years of unwavering support from the Wallace daughters and their families, Vivian's last days were spent in her own bed, surrounded by her children and grandchildren, her head on her own pillow in the place she called home.

Before Bill and Vivian Wallace, I was just another kid from India who came to America to seek out his fortune. Bill's tragic situation opened my eyes to a reality I didn't anticipate in a place I didn't expect to confront it: the richest country in the world. What happened to Bill, and what happens to millions of middle-class Americans just like him, was a reality I couldn't unsee. It was a reality no one was talking about.

My intention was never to go to battle. The battle came to me. So, I did what people do in battle—I started fighting. First, I fought for Bill Wallace, and then I fought for every frail, sick, and frightened person who came to my elder law firm for help. In the process, I discovered the ridiculousness of a broken system that fails families at every turn.

Why were so many people ending up like Bill?

Why didn't anyone seem to notice ... or care?

How could I make things better for them?

I have dedicated my life to answering these questions, and this is my story.

INTRODUCTION

What are your biggest hopes and dreams for your retirement years? I've asked a variation of this question thousands of times—on stage at seminars, on camera at webinars, on the radio, and on television.

Most of us have a good idea about the things we want from retirement. Almost everyone can articulate their hopes and dreams. The people I interact with on this question seldom have trouble painting a vivid picture of how they want life to be. They raise their hands and articulate their ideas like eager children in a classroom, thrilled because they know the right answers. Answers like travel, new hobbies, time with family, and adventures always end up on the list. I can see the excitement in their eyes.

While I love hearing about the fun things people plan to do with their retirement years, that's not what interests me most. Their excitement isn't the reason they signed up to hear me speak.

They signed up because they were afraid.

Would you attend a retirement planning lecture because you're confident? No. You show up because, like millions of other people, you have doubts. There's a niggling fear that you can't quite articulate; there's an anxiety you can't quite shake.

Anxiety about the retirement years is what motivates people to listen to what I have to say.

After everyone has listed the exciting who, what, and where of their plans for their retirement years, I pivot to the real reason people came to hear me.

I want to know what they fear most about retirement. This is where the conversation gets real.

The things we hope to avoid in retirement don't get talked about very often. Almost no one focuses on what we want to avoid, because doing so means confronting realities that most Americans would rather not talk about—things like declining health, loss of control, frailty, and death.

So, when I ask this question—*What do you fear most about retirement?*—there is usually a long pause before anyone is brave enough to answer.

However, after the first courageous person speaks up, the floodgates usually open.

So now I ask you, the reader, what do you fear most?

Over the last two decades, tens of thousands of people in my seminars, webinars, and workshops have answered this question.

Their answers boil down to three things:

1. They are terrified they will end up in a nursing home.
2. They are afraid they will outlive their money.
3. They are afraid they will be a burden on their family.

Do you have these fears?

Should you be afraid?

Researchers say the answer is *yes*.

Though most Americans hope to be able to live out their lives in their own home, the reality is that less than 30 percent will be able to do so.[1] There's a 70 percent chance that you will not be at home when you are taking your last breath. You will likely be in a care facility, a place almost no one wants to end up. There's a 69 percent chance that when you fall ill you will become a burden on your family,[2] something nearly everyone wants to avoid. And lastly, many people who deal with incapacity will have reason to worry about losing their hard-earned assets to uncovered long-term care costs,[3] an outcome no one wants.

How can so many Americans be experiencing such dismal results? And, more importantly, why is there a deafening silence when it comes to planning around these issues?

That's the question I will be answering in this book. The way we define success in retirement is largely based on a marketing bait-and-switch scheme. The photoshopped images of older people living the dream as often depicted in glossy retirement planning brochures don't paint an honest or realistic picture.

Where are the brochures selling retirement dreams that include older adults in the throes of cognitive decline who have set fire to their house yet again, lost thousands of dollars to scam artists, or have taken a wrong turn on their way to the grocery store? Where are the photoshopped images of older adults learning to walk again in rehab after suffering a stroke? Where are the promotional images of older adults whose needs are consuming the lives of their family members?

You won't see those images because that's not what retirement planning is about in this country. Retirement planning the way it's done today is based on the false notion that your later years will unfold in one gleeful, adventure-filled phase. The retirement dream is that you will live a healthy and active life until you die in your sleep.

Unfortunately, that is only a dream for most of us. Most of us will spend some (possibly many) of our retirement years dealing with health problems that gradually increase our dependence on others.

Yes, a few people will go out with a bang. They will be the lucky ones. For the rest of us, retirement will be a long, slow, downward skid toward an undignified end.

Broke. A burden. Stuck in a nursing home. All of these outcomes can be avoided with proper planning.

That's what makes today's approach to retirement planning such a tragedy. We aren't planning for the reality of sickness and frailty, yet most of us will experience these things. If success in retirement is pitched as having the money to live your best life when you're healthy, shouldn't that best life include the years you spend in failing health? Wouldn't you want to have control over where you live, how your affairs are managed, how your money is used, and how your needs impact the lives of your loved ones even as your independence is waning?

If your retirement plan is successful, you should be able to live where you choose until the moment you take your last breath, even if your health fails, without being forced to move to an institutional care setting like a nursing home. You should be able to protect your nest egg from unplanned long-term care costs, so you don't end up broke. You should be able to grow old without becoming a burden on your family, or a source of conflict and disorder among your family members.

If you can nail those three things, you've grabbed the brass ring.

Why will so few of us accomplish this?

The moment you lose your health, your retirement dreams will turn into retirement nightmares. There is no escaping it. You can't wish it away. You can't talk it away.

This is the reason people come to my seminars, webinars, and work-shops. This is the reason people choose to work with me—to develop a plan to avoid the negative outcomes that traditional planning fails to address.

It's not that we don't plan for life in retirement. Americans do more planning than just about anyone else, yet most of us are unable to achieve our basic retirement wishes.

The traditionally accepted planning formula for retirement success is focused on money. Conventional wisdom says that if you have a paid-for home and a hefty nest egg by the time retirement rolls around, you should be okay. Social Security will provide additional monthly income. Maybe you even have a long-term care insurance policy to foot the bill for future long-term care costs. Other than possibly moving to a sunny climate, most Americans don't do any special planning for their housing in retirement. More than three-quarters of Americans plan to age in their own homes.[4] Planning for health care in retirement focuses around enrolling in Medicare and possibly getting a supplemental policy. Legal planning for retirement means getting estate planning documents such as Wills, Trusts, Powers of Attorney, and Advance Directives.

You have a financial plan. You have an estate plan. You have Medicare.

Will this planning keep you from being forced into a nursing home, going broke, or becoming a burden when your health fails?

Probably not.

In the coming chapters, I will show you why this happens to millions of people who thought they had a solid plan for retirement.

This book is written for anyone with retirement on their mind, whether they're thinking of their own retirement or that of a loved one. Though I cite research and statistics, this is not a lofty academic work. My goal is to present the realities of retirement planning using language that anyone can understand.

Part 1 of this book begins with a personal story. You'll read about my journey of my expanding awareness and increasing horror as I searched for the root cause of a retirement plan failure that hit close to home. You will read my analysis of the problems inherent in our nation's retirement planning system, a carefully hidden but very real American disgrace. Along the way, you will learn my story and the stories of the thousands of clients I've worked with over the years. You will discover, as I did, that there is a little-known yet immensely powerful disconnect between the goals you have for your life as you age and the goals professionals in the retirement planning industry have for their clients.

In Part 2, I suggest a radically different way to think about retirement planning that empowers you to harness what is good in the American system so it works for you, while taking control of the planning process (and the professionals you trust to guide you) in a way you never dreamed possible.

The book closes with a list of resources you can use to create a better plan for your retirement, one that gives you a fighting chance of living out your years on your own terms, with dignity and independence.

PART 1:

WHY RETIREMENT PLANS DON'T WORK

CHAPTER 1

THE STORY
OF BILL AND VIVIAN

Beginnings

Why is a guy who was born in India talking about the way Americans plan for retirement?

Before I answer that question, let me tell you a little bit about myself. I was born in the plains of India, southwest of New Delhi. My family lived together with my uncle's family and my grandparents in a large compound that was a lot like sharing space in a big hotel. This living arrangement—called the joint family system, where several families live together in separate wings of a large home—is common in India. Thanks to the joint family system, I grew up in the same household as my aunts, uncles, cousins, and grandparents. It was noisy and chaotic, and it was home.

I came to America in 1982 to attend college. Like just about every person not born in this country, I had a vision of what life was like here. I thought the streets were paved with gold. The only ingredients necessary for success in America were hard work, perseverance, and a desire to play by the rules.

As far as I'm concerned, America has certainly lived up to its reputation as the land of opportunity. You'll get no complaints from me. I have had my share of both setbacks and successes. What I didn't realize was that I also had expectations of America being great in ways it turned out not to be.

One of the biggest surprises involved how Americans handle the care of their oldest and most vulnerable. In the U.S., long-term care facilities are everywhere. They go by a variety of names—nursing homes, rehabilitation centers, assisted living facilities, and memory care communities are just a few—but they all have one thing in common: they are all institutions.

Where I grew up, there were no old people living in institutions. There were no long-term care facilities, nursing homes, or memory care communities that I was aware of. Elderly relatives lived with their extended family until they died.

How did I become aware of this profound difference? It happened many years after I came to America. That's when I encountered the people who would change the course of my life. I tell the story of this family—the story of Bill and Vivian Wallace—at every seminar, webinar, and workshop I conduct.

Bill and Vivian – The Early Years

The story of Bill and Vivian began long before I entered their lives. Bill Wallace was born in Colbert, Washington, a small town north of Spokane. Bill met Vivian Clark while she was attending a nurses' training program in Spokane. Like many young men of his generation, Bill decided to serve his country, enlisting in the Air Force.

After a whirlwind courtship, it was time for Bill to go to pilot training. From the nurses' station of the downtown hospital, Vivian heard the whistle blow as Bill's train left Spokane, and she knew she was in love.

Bill's stint in the service didn't last long. During basic training, Bill learned that he had a horseshoe-shaped kidney. Bill was medically discharged from the Air Force, and he hurried back to Spokane to marry Vivian.

The day after their wedding, they left for Petersburg, Alaska. Vivian worked as a registered nurse in a ten-bed, one-doctor hospital while Bill worked as a fisherman. Three of their five children—Pam, Jan, and Rondy—were born during the time the couple lived in Alaska.

After ten years in Alaska, Bill and Vivian decided to move back to Spokane to raise their family. They paid cash for their first home, a small two-bedroom, one-bathroom house on a spacious lot on Sullivan Street surrounded by meadows in the valley outside Spokane. Bill got a job as a mail carrier working for the U.S. Postal Service, while Vivian remained employed as a nurse.

Soon, two more girls were added to the Wallace family: Sherry and Jamie. A one-bathroom home soon became too small for their growing family. Bill and Vivian did what most parents would do: they moved their family to a larger home. Their new place was situated on a five-acre parcel of land about a mile away on Broadway Road.

Bill, Vivian, and their five daughters lived comfortably, navigating life's ups and downs like any normal middle-class family. While the children were young, Bill and Vivian focused on giving them a proper education. It was only when their youngest, Jamie, left for college that they started thinking ahead to retirement.

Like many Americans of their generation, Bill and Vivian built their plans for retirement around a simple notion: if they had their house paid for and a few hundred thousand dollars in the bank, surely between Social Security, Medicare, and a debt-free lifestyle, they should be able to lead a comfortable retirement. They planned on exploring America by RV after Bill retired. Their retirement dreams were set.

The Diagnosis

Unfortunately, the RV never left the driveway. Most of their retirement dreams were never realized because Bill was diagnosed with Alzheimer's disease during the last year of his work life.

Vivian spent the next few years keeping Bill's diagnosis a secret from all but one of their five daughters, Jan, who also lived in Spokane. Vivian didn't want to burden the other daughters, but her burdens were only just beginning. As the disease progressed, there were many days when Bill didn't recognize Vivian.

"Who are you?" Bill would ask. "Where is my wife?"

As these symptoms occurred more frequently, Vivian realized that she could no longer meet Bill's needs while managing a five-acre mini ranch with crops like hay and corn, and a menagerie of chickens, peacocks, dogs, and other animals to care for.

When Vivian finally opened up to her daughters about the situation, the girls came together in Spokane to discuss the issue. Vivian had an important decision to make. Should she and Bill continue living in the house they had called home for so many years? If she stayed there, Bill would need to be moved to a nursing home. If she wanted to keep Bill out of the nursing home, she would need to downsize to a smaller home so she could focus her energies on caring for him.

Vivian decided to downsize. It was worth it to help Bill avoid the nursing home.

Their five-acre homestead sold quickly, and Vivian bought a small house on the Spokane River that required far less upkeep. For the few maintenance tasks that remained, things like lawn mowing, landscaping, and repairs, Vivian hired a local service and received help from her family in Spokane. Free from the burdens of maintaining a home, she focused on caring for her husband.

Within just a few days of moving into their new home, however, the flaws in their plan became evident. Bill's condition had deteriorated to the point where he was no longer recognizing Vivian most days. Bill wasn't recognizing his home, either, since he had been uprooted from the surroundings he knew. Almost immediately, Bill started wandering, looking for his wife and his home. Vivian ended up calling 911 on several occasions.

Despite the challenges, Vivian was determined to keep Bill at home. It wasn't easy, but she managed it for several years.

One night, Bill woke up. He didn't recognize Vivian. Thinking she was an intruder, he started to choke her. Thankfully, their daughter, Sherry, was home to help that night. Awakened from the guest bedroom by the commotion, she called 911 and was able to help Vivian break away.

After explaining the situation to the police, Vivian was able to avoid having Bill arrested on assault charges. The police officers agreed to transport Bill to the psychiatric ward for evaluation.

The next morning, Vivian called their family doctor and asked for help.

"You're a nurse and you already know the answer," the doctor told Vivian. "There's only one solution and that's to put Bill in a nursing home."

Vivian's long quest to keep Bill at home was over. She had lost the battle.

She would also lose the war, but we wouldn't discover that until much later.

These weren't easy times for the Wallace family. Bill was in a nursing home, and Vivian was lost. Without her daughters, especially Jan, who lived in Spokane, Vivian wouldn't have been able to face each new day.

It is around this time that I enter the story. The way I came to be in Bill and Vivian's lives was through Jamie, their youngest daughter. I was working for Allstate Insurance Company as a sales manager, and Jamie was an Allstate client. She had totaled her car in an accident and the claim was not going her way. Jamie's Allstate agent had just retired, so her file landed on my desk. The year was 1989.

"Where are you from?" Jamie asked during one of our phone conversations.

"I'm from India," I replied.

"I thought that might be the case," Jamie said. "I have an in-law from India. I recognize the accent."

Her comment opened the door to a personal conversation, and then another, and another. After the claim was settled, I asked Jamie to marry me. She surprised me when she said yes.

Welcome to the Family ... and the Nursing Home

Jamie wanted me to meet her family. We left Seattle on a Friday evening and stayed with her mother when we arrived in Spokane. On Saturday, I met Jamie's sister and her sister's family. On Sunday, as we were getting ready to drive back to Seattle, Jamie asked if we could stop at the nursing home so she could see her dad. By now, I knew that Bill had Alzheimer's, though I had only a vague idea of what that was. I knew her dad was living in a nursing home, a concept I knew nothing about. As I mentioned earlier, there were no nursing homes in India, at least not like they exist here in the U.S. In India, the term "nursing home" refers to a place for a short-term stay after a surgery or health event. It's a place you'll come home from after a few days or weeks, not a place you'll stay forever.

I'll never forget what happened that day. As we entered the nursing home, all I could see were elderly people unable to care for themselves.

It was like a junkyard for old people who were no longer functional, like discarded cars too old to run on the road. We passed this spectacle as we made our way to Bill's room.

When we walked in, Bill recognized Jamie immediately. Although he had lost his ability to speak, he burst into the biggest of grins. Jamie was both happy and heartbroken to see her dad in this setting.

It was difficult for me to watch.

We spent two awkward hours in the nursing home interacting with Bill. When we were ready to leave, Jamie gave her dad a hug and told him she would be back. Thinking Jamie was taking him home, Bill clung to her arm and started walking to the door with her. He didn't let go.

Jamie started to cry. A nursing home employee saw what was happening and came from behind to tap Bill on his shoulder. Bill was distracted long enough for us to enter the key code to unlock the door, leaving Bill behind.

This was a traumatic experience for Jamie, and a surreal experience for me. For the first time, after so many years in America, I asked myself, how can the richest country in the entire world take care of their old people this way when they can no longer care for themselves?

This was a logical question for me, a person observing the situation through third-world eyes. At home in India, I had seen all four of my grandparents take their last breaths with their heads laying on their own pillows in their own homes, surrounded by their loved ones. All were dealing with incapacity in one form or another, yet there was never any question about whether they would be cared for in the home they knew and loved. They didn't have to worry about being sent to a long-term care facility. Not once did I hear my relatives fret about how they would manage.

Surely this wasn't the best America could do.

Or was it?

Bill and Vivian Relocate

Jamie and I married on July 22, 1995. Bill did not walk Jamie down the aisle. Shortly after the wedding, we invited Vivian to move out of her home in Spokane and come live with us. She hemmed and hawed for about six months.

We kept asking. She kept putting us off.

One day the truth came out. "I don't want to be a burden," Vivian admitted.

I started laughing. "Burden?" I said, "What kind of burden are you talking about? I grew up with sixteen people in the same house. There's not enough of you to make it a burden for me."

Finally, she agreed to move in with us.

After Vivian was settled, we set about relocating Bill to a nursing home in the Seattle area. Though there were four nursing homes within five minutes of our home in Federal Way, we elected to place Bill in a facility eleven miles away in the town of Des Moines.

Why didn't we choose a facility closer to home? Each nursing home had a shiny brochure, glowing references, and five-star ratings. Our decision boiled down to one very simple and highly scientific approach: the smell test. The nursing home in Des Moines appeared to be cleaner and better maintained than those we visited in Federal Way. It was the best of all the nursing homes we visited.

Once Bill was settled into his new home, I visited him every day. By this time, he had lost the ability to walk and was confined to his bed and his wheelchair.

The more time I spent with Bill, the more I wondered, and the more questions I had. Why was Bill in a nursing home? He wasn't a threat to himself or anyone else.

The answer: Bill was incontinent and nonambulatory. He needed care.

Really? Millions of people in other parts of the world suffered the same issues, and they weren't forced to move into nursing homes. In fact, four-fifths of the world's population lives in either second- or third-world countries, places where there are no long-term care facilities. Just because somebody becomes incontinent and is no longer able to get around on their own, it doesn't mean that they can't receive care at home. This belief that incapacitated older people are better off in institutions seemed to me a uniquely American phenomenon.

If people in other countries could care for their incapacitated loved ones at home, why would Americans believe that it was beyond the ability of family members or noninstitutional care staff to address these issues at home? What was so different about Bill's situation? What was so different about growing old in America?

Keep in mind that I was approaching this situation from the perspective of a person who grew up in India. I already knew that there was nothing extraordinary about how we grow old in America. The years accumulate for us in the same way they accumulate for every other human being in the world. People grow sick and frail as they age.

The difference isn't in how we age, but rather in how we meet the needs of those who are aging. The difference is in how America deals with people affected by the sickness and frailty of old age. Americans seem quite comfortable warehousing their elderly population in long-term care facilities.

I didn't want it to be this way for Bill. It wouldn't be this way for my parents, and this isn't what I wanted for my father-in-law, so Jamie and I decided to look into bringing Bill back home to live with us.

An Unwelcome Discovery

Once Bill was placed in the nursing home in Spokane, Vivian paid for his care out of pocket, unaware that there was any other way to foot the bill. In the long-term care world, paying out of pocket is called "private pay."

When their money was gone, someone in the nursing home suggested to Vivian that she should now consider qualifying Bill for Medicaid benefits. Left with little more than the value of their small home in Spokane, Bill easily qualified for the program. Though I didn't know it at the time, Vivian had inquired about Medicaid earlier, but had been told that they were "too rich" to qualify. Once Medicaid benefits started, the government paid about $5,500 every month to the nursing home in Des Moines.

Surely $5,500 per month had to be more than enough to pay for Bill's care at home.

I started looking into the cost of home care and discovered that the amount you pay depends on the amount of help you get. In a nursing home, you're paying for round-the-clock care. In reality, most people don't need that much care, nor do they get it, even in a nursing home.

Between Jamie, Vivian, and me, we were three adults who could help Bill if he lived at home. We also had Jamie's sister Jan and her husband, who were willing to come to Seattle to help. As I figured it, we wouldn't need all that much assistance. We could hire professional caregivers to help us get Bill up in the morning, take him to the shower, and get him ready for the day. After that, they could go. Another caregiver or two could come back for a few hours in the evening to get Bill ready for bed.

I looked at what kind of care Bill was receiving in the nursing home and calculated how much it would cost to contract care providers to bring that care into our home. My estimates showed that for about half the amount of money our government was paying to keep Bill in the nursing home, we could provide the same care for Bill in our own home.

This was exciting news. I figured we would just call Medicaid and tell them what we wanted to do. "We're going to save you money and take Bill back home," I would tell them. This would be the first time anyone had called Medicaid with this proposition, and I assumed they would be delighted to hear it.

However, when we brought the idea to the social worker serving as our Medicaid liaison at the nursing home, we were informed that the program Bill was on allowed him to access care only in a nursing home setting. If we took him back home, we would have to pay for any care he needed out of our own pocket.

I couldn't believe it. Surely this wasn't the way the most progressive country in the world functions. Was I understanding this correctly? We, as a society, were willing to pay twice as much to keep a man in a place he didn't want to be, a place he didn't need to be since our family wanted to bring him home. We, as a society, were willing to pay double what was necessary, just to follow Medicaid's rules.

This didn't make any sense, so I decided to look for legal help. Maybe a lawyer could explain things.

I found a law firm and made an appointment. The attorney I selected divided his time between serving as a part-time judge in a local municipal court and private practice with his son and daughter. I felt certain that a judge in private practice would have the answers we needed.

The attorney listened closely as I shared my story. "Rajiv, I know what Medicaid is," he said, "but I have not a clue how to get Medicaid to bring your dad back home."

No one could explain why. No one seemed to care.

This is what sent me to law school in 1999. I knew there was something terribly wrong.

I'll tell you that story soon.

For now, let's fast forward to May 2001, my second year in law school.

I was almost finished with my last final exam when the cell phone in my pocket began to buzz. I glanced at the caller ID to see that it was my wife, Jamie.

I took the call. "They say Dad won't live through the night," she whispered, her voice wavering. "You'd better come."

After the exam, I headed to the nursing home. I couldn't help but reflect on everything that had happened. Like most middle-class Americans, Bill and Vivian probably had visions of a long and pleasant retirement. Their plans did not include being forced into a nursing home, running out of financial resources, or being a burden on others.

I arrived at the nursing home to find Vivian, Jamie, and our two little ones gathered around Bill's bed. After sitting with them for a while, I suggested they go home to get some rest. I told them that I would stay with Bill.

I sat with him all night. When morning came, the nurse encouraged me to go home and rest as well. I left with plans to take a quick shower and then come right back.

Bill took his last breath soon after, alone in the nursing home. He died before I could return.

Vivian lived with us for another six years after Bill's passing. She died of a form of kidney cancer that had metastasized to her bones. If you've been around anyone who has suffered from bone cancer, you already know that Vivian faced incapacity issues that would have likely warranted institutional care. She was incontinent. She was nonambulatory. She was unable to care for herself. Vivian was a poster child example of a human being who, under America's long-term care system, should have spent six months or more in a long-term care facility.

She didn't. That's not what we wanted for Vivian. The extended Wallace family made it possible for Vivian to stay in the home she knew and loved. For several years, Jamie's sister, Jan, and her husband spent time in our home to give Jamie and me a break from our caregiving duties. Jamie's sister, Rondy, transported Vivian to every cancer treatment and medical appointment. Jamie's sister, Sherry, traveled from Canada to help as often as she could. This loving care made it possible for Vivian to draw her last breath on the same pillow she had always slept on, surrounded by her loved ones. The amazing part of Vivian's story is not that she was able to die at home. It's that not for a single day did we look to Medicaid for assistance.

Bill and Vivian had planned for their retirement exactly as they were told, yet their lives ended very differently.

There Has to Be a Way

As I would soon discover, Bill's story wasn't unusual. From Bill being moved to a nursing home despite Vivian's willingness and desire to care for him, to the complete annihilation of their combined net worth, the commonness of this story was what I found so appalling.

I knew that I was witnessing a catastrophic breakdown of some kind. Bill's plan for his retirement had failed in some fundamental way, that much I knew.

What I didn't know at the time was that what happened to Bill happens to 70 percent of older Americans. I wouldn't discover that until much later.

One of the worst parts was that the professionals we were told to trust seemed unable to help. Nobody had answers—not the financial planners, not the doctors, not the lawyers—and nobody seemed to know what to do. Though each professional wanted to do right by us, in the end, the advice they provided was just one piece of a big puzzle that no one seemed to know how to solve. In the end, every professional did their job exactly as they were trained to do, yet the outcome for our family (and millions of others, I would soon discover) was tragic.

I simply refused to believe that we were living in an America with rules that punished our family for wanting to do the right thing by Bill. I refused to believe that I lived in a country that was okay with charging taxpayers double the costs for care that our family didn't want in the first place.

What could I do to change things?

At that time, before law school, I was still a manager at Allstate Insurance Company, and I met with an estate planning attorney my company used to provide training programs to our agents.

I explained what had happened with Bill. "People are being forced into nursing homes when they would be better off staying at home," I said. "We could create a training program that teaches people how to keep their loved ones at home. I could offer a non-lawyer's perspective, and you could offer the attorney's perspective. We could work together."

"Oh, I could never do that," he said flatly.

"Why not?"

"Because the ethical rules of professional conduct prohibit me from working with any non-lawyer."

His unwillingness to help was disappointing, but it didn't discourage me.

I was determined to help people in Bill's shoes find better answers, but how would I do that without legal training?

And then it hit me.

Why not go to law school? Why not try to solve this puzzle—this problem—from inside the system?

It was a big decision. I had been successful in the insurance world. Since joining Allstate in 1989, I had moved up the ranks quickly. It took me just two years to be promoted to management. I had done things no one else had done, such as managing more than one market at a time. My bosses were telling me that a senior management role was in my future if I continued to perform at a high level.

I liked my work at Allstate, but I was feeling the desire to do something more meaningful. The experience with Bill had changed me. I wanted to save Bill and the millions of older adults just like him. I couldn't do that without a law degree.

When I was pondering how to fit law school into my life and my budget, I remembered that Allstate had an education policy. If a manager wanted to go back to school, Allstate would pay for it.

I went to Chuck, my boss.

"I want to go back to law school and here's why," I said. I told him the whole story about Bill and Vivian. "Many of our clients will be facing this same problem. We can help them avoid it with the right education. I can provide that education."

"But you won't be working in the sales department," Chuck said. "You would be working in some other department. You don't want to do that."

I could see where he was going. My law school education wouldn't benefit his organization. My heart sank.

"If you want to take some other class, I would probably pay for it, but not law school," Chuck continued. "Oh, and if you leave this job, you won't get any promotional chances with this company ever again. Just keep that in mind."

I left that meeting determined to find a way to get to law school. After talking it over with Jamie, I decided to fund law school on my own. I applied to the law program at Seattle University and was accepted. After completing my first semester, something unexpected happened.

I was at work when the phone rang. It was Chuck.

"Rajiv, I've been thinking," he said. "Why don't you go up to Alaska for a year?"

For decades, Alaska had been one of Allstate's most profitable regions, but that status was in jeopardy because State Farm had recently expanded into the region. State Farm was undercutting Allstate's business and the manager of the Alaska market, under fire for the losses, had suddenly quit, leaving the region in disarray.

"You want to go to law school," Chuck said. "Go to Alaska for a year. Stabilize that market and I'll pay for your law school by giving you a bonus."

It took me a moment to process what he was saying.

"Yes!" I said, "I'll do it."

Seattle University Law School agreed to hold my place until I returned. I moved Jamie and baby Sid to Alaska. Vivian stayed back in Federal

Way, living in our house and looking after Bill, who was still in the nursing home.

A year later, as promised, Chuck gave me that bonus. To create space in my life for law school, I gave up my sales management role with Allstate and moved into direct sales. I bought an insurance agency and became an agent once again, selling insurance by day and attending law school at night.

Focus on Elder Law

During the more than three years I spent in law school, I took classes on many topics, but the program offered just one course in elder law. This course explained how government programs like VA benefits, Medicare, and Medicaid work. I looked forward to every session, listening carefully for insights that would help me understand what had happened to Bill and Vivian. During the lectures on Medicaid, I realized that Bill could have easily qualified for the COPES program with a Spousal Trust, a simple estate planning tool available at that time.

How could Bill's attorney not have known about this? Could it be that we had been working with the wrong attorneys?

The more I learned during my time in law school, the more I understood. My classes on estate planning were especially revealing. Why were rich people allowed to protect their money from estate taxes while middle-class Americans had to jump through hoops to protect their money from Medicaid? Everyone knew how estate taxes diminish the estates of the wealthy, but few seemed to know about the impact that long-term care costs were having on the estates of middle-class Americans.

I vividly remember Jamie and I having phone conversations after Vivian had learned about the COPES program. The Community Options Program Entry System (COPES, for short) is a Washington State

Medicaid waiver program designed to enable individuals who require nursing home-level care to receive that care in their home or an alternative care environment, such as an assisted living residence.

It sounded like the perfect solution for Bill. When Vivian tried to apply, she was told that Bill didn't qualify because he had too much money.

The professionals who were advising Bill were no help. "That's the way the system works," they told her. Even though I was learning that this is *not* the way the system works, it is the way most laypeople and professionals *think* the system works.

There had to be something missing. I wasn't quite sure what it was, but I believed that with the legal knowledge I was gaining, I would be able to figure it out.

Eager for Experience

During my second year as a law student, I was starting to understand what elder law was and what it could do. I wanted to learn more about what an elder law practice was all about by getting hands-on experience in the field, so I started looking for elder law attorneys in my area. In the process, I discovered the National Academy of Elder Law Attorneys (NAELA), which had a directory listing all elder law attorneys in the country, by state and city. That's how I found Preston Johnson, a NAELA member attorney in my hometown of Federal Way, Washington. He was one of the hundreds of attorneys across the country who practiced elder law, a specialty few outside of elder law circles have even heard of.

To get some hands-on experience working in an elder law firm, I went to see Preston. "I want to come work for you," I announced as I walked into his office.

He looked up. "We're not hiring," he said. "Besides, I'm transitioning my practice to a lawyer named Sandra Wilton. You can talk to her and see if she wants to hire you."

I tracked down Sandra Wilton and gave her a call. "I want to work for you when you acquire Preston's practice," I said.

"It's a small practice," she said. "There's not enough revenue to hire you."

"Then why don't you just let me work there for free?"

Sandra Wilton still wasn't interested.

There had to be a way, so I went to see Preston again. "Why don't you sell your practice to me?" I asked.

"I'm transferring my practice to Sandra," he said. "It's already decided."

"I'll pay you," I offered.

He shook his head. "I already have an agreement with Sandra. The answer is no."

I looked at him for a long moment, then turned to leave.

"Rajiv," Preston said suddenly. "There is one thing I can do. While I'm still running this practice, you can shadow me. I'll show you what I do and how I do it."

That is how I got my first opportunity to work in an elder law attorney's office. It wasn't a paying gig, at least not initially, but I didn't care. I was a third-year law student by that point, and I was eager to learn.

Preston was a godsend. He taught me. He coached me. He opened his law library to me. He introduced me to attorneys across the country who were members of NAELA. These introductions expedited the development of my network, both in the Seattle area and nationally. Thanks to Preston's connections, relationships that would have taken decades to unfold developed in only a matter of months. I was like a sponge, soaking up information and learning from the most experienced and respected elder law attorneys in the nation.

I can't overstate the influence of NAELA in my development as an attorney. I was so impressed that I joined as a student member during my second year of law school. Eventually, I was even elected to the organization's board of directors, the only person who started off as a student with the organization, I was told.

After finishing law school, I kept the insurance agency for a few years while working for Preston Johnson in his law firm.

One day in 2004, my phone rang. It was Sandra Wilton.

"I decided not to take on Preston's practice," she said. "If you want it, it's yours."

I had offered to buy his practice from him, and that is what I did. Preston and I struck a deal. For seven years, he stayed with me, helping me when I needed help.

Once the law practice was on its feet, I sold my insurance practice and bought a building where my law firm, now called Life Point Law, exists to this day.

Could This Be the Solution?

During my second year of law school, I read an article in a NAELA newsletter that changed the trajectory of my career.

The author was Tim Takacs, an attorney in Tennessee who suggested that the elder law attorney's legal answer to an older client's problem, by itself, is an incomplete answer. Creating legal documents and helping clients qualify for Medicaid isn't enough, Tim asserted. You can't have a complete solution for clients without a geriatric care manager, a professional who helps clients coordinate care and make decisions throughout the long-term care journey. As Tim saw it, elder law wasn't really about the law at all. Elder law was about life.

I remember reading those sentences again and again, underlining and highlighting them.

Finally, I thought. Someone else out there gets it.

Tim was doing something considered radical in those days. He had added non-legal professionals to his staff to provide care management services. The concept of a geriatric care manager working inside an elder law firm to provide case management was a controversial idea. Not everyone in NAELA was a fan, but I was. Even today, there are many detractors to the idea of non-legal professionals "polluting" the sanctity of the legal profession. It is this type of thinking that limits innovation and prevents consumers from getting better answers from professionals. My experience with Bill's lawyer was the foundation for this belief. Despite having a lawyer to guide his planning, Bill ended up with poor results. If a geriatric care manager had been involved in Bill's care, could he have avoided the nursing home?

Was this the missing piece of the puzzle I had been trying to solve?

Eventually, I ran into Tim Takacs at a NAELA conference where he presented a program on Life Care Planning, the term he had coined to describe his new approach. I couldn't wait for the talk to be done so I could chase him down.

Tim told me about his plans to create an association of law firms that were interested in adopting this practice model. The Life Care Planning Law Firms Association launched later that year, and Tim was its first president.

I can't overstate how influential Tim was in the development of my way of practicing elder law. By then, I was a working attorney. I was fluent in the practice of traditional estate legal planning—Wills, Trusts, Powers of Attorney, and the like—for older adults in crisis. I was also skilled in the area of crisis planning. Crisis planning is a focused response to an older adult's sudden debilitating illness or traumatic injury that ensures their needs for medical care and long-term care are met without impoverishing either the elder or the family.

Tim introduced me to the possibility that a law firm could do more than just handle legal documents and Medicaid qualifications. An elder law firm could employ social workers, registered nurses, and other professionals capable of delivering the care management services families so desperately needed. I will be forever grateful to Tim for his insight.

Determined to offer Life Care Planning to my clients at Preston's law firm, I joined the Life Care Planning Law Firms Association, eventually becoming its second president.

I didn't follow the Tim Takacs formula to the letter in the way most Life Care Planning acolytes did. Instead of hiring my care manager as an employee of the law firm, I networked with care managers in the community. I formed a partnership, if you will. Whenever I would get a client who looked like a good prospect for a Life Care Plan, I did the legal work and the Medicaid application, and I would have a care manager work alongside me to help the family figure out how to use the financial resources to keep their loved one away from institutional care settings, or to improve their lives if they did choose institutional care. "If there's any way to keep them at home, we're going to try to keep them at home," I would remind the care manager before each home visit. My goal for each client was to accomplish what I had wanted for Bill Wallace—but hadn't been able to accomplish at the time. I wanted each of my clients to have the dignity of being able to age at home without going broke or becoming a burden on their families.

As I worked with various care managers, I discovered something I didn't expect. Some of the care managers seemed to be biased toward institutional care. They discouraged care at home.

I discovered this unsettling fact as I started working with different care managers as my Life Care Planning caseload expanded. One situation stands out. The client was an older lady who was living at home and wanted to stay there. Confident that a good care plan and financial resources through Medicaid could allow for this outcome, I contacted a care manager and charged her with the task of developing a plan that would allow my client to access care at home. I was specific in my ask. "Your role is to find out what it will take for this lady to be able to stay at home," I recall directing her.

The care manager went to see the client and her family, and then gave me her report.

I sat down to read it. Three sentences in, I couldn't believe my eyes. "This person should not be living at home," the care manager had written. "She needs to be in institutional care."

The care manager listed all the reasons why she thought a care facility was the best place for our client, along with a detailed description of her care needs and the types of facilities that would be appropriate for her.

When I met with the care manager, I was direct. "I had given you a very specific task," I told her. "I needed you to help me figure out what it will take for this person to stay at home. If we can keep people at home in India, then surely, in the richest country in the world, we should be able to figure out a way to do the same."

Without blinking an eye, the care manager retorted, "This is not India, Mr. Nagaich. Maybe you need to be practicing law in India and not America."

That's when it dawned on me that so much of what we're dealing with is a matter of perspective. If the professionals we count on to help guide us in our planning quest do not believe in the goal of aging at home, how can the public have any chance to accomplish that outcome? It was never the care manager's place to say, "You should be able to stay at home." It's the care manager's role to say, "This, in my opinion, is what it will take for you to stay at home. Let's say you'll need three professional caregivers, and it will cost you this much per month. If you don't want to stay at home, then these are your choices."

For this care manager, like so many others, the baseline assumption is that an institution is the best place for an older person, so they don't bother to think through what it would take to keep that person at home.

That's when I realized that I couldn't work with just any care manager. I needed to have my own staff who was committed to the same perspective that I was. This is likely the reason Tim Takacs had been advocating for elder law attorneys to hire care managers rather than work with someone who wasn't an employee of the firm. I understood that I needed to work with people who saw institutional care as a last resort, not the first.

Over time, we were successful. The Life Care Plans we created helped many of our elderly clients remain at home. As satisfying as it was to help families through these exceedingly difficult situations, I still felt like something was missing. Outside of those I had the fortune to work with, I continued to see that a majority of older adults who had hoped to grow old in familiar surroundings found themselves forced into long-term care facilities when their health failed. All but the wealthiest found their life savings decimated by the high cost of care. And all the families I worked with, even the most affluent, found themselves facing heavy burdens—financial, legal, and personal—as they struggled to manage their loved ones' lives. For my clients, I was able to ease the challenges, not eliminate them.

Why does this happen? I was determined to find out.

CHAPTER 2

WHAT GOES WRONG

S adly, Bill Wallace's story is a common one for many Americans. No one begins their retirement hoping to become a burden on loved ones or expecting to go broke paying for uncovered care costs, yet just about every older adult is at risk of being institutionalized and burdening their relatives. Families with small to medium size estates run the added risk of financial ruin, despite a lifetime of saving for retirement. Unfortunately, most of these families will be unprepared, just as my father-in-law's family was, because this is likely the first time they will deal with a loved one's incapacity. And they will be unprepared not because they did not plan, but despite having planned.

Bill and Vivian Followed Traditional Advice

Traditional retirement planning in America, it seems to me, is built on the fairy-tale notion that we live and then we die peacefully in our sleep. According to this planning perspective, the most important issues to address involve amassing wealth which can be used to allow us to live the fairy-tale lives depicted in glossy brochures, and to ease the challenges loved ones will have to deal with when one eventually dies. If you are lucky enough to die in your sleep, traditional planning will serve you and your loved ones well.

However, that's not how life will unfold for most of us. Most of us won't die in our sleep. Most people get sick and find themselves unable to manage their daily activities without assistance.

Facts from the Alzheimer's Association tell the tale. Someone in America develops Alzheimer's every 67 seconds, and it is estimated that nearly 500,000 new cases of Alzheimer's disease will be diagnosed in 2022 alone. One in three older adults dies with dementia or Alzheimer's disease.[5] One in eight Americans over age 65 and almost half of all Americans over age 85 will be unable to manage their own activities of daily living without the assistance of others.[6]

For these people, traditional retirement planning is little more than a false promise; it is a recipe for disaster, as it was for Bill and Vivian.

If you are diagnosed with a chronic illness or disability, no matter how much you hoped not to become a burden on others, your family will inevitably be dragged into the situation. The only question will be this: how prepared will your family be to deal with your problem, and how much time will they have to devote to it? They will be the ones who will be coordinating your health care needs, trying to understand your housing options, working with medical providers, trying to manage your affairs when you can't, and contacting lawyers to get a handle on how to pay for the long-term care you now need. What will start as a health issue will soon turn into a housing, financial, and legal issue, and all along the way the process will be a family affair.

Given that reality, let's look at the traditional planning actions that Bill and Vivian took to prepare for retirement. According to the advice dispensed by professionals today, Bill and Vivian did everything right.

- **When they turned 65, Bill signed up for a Medicare-like health program for retired government employees so he and Vivian could access health care services in their old**

age. Enrolling in Medicare or a Medicare-equivalent program like Bill did, followed by purchasing a supplemental insurance policy, is how most people today plan for their health care needs in retirement.

- **Bill and Vivian paid off their home before they retired.** Their goal was to live out their lives in the place where they had raised their children. They loved their family home, and it was where they hoped to draw their last breath. If something happened and they needed to move, they would figure it out then. This is how most older Americans plan for housing in retirement.

- **They worked with a financial advisor who helped them invest their retirement nest egg** so they would have a secure financial future—or so they thought. This is where most of their planning was focused. It was all about the finances. Their goal was to accumulate the largest retirement nest egg they could, retire debt free, and have a reasonable income to supplement Social Security benefits. Bill and Vivian didn't have long-term care insurance. I'm not sure why they didn't buy it.

- **In addition to creating their financial plan, Bill and Vivian worked with a lawyer to create all the legal documents that people are advised to have.** This included a Will, a Power of Attorney, and a Living Will. Armed with these documents, they considered their legal planning to be complete.

In short, Bill and Vivian had done exactly as they had been told to prepare for retirement. They had a doctor, an expectation to live out their lives in the home they built and paid for, a financial advisor, and a lawyer. Despite this planning, Bill ended up forced into institutional care even though Vivian, Jamie, I, and Bill's other children wanted to care for him at home.

Clearly, it wasn't that our family had given up on wanting to take care of Bill at home. We were totally willing and able to do it, yet Vivian was forced to spend all their assets paying for his care in an institution.

The shortcomings of traditional planning were apparent in Bill and Vivian's story. Was the problem embedded in their unique set of circumstances? Are things different for others? What about people who aren't married? What about people who don't have children, or whose children aren't willing or able to help? Are things different for them?

Unfortunately, the answer is no. As an attorney, I'm looking at the fact patterns, and I have learned through many years of experience that the story often plays out the same for everyone: married or single; kids or no kids; friends or no friends.

If you still have doubts, let's take a look at another story.

The Story of Susie

A woman in her sixties—let's call her Susie—is sitting at home watching her favorite TV show. Out of the blue, Susie experiences a massive headache. Instantly, she knows that this is not an ordinary Tylenol headache. She dials 911. When the EMTs enter Susie's residence, they determine she suffered a stroke and rush her to a hospital.

The U.S. Centers for Disease Control and Prevention report that an estimated 795,000 people will suffer a new or recurrent stroke each year.[7] Provided they get medical treatment within three hours of the first onset of symptoms, chances that a person in America will survive a stroke today are better than ever before. However, surviving is not the same as thriving.[8]

Susie's episode starts out as a medical issue.

The treating physician advises Susie that she should improve her eating habits, exercise, and lose some weight. That's great advice for preventing the next stroke, but it doesn't help much with this one.

A few days into this episode, the doctor tells Susie that she no longer needs to be hospitalized, which sounds like great news. It's not. Susie isn't yet strong enough to live at home on her own, so the physician signs discharge papers that send her to a rehab center to receive physical, speech, and occupational therapy.

Let me pause Susie's story for a moment to give you some context. In my work with clients, I've seen again and again that people who are able and healthy simply cannot fathom what things will be like when they're on the verge of being sent to a long-term care facility. When you're healthy, you have no problem telling yourself (and others) that when your health fails, you'll move to a facility if that's what's required. After all, you don't want to be a burden.

It sounds good in theory, but it rarely works that way in practice. As your health deteriorates, as you spend more time in hospitals, the more it dawns on you why people don't like living in institutional care settings. It's not like room service at a hotel where people are falling over themselves to wait on you. You push the call button, and no one comes. You can't get to the bathroom on your own, and it takes a long time for help to show up.

Poor service isn't the only problem. It's the environment in which this service is delivered that makes the experience even worse. You're dealing with a bunch of people you don't know, people who will be telling you what to do and when to do it. You've lost just about all control over your life.

The horror created by this loss of agency doesn't become real until you have lived it yourself. Once you've experienced it, you will do whatever you can to avoid it. My clients who are still healthy look at me like I'm insane when I tell them what will happen. "You'll be going to a place where you don't know anyone. Everyone else will tell you what to do, and you'll have no control over your life," I tell them. Most of them just look at me and say, "Yes, and....?" They just don't get it.

You may think that living in an institution is no big deal, but that's not the tune you'll be singing when you're about to be admitted to a long-term care facility and it dawns on you that life as you've always known it is coming to an end.

That's what was on Susie's mind as she was laying in her hospital bed with her family gathered around her, trying to decide which rehab center to choose. Susie hadn't planned for this. She didn't think she needed to. She was expecting to die in her sleep—at home. Why study up on rehab center options when you're certain you won't ever need one?

Even though Susie and her family don't know which rehab center to choose, the discharge planner insists they pick one. The hospital staff is not permitted to make a recommendation. How does Susie's family decide?

They flip a coin.

There's another problem, though Susie doesn't realize it just yet. She doesn't know that in America, the terms "rehab center" and "nursing home" are effectively synonymous. Technically speaking, a rehab center is a place where you go for short-term care following an illness or accident. A nursing home is for long-term care. People check out of rehab centers; most people who go to nursing homes don't come out. That's the American view. And while this is how things play out in most cases, it is not a guaranteed outcome that you will return home from a rehab center.

When I'm viewing this situation through Indian eyes, I look at it this way: You took me to the hospital. Thank you, hospital, for saving my life. I'm grateful, but please don't send me to a place where I don't know anyone, where everyone's going to tell me what to do, and where I have no control over my life. I would much rather go to the familiarity of my home, where at least I know what is where.

Susie doesn't have that perspective. At first, she views the rehab center as an extension of the hospital, simply a continuation of the medical care she has been receiving all along. However, shortly after entering the rehab center, there's no hiding from the fact that she is in some form of a nursing home. She can hear it. She can see it. She can smell it.

Susie, like most Americans, never wanted to see the inside of a nursing home as a patient. If Susie knew about the study that revealed that 61 percent of Americans would rather die than live in a nursing home, she would count herself in that group.[9]

She starts to rationalize. *This is a temporary arrangement required by special circumstances*, Susie tells herself. *It won't last forever. It can't last forever.*

For the first two or three weeks, Susie is confident things will get better. She works hard in therapy. She's determined. But as more weeks go by, the rehab center experience starts to get old. She wants out.

When Susie's husband, Frank, comes to visit, she is impatient.

Frank asks, "How are you doing?"

"Who cares how I'm doing," Susie snaps. "Just tell me when I'm getting out of here!"

What Susie doesn't yet know is that Frank has just talked to her doctor. Because her physical limitations are severe, it will be difficult for her to go home. Her wheelchair won't fit through the narrow doorways in their house, and it won't work at all on the stairs.

Susie's medical problem has created a housing issue—but not just for her. She is exactly where she needs to be after a stroke, even though she has no desire to be there. What no one realizes just yet is that Susie's housing problem will have to be solved by her family, the very people she vowed never to burden.

Frank and Susie don't panic just yet. No matter how tired Susie is of being in the nursing home, at least the cost is being covered by Medicare.

Susie and Frank expect Medicare to cover the bill for 100 days, because the booklet from the Department of Health & Human Services on Medicare Coverage of Skilled Nursing Facility Care says on page 14 that you can get up to 100 days of Skilled Nursing Facility coverage.[10]

Susie and Frank, unaware that "up to" means that the number can be significantly less than 100 days, are surprised when on day 33 (it could be any day, and ironically, it's usually a Friday), a social worker walks into Susie's room and announces that Medicare is going to stop paying for care starting Monday.

Susie and Frank are surprised. They didn't realize that Medicare will only pay for care if Susie's condition is improving. Her doctors have determined that she's progressed as much as she can, which means that Medicare will no longer cover her rehab stay.

What Susie doesn't know is that she's not getting the whole truth. The rule about how much skilled nursing care will be covered by Medicare was clarified in 2013 after a class action lawsuit.[11] The rule states that facilities cannot refuse people Medicare because they have stopped making progress. The rule has always been that if therapy and rehab are needed to maintain a person's current status, or prevent further deterioration, then the facility must continue to provide Medicare-covered skilled services.

That's not how this rule is often applied. In many cases, as soon as the facility determines you've stopped making progress, they decide that your Medicare coverage will end. This is an arbitrary decision on the facility's part. Medicare doesn't have any say in the matter; they are relying on the rehab facility's incorrect interpretation of the rule—and of Susie's progress. As a result of this faulty interpretation, Susie is refused rehab care under Medicare well before her 100 days are up.

Now, Susie and her family have less than 48 hours to make other arrangements.

What should they do?

Susie can't go home. She can't safely navigate in her home. That leaves one option. Susie can remain in the nursing home and pay privately.

Frank and Susie resign themselves to this option, to pay privately—that is until the social worker tells them how much it will cost. In the Seattle area, the private pay rate for "rehab" in a nursing home ranges from $15,000 to $18,000 per month. When Susie and Frank hear this news, they gasp. Who has that kind of money laying around? They certainly don't. They could opt to forego rehab and move to the nursing home part of the same building, but the cost for long-term care in that setting isn't much cheaper. It's $9,000 to $12,000 a month and rising each year.

In addition to the housing problem, Susie's stroke has now created a financial problem.

Keep in mind that creating a financial plan was the main thing Susie and Frank did to plan for retirement. They had a house they owned free and clear. They saved money. They bought the right insurance policies.

None of it matters now. Despite all that planning, Susie's health problem may just bankrupt the family.

One of Susie's friends hears about what happened and calls her at the rehab center.

"You need to see an elder law attorney," the friend says.

Susie objects. "Why do I need to see a lawyer?" she asks. "I have a lawyer. I have a Trust. My kids won't go through Probate. I have a Power of Attorney. I have all the legal documents a lawyer can help me with."

"Elder law attorneys do different work," the friend says patiently. "If you go to an elder law attorney, they will help you find a way to pay for the long-term care you need without burning through all your assets. An elder law attorney can help you apply for Medicaid or VA benefits, but even more than that, the right elder law attorney can help guide you through the maze of our medical system and help you build a plan that will allow you to live as good a life as possible under the circumstances, without your family losing their sanity in the process."

Susie is confused. Why hadn't the attorney who worked on her estate plan advised her about these issues? Why hadn't her attorney told her that Medicare did not need to end in 33 days, or that Medicaid or VA benefits could pay for her care costs once Medicare ends? Why hadn't her attorney told her that it was possible to organize care at home and not in a rehab center or nursing home?

Unfortunately, most estate planning attorneys are unaware of the options they can offer their aging clients. Most people who don't have a long-term care insurance policy, or those with one that doesn't provide enough benefits, don't know that they can plan for the day they might need Medicaid to pay for long-term care before catastrophe strikes. Many general practice attorneys aren't aware of this, either. Without that knowledge, Susie's attorney is limited in what she can do.

This does not make the attorney a bad attorney, just one who can't be expected to give advice on topics they are not familiar with.

So, despite having a lawyer, Susie and Frank now have a legal issue on their hands, something they may not even recognize unless they are lucky to have someone give them this insight, as Susie's friend did.

Finally, Frank, frustrated and overwhelmed, informs his children that he needs help caring for Susie. When Susie was in the nursing home, Frank believed he had the situation under control. Now, he doesn't know where to turn.

His children, unaware of the severity of the problem, are suddenly faced with decisions about caring for their mother that they were not prepared to make; decisions about finances, caregiving, housing, and legal affairs.

This issue has now become a burden to the family, a scenario Frank and Susie wanted to avoid at all costs.

All it takes is one health problem to unravel all your carefully laid retirement plans.

This is why I say that traditional planning is a recipe for disaster for most retirees. It leaves you with a false sense of security that you have done all you are called upon to do to live a happy and secure future, when, in fact, you have a lot of holes in your plan.

The Problem of Fragmentation

Both the real-life Bill and the fictional Susie saw their physicians regularly, consulted with financial planners, paid off their homes before retiring, and created all the estate planning documents experts recommend.

How could all this planning end up in such a mess?

As I worked with clients amid a long-term care crisis, I started to see a common theme.

It wasn't that people weren't planning for retirement. They were. The problem was that they did their planning for health, housing, finances, and legal issues in silos, and they didn't plan at all for the roles their family members would play. Their planning was fragmented. They engaged in what I refer to as bumble bee planning. People flit from one professional to another, from one topic to another, never coordinating the plans they create with each professional. This is how we are taught to plan for retirement, even though the things we need to plan for—health, housing, finance, legal, and family issues in retirement—are all part of a single puzzle.

The shortcomings of this bumble bee planning won't become evident until you're incapacitated by a health care crisis later in life.

No one is connecting being "broke, a burden, and stuck in a nursing home" to the way they plan for retirement. Instead, we settle for the notion that being "broke, a burden, and stuck in a nursing home" is just what happens to others, not us. Or, it will happen only to those who aren't lucky enough to die in their sleep. Even though the statistics paint a different reality.

My view is that today's recipe for retirement planning practically guarantees that the plans you create, even with the help of a professional, or several professionals, will be full of gaps and holes. Even worse, the plan you created with one professional is likely to conflict with the plan you created with another professional. And you will have no idea. Think about it. When is the last time you had your financial planner, your lawyer, your doctor, and your real estate agent sit around a table and discuss the advice they are giving you to ensure that there is nothing in that advice that will come back to thwart the plan you are carefully pulling together?

This doesn't happen. Nor does the retirement planning industry deem it to be a necessary part of the planning process.

So, what is missing? By way of analogy, we can look at a different catastrophe … the flying of airplanes by terrorists into the Twin Towers.

> The 9/11 Commission detailed a second theory of intelligence failure, failure of management, or more precisely, failure of coordination. The Commission's report notes "information was not shared, sometimes inadvertently or because of legal misunderstandings. Analysis was not pooled. Effective operations were not launched."

The report goes on to make an analogy of the intelligence community as a hospital full of specialists with no attending physician to ensure unity of effort.[12]

It is not hard to see the similarity between the 9/11 Commission findings and why things go wrong in the lives of people when incapacity strikes a member of the family.

Let's take a look at Susie's interactions with professionals, starting with her health care team.

The health care team saved her life, but is the doctor to blame for Susie's crisis? Susie's doctor did his job. He provided care and medications to help her recover, and then he sent her to a rehab center. The doctor is doing exactly what a physician is expected to do: provide health care.

How much thought does a physician give to the impact of such a discharge on Susie's finances, given that Medicare could end their coverage? None. That's Susie's job.

Susie can't go home because the home her real estate agent helped her buy a decade ago is unsuitable for a person recovering from a stroke. Is the realtor to blame for Susie's crisis? The fact that Susie didn't consider whether the home she had purchased would be suitable if she was incapacitated isn't the realtor's job. It's Susie's job.

Is Susie's financial planner to blame for her crisis? The professional who helped Susie build her retirement nest egg did nothing wrong. In fact, this financial planner gave Susie advice that she didn't take. Susie's financial planner told her to buy a long-term care insurance policy, but Susie refused. It was too expensive, and she might never need it, she told her financial planner at the time. So, the financial planner is not to be blamed. And even if she had purchased a long-term care insurance policy, the fact is that no policy could have guaranteed that she would not end up in a rehab center, it would have only paid for the cost.

How about Susie's accountant who helps her file her tax returns, or the insurance broker who helped her buy her Medicare supplemental policy? Well, they are even more removed from her financial advisor when it comes to helping Susie with housing or incapacity issues.

Is Susie's lawyer to blame for her crisis? He provided services exactly as he was trained to do in law school. He created a Will or Trust, Powers of Attorney, and Living Will documents. The attorney did nothing wrong.

Every professional was doing his or her job, yet nobody's solution helped Susie in the end. Nobody can claim to have done a good job helping Susie and Frank get ready for retirement in an effective manner. And it is not their fault. It is just how planning has evolved and become accepted in our society, leading to almost ready acceptance of the burden, broke, or nursing home reality we live with.

There's also a family component to fragmentation. The impact that eventually returning home will have on Susie's husband, and on her children who live several states away and must travel to support her, is Susie's responsibility. Like so many of us, Susie has probably never talked to her children about how her failing health might impact them, or at least not in an effective manner.

Ultimately, Susie has no one to blame but herself for this debacle that has now taken over the lives of everyone in her family.

This is a bitter pill for anyone to swallow, so let's make it less distasteful.

Susie didn't know any better. Few, if any, of us do. Susie did exactly what the experts advised her to do.

When someone develops a long-term illness, the health issue creates an interconnected set of housing, financial, legal, and family issues that traditional retirement planning neither recognizes nor addresses. People are living longer than ever, and these long life spans are creating new issues that professionals in general and society at large are just starting to grapple with. But, it is still startling to me that there has been almost no innovation on how retirement planning is done. Each profession is settled and content with how it offers retirement planning guidance, and the public has not risen to revolt against that way of planning.

To me, planning for retirement in a way that addresses these interconnected variables is a lot like building a house. You have an architect draw up the plans, then you get a general contractor who agrees to oversee the project. The general contractor hires subcontractors, each of whom does their part to build the structure. The general contractor is monitoring cost, quality, and speed, and making sure the product meets its stated goal.

Why is it that the retirement plans that most people create don't work out?

It's because there was no architect to draw up a plan that coordinates the health, housing, financial, legal, and family issues people face in retirement, especially after a health crisis. There's no general contractor to oversee the professionals working in each fragmented area.

Your doctor, your financial planner, your attorney, and others are the subcontractors. They are each doing their part.

Who is overseeing the project?

Your doctor isn't. Your lawyer isn't. Your financial planner may say he is, but he's not.

The architect is supposed to be you. The general contractor is supposed to be you.

No one tells you this.

No one teaches this.

This is the root cause of retirement plan failure.

The Research on Retirement Plan Failure

After several years as a lawyer, I started seeing the limits of my elder law practice's ability to help people.

Most adults who became my clients were people like Bill and Susie; people dealing with what is known in elder law circles as the "elder care crisis." An elder care crisis is what happens when immediate arrangements need to be made for an older adult's housing because their current environment is no longer safe or appropriate.

When these people came to me, I did what I was trained to do in law school. I helped them get the appropriate estate planning documents. I helped them qualify for Medicaid and VA benefits to pay for long-term care while protecting family assets as much as possible.

I had a steady stream of clients just like this. It was a constant parade of Bills and Vivians. An older adult's health was failing and the family couldn't manage things anymore, so the person needed to be placed somewhere. In some cases, family members had been caring for the older adult at home, often for many, many years. By the time they found their way to my office, the family was in disarray. In some cases, the primary caregiver had become sick or died.

It was the same situation again and again. It started feeling like Ground-hog Day.

The legal solutions I could offer to address their problems were limited at best. Even with the addition of a geriatric care manager, I felt constrained in my ability to help. Was there really a way to fix this from within the legal system? I was having my doubts.

How could so many older adults be ending up in this situation?

Had anyone done research?

This is what I have been doing with my evenings since 2004. While other people were reading novels, I was sitting at the computer conducting research. In the process, I stumbled upon statistics that shocked me. I was surprised to discover that a substantial amount of research had been done on this subject by government agencies and universities. I've already cited some of the research I discovered.

As I looked at the data, I could see that the problem was much bigger than I ever imagined.

Why didn't the average person know about this research?

Here's my theory: When you're an average person handling the care of an older relative on your own, you're simply trying to get through each day. You're just trying to figure out what your loved one needs and how to keep them safe. You go through this once or twice in your life. After your loved one dies, you move on. You don't think to analyze your experience or look for research. You get on with your life.

For every family caregiver who is unaware of the research that points to the dismal results of retirement planning in this country, there is an entrepreneur, a long-term care insurance company, or the builder of long-term care facilities who is using that research to create a business that will generate revenue from people whose retirement plans have failed.

Look around you. How many long-term care facilities are going up in your community? I'm willing to bet it's more than a few. The companies building these long-term care facilities are using this research to prove the viability of their business.

I want to share this research with you so you can avoid retirement plan failure.

Let's start with the big picture. In the United States, more than 10,000 individuals turn 65 every day.[13] In 2015, people aged 65 and over accounted for one in ten individuals in our society.[14] In 2019, people 65 and older represented 16 percent of the population, more than one in every seven Americans. By 2030, that number will increase to almost one in four.[15] By the year 2035, the number of American households with someone over age 80 will have doubled.[16]

Though most Americans hope to be able to live out their lives in their own home, the reality is that less than 30 percent will be able to achieve this hope.[17] Research shows that about 70 percent of people 65 or older will need long-term care services at some point in their lifetime.[18]

Where will the money come from to pay for all that care? The median income of the 65+ population in 2019 was $27,398,[19] and in the same year, 33 percent of older Americans had incomes of under $50,000.[20] The average Medicaid-covered cost of long-term care services provided to older adults (65+) in an institutional care setting was $51,403. In comparison, the cost for Home and Community Based Services was $28,778.[21] In 2015, only 5 percent of the total population over the age of 40 had a long-term care insurance policy.[22] As a result, the bulk of provided care was uncompensated care provided by family members.[23]

If you have planned for your retirement in the usual way, and you are counting on Medicare to cover your medical costs and pick up the tab for any long-term care you might need, you will be in for a rude awakening.[24] If you are one of the millions of Americans with a small to medium size estate, the biggest threat to your financial well-being in retirement will be uncovered long-term care costs. This reality is turning Medicaid into a program not just for the poor, but a program that you will be forced to rely on in retirement. Estate planning, the way it is done today, completely ignores this reality.

The statistics reveal a cold hard truth. Sixty-nine percent of people over age 65 will deal with incapacity of some sort which will render them dependent on others for assistance with many activities of daily living.[25] Many people dealing with incapacity will have reason to worry about losing their hard-earned assets to uncovered long-term care costs,[26] while at the same time becoming a burden on loved ones.[27]

If there wasn't a way to describe your free-floating anxiety about retirement before, there should be one now.

The problem is in the planning.

CHAPTER 3

THE PROBLEM WITH HOUSING

Why is a Lawyer Talking about Housing?

I am an elder law attorney. I practice a type of law that often involves helping people pay for long-term care. Since I'm often intimately involved in the process of determining where an older adult will live, I consider myself also in the housing business.

Remember earlier when I wrote that an older adult's health problem almost always creates a housing problem when he or she can't return home? This is the point when people usually find their way to me, so the topic of housing is where I want to start in this deep dive into what's wrong with the way Americans plan for retirement.

For most Americans, housing is the single most under-planned issue. This creates a pressing planning opportunity, yet there is no professional group that is discussing this issue with their clients in any actionable way. Physicians don't discuss this. Financial advisors don't discuss this. Realtors don't discuss this. Neither do lawyers.

People aren't talking about this with the professionals they are relying on to help them plan for retirement, yet about 90 percent of Americans say they want to remain at home[28] as they age. Information published by Stanford University shows that even though well over 80 percent of the people polled expressed a strong preference to be able to die at home, less than 30 percent of Americans actually get to experience that ending.[29] Around 70 percent of all Americans will die in either hospitals, convalescent homes, nursing homes, assisted living facilities, adult family homes, or boarding homes—someplace other than where they wanted to be during their last moments on earth.

I also think that most Americans understand that though they may want to stay home, they may not be able to if they become incapacitated and their care needs cannot be met at home. In my opinion, there's a collective sense of resignation—a belief that nothing can be done. Nobody wants to move to a care facility, yet most accept that this is likely their future. That's just the way it is.

If you haven't already figured this out by now, I'm always asking the question "why?" What's the root cause? I'm not content with the status quo if it creates suffering for my clients.

Nowhere is my desire for answers stronger than on the subject of housing. Part of my relentlessness comes from my radically different cultural perspective on the aging issue. As I described earlier in the book, I grew up in India in a large home with most of my extended family under the same roof. I lived with my grandparents, and I saw them dealing with issues similar to those we deal with in the U.S. As my grandparents grew older, they developed the same issues that older adults develop here in America. However, despite their incontinence, their inability to get around, and their inability to care for themselves, in India, we didn't put them in a nursing home. The family manages their elderly loved ones' needs at home by bringing in outside help.

As I worked with clients in my elder law practice, I started paying close attention to the housing choices they were given. I started watching where they ended up. For most, their final destination was a nursing home, a memory care facility, or a similar setting.

Why were none of my elder law colleagues talking about this? Why did no one else view this as a problem? Why did I see things differently?

The answer lies in my perspective.

My colleagues in the elder law community had the American perspective. My perspective was that of a person born in India, a place where there were no nursing homes.

This differing perspective has made things interesting for me, to say the least. Thanks to my different perspective, I push back. I don't always quietly accept the status quo, and this makes waves.

In the process, people have drawn all sorts of conclusions about me. Among other things, I've been accused of being opposed to putting anyone in a nursing home at any time for any reason.

While that's not true, I can't hide my bias toward caring for elderly loved ones in the home if it's at all possible.

During a legal conference in 2021, one of the attending elder law attorneys gave a presentation that included a story about moving his frail elderly father into his home. "This is what we elder law attorneys should do," I remember thinking as I listened to him speak. Then, the attorney said that his father needed too much care, so he placed him in a facility. Though this attorney discussed in detail how difficult this decision was, he failed to mention whether his dad went willingly.

I thought to myself, "You're normalizing something that is abnormal to every older human being."

Was I the only one having these thoughts? There was more than enough empathy in the room for this attorney, and almost none for his father. The general reaction after this attorney's presentation was, "You poor guy. You did so much. You did the right thing."

It seemed to me that even elder law attorneys were normalizing institutional care in America, and it didn't sit well with me.

I couldn't find any empathy for this attorney. After his presentation, I tracked him down.

"This is a cultural issue," I said. "Elder law attorneys are the ones people should be able to look up to when it comes to finding ways to avoid institutional care. We should be setting a higher standard. We should be the ones saying that institutional care is not normal, yet we make it normal."

Several years ago, I was at a retreat with a group of attorneys. Between sessions, I went out for a walk with an attorney whom I greatly respect.

"Why do you rail so much against nursing homes?" this attorney asked me. "I just put my mom in a nursing home. I couldn't take care of her. What's wrong with that?"

"Oh, there's nothing wrong with it," I replied. "It's fine. The only thing I worry about is when your time comes to go to the nursing home, will you go willingly, or will you fight it?"

She never did answer my question.

Aging in an institution is now considered the norm, even by elder law attorneys. Yet, if you ask any older adult—attorneys included—where they want to live as they age, none will reply that they hope to end up in an institution.

If the professionals charged with advising families can't offer a pathway to a different housing option, who can blame the general population for thinking nursing home care is inevitable?

The Problem of Housing during a Health Crisis

The day your health fails is a bad day. You have a stroke or a heart attack. You cause an accident. You start a fire. You're wandering or lost. You can no longer take care of yourself.

That day is probably one of the worst days of your life.

If your plan for housing is "I want to stay in my home as long as I can, and when I can't, I will move," you're not going to like how things turn out.

Here's how it usually happens.

On the day your health fails, you will likely end up in an institution of some kind, a place that's the opposite of home. You won't know anyone. You won't know where anything is. Everyone's going to be telling you what to do. You will have zero privacy and even less control over your life.

Your misery will be a thousand times worse than it would be if you were dealing with your health issue at home.

After decades of practicing law, I can say with total confidence that what sounds logical today is the exact opposite of what you'll be doing the day that you realize that home is no longer an option.

You will fight it. Over the years, I have seen patterns emerge. One that repeats itself over and over is this: very few people willingly embrace institutional care.

When we say this:

"I want to stay in my house as long as I can..."

What we really mean is this:

"When my health fails, I want the care to come to me without creating burdens for my family or going broke in the process."

When the health crisis arrives, your vague hope to "stay at home until you can't" turns into a one-way trip to the nursing home because you didn't think through the mechanics of what it would take for your family to bring you back home after a health crisis.

The Problem with Getting Care at Home

Are you assuming that your family will bring you home once you're discharged from the hospital after a health crisis during your retirement years? If the answer is *yes*, prepare for disappointment. There will be pressure on your family to move you to a facility once the immediate crisis has passed. Most health care providers believe that older people are safest in institutions.

What if you want to come home?

When Bill was in the nursing home, I tried to bring him back home. Every time I brought it up, the social worker threw up a red flag.

"You'll be taking him against medical advice because we don't suggest that he should go back home." This was the social worker's reply every time I asked about bringing Bill home.

Why did this stop us? The answer is a frustrating but simple one: If you take somebody home against medical advice, you risk being no longer qualified to receive Medicare benefits. That reality paralyzed me at the time. I wasn't an attorney then and I didn't understand the law.

I also didn't know that there's an industry that will do everything it can to help you take your last breaths at home. You've probably heard of it. Hospice does everything it can to make your dream of dying in your own home come true. However, you won't be able to access hospice care unless you have less than six months to live.

Maybe you know someone who has received hospice care. It's a comprehensive approach to care that involves a multidisciplinary medical team, usually headed by an occupational therapist, physical therapist, or social worker. This team offers a single point of access for everything you need. They visit the home to do an assessment. They identify adaptive equipment that will help you live more safely at home—things like a hospital bed, a respirator, a grab bar, safety equipment, and the like. They will order what you need and get it set up in your home. If you need the support of a nurse to attend to your medication needs, hospice will arrange for this. If you need a bath aid to attend to your hygiene needs, hospice will provide one. If you need a spiritual advisor to help counsel you and your family through this difficult time, hospice will handle it. Hospice will also make sure that every family member who will be supporting you during your last six months at home has access to a toll-free number that they can call 24/7.

Jamie and I used hospice services during Vivian's last months. Nurses came regularly to manage her medical needs. Bath aids came to attend to her hygiene needs, and a spiritual advisor was at hand to help her transition to the next phase of her life. Most importantly, hospice provided us with a 24-hour support system. We used that toll-free number on more than one occasion.

After going through this experience with Vivian, I was left with many questions. Why was the hospice approach to care at home not available to families at an earlier point? Or to those who did not have a diagnosis of being terminally ill? What if it could be? Might that be a way to bring people home?

The Problem with Making Housing Decisions Under Pressure

You have seen how a health problem can create a housing crisis if you can't come home because you are incapacitated by an illness or injury. What is the lawyer's solution to this crisis? It's a legal document called the Power of Attorney, and it grants your named agents the legal authority to do whatever they deem appropriate to ensure your safety and well-being. The Power of Attorney comes in a variety of forms: the Financial Power of Attorney and the Healthcare Power of Attorney are two of the most common.

The Power of Attorney plays a significant role in housing decisions. Fast forward to the day your health fails. You have a stroke and you're in the hospital.

What does the Power of Attorney document tell your agent to do when you end up in the hospital?

Nothing! Cue the crickets.

Your Power of Attorney gives your agent authority and responsibility, but absolutely no direction. For that, your agent will be forced to read between the lines, and when they do, they will find an assumption:

I love you. I trust that when you come to my aid, you will figure it out.

Figure what out?

The "it" is never stated in the document.

Let that sink in.

How does this play out in real-life housing decisions after a health crisis?

Let's come back to your stroke scenario. You've been in the hospital for a while and you're making a good recovery. The social worker comes to the agent you named in your Power of Attorney—let's say it's your daughter—and says, "It's time to discharge your parent. Which rehab center do you choose?"

What does the Power of Attorney paperwork say about how your daughter is to handle this situation?

Nothing.

To make matters worse, if you're like most Americans, you've never actually talked to your daughter about what she should do in this situation, at least not in a way that will bring clarity to what she must do at the time. Your plan for housing is built on the shaky foundation of assumption and hope. You assume that your daughter knows that you don't want to go to a nursing home, and you hope that your daughter will figure out a way to make that happen. Perhaps your daughter had assured you in the past that she would not allow you to end up in a nursing home. But, there was no plan on how she would achieve that outcome without becoming your unpaid caregiver. So, there's probably a prayer somewhere in there, too.

What decision will your daughter make?

Which rehab center?

The social worker is tapping her foot, waiting for an answer.

Remember, your daughter doesn't have any instructions on how to handle this situation. She has no way of knowing that the choices she is being given (choosing a rehab center among several from a list) are reflective of the medical system's preference for institutional care as the best option for older people when there is concern about safety in the home.

"Which rehab center?" The social worker asks the question again.

What will your daughter say?

The response is likely to be, "What do you suggest?"

If you're lucky, your daughter will say, "I will do some research and get back to you."

Most people in your shoes aren't so lucky. In the end, more likely than not, your daughter will look to your health care provider for direction. Your daughter probably won't push back against the hospital's desire to put you in rehab.

Why does this happen? Here are a few reasons:

1. Your daughter probably has no idea that pushing back is even an option because most of us are accustomed to following the direction of health care providers.

2. Your daughter may think that her decision is only between "*this* rehab center or *that* rehab center," not "rehab center or *home*."

3. Your daughter may not have the time or the willingness to do the research needed to make a decision.

There will be no discussion about the possibility of your receiving care at home because you have done no planning around this issue. You never imagined that you would need to be rescued from the hospital, and you were assuming that your Power of Attorney document would be sufficient. You might even accept that rehab in a rehab facility is a good idea given the care needs you may face at the time, not recognizing that the same care could be arranged at home.

You won't be alone in this quandary. This is what happens to most Americans.

Simply *hoping* to live out your life in your own home is *not* a reliable plan. Praying that your agents make the right decision without giving them the tools to do so is little more than wishful thinking. Hoping and praying that you'll be able to come back home without a plan to make it happen almost certainly guarantees that you will be forced into institutional care against your wishes.

The Problem with Thinking Money Is the Answer

If you're reading this chapter and you're thinking that nothing I've said so far applies to you because you're financially well-endowed, this is where you should start paying attention.

Having a lot of money is no guarantee that you won't be forced into a nursing home or end up a burden on your family. It's not even a guarantee that you won't go broke. Money doesn't solve every problem, especially when it comes to housing in old age. In fact, rich and famous people whose names you would recognize routinely end up forced into institutional care, even though that's not what they wanted. Retirement plan failure isn't something that just happens to people of limited means. Retirement plan failure happens in every tax bracket. Without a plan to use your money after a health crisis, old age can turn into a nightmare, even for the super-rich.

If you're wealthy, consider the stories that follow to be cautionary tales.

Casey Kasem

Is an $80 million fortune enough to avoid being forced into institutional care? It wasn't for *American Top 40* radio personality Casey Kasem. Despite all that money, Casey Kasem was unable to take his last breath at home. He was dragged from California through Oregon to die on the third floor of St. Anthony's Hospital in Gig Harbor, Washington. He died away from his home while his loved ones were embroiled in conflicts over access and care. "My father wanted to be at home," Casey's daughter, Kerri, told me. "He had enough money to have caretakers around the clock, yet he was moved from facility to facility. We couldn't find him, so we couldn't visit. He was alone, sick, and scared."

Ronald Reagan & John O'Connor

In 1994, a few years after Ronald Reagan finished his second term as President of the United States, he announced in a handwritten note to the nation that he had been diagnosed with Alzheimer's disease.[30] Reagan's public appearances became less and less frequent until 2001, when his family determined that he would live in semi-isolation. Despite at least ten years of battling against the ravages of Alzheimer's, he never spent a day in institutional care.[31]

John O'Connor, the husband of Supreme Court Justice Sandra Day O'Connor, was ravaged by the same illness, but unlike Ronald Reagan, he ended up spending several years in an institutional care setting.[32] In the summer of 2006, after John's condition had deteriorated and after Justice Sandra Day O'Connor had retired from the bench to care for him, John was placed in a care center located near their home in Phoenix.

There is a lot that can be learned from these two scenarios as to what it takes to allow one to be able to avoid institutional care. It takes resources, an accessible home, and the support of someone who will make it possible to avoid being institutionalized.

Both Reagan and O'Connor were financially successful and had the means to be able to afford care at home. Both had residences that could accommodate home care without difficulty or could have made the necessary modifications with the resources available. The difference is that only one had the support of a family member who vowed never to see her husband in an institutional care setting—Ronald Reagan had Nancy as that guardian.

That does not make the O'Connors somehow less. It just means that the decision to accept institutional care is a question of personal choice. There is little information available on whether John O'Connor would have preferred to stay in his own home with his family, but there is a strong indication that Nancy Reagan was the one who was determined to keep Ronald Reagan out of an institutional care setting all the way to the end.[33]

I wrote letters to both Nancy Reagan and Sandra Day O'Connor. I wanted to know their thinking about the housing issue. I asked them how they made their decisions about where their husbands would live as their Alzheimer's disease progressed. I didn't hear back from Nancy Reagan, but Justice Sandra Day O'Connor wrote back to tell me that she wasn't ready to talk about it just yet, but she would someday. That someday never came, because she is now incapacitated by Alzheimer's disease.

The Smith Family

A few years ago, I worked with a couple that I'll call the Smiths. Dan and Susan were both high-level executives in their respective fields, and were well-situated financially. There were no children. I was helping them create their *LifePlan* for retirement.

Susan called me one day. "We have to put our planning on hold," she said. "I need your help with my dad."

She told me the story. Max, her elderly father, had fallen ill and was admitted to the hospital. From there, he was discharged to a rehab center. That's where I met the family. The doctors were recommending that Max be sent to a nursing home.

This was the classic crisis planning case that I see every day as an elder law attorney. Through her work with me, Susan knew that I could help the family avoid this outcome for Max, so she asked for my help.

I met Susan and a few of Max's family at the rehab center. Her mom (let's call her Doris) was there, along with two of Susan's brothers. As I sat with the family, I noticed that Doris was looking at a stack of brochures from companies that make money by placing older adults in long-term care facilities.

"What are your goals for Max?" I asked Doris.

"We want to be able to bring him back home," she said. "I don't know how that's going to work out. Everyone's telling us Max won't be safe at home."

After a thorough analysis of her financial situation, I could see that this was a very wealthy family. They would have no trouble paying for the care Max needed, for as long as he needed it. "The doctors tell us that Max could live two months or two years," Doris told me.

After visiting the family, I went to see Max. He was intubated and couldn't speak. Afterward, I met with Doris and her family. "We can arrange for care in the home if that's what you really want," I told her. "Before you make a decision, let me bring Jan, my geriatric care manager, to your home so she can complete an assessment of what it will take to bring Max back home. Then, you and the family can decide what you want to do. Remember, I want all family members to be there for the meeting."

On the day of the appointment, Jan and I pulled up to a palatial residence with a sweeping 180-degree view of the Pacific Ocean.

Jan walked through the house to determine how suitable it would be for Max. Like most homes, it was not age-friendly. There was no bedroom on the main floor. "We could make this dining room into a very livable, temporary bedroom on the ground floor," she said. Before the meeting, Jan told me privately that she had reviewed Max's medical records. It was doubtful that he would live more than a month or two. This temporary solution would likely be sufficient.

After the assessment, the family gathered to hear Jan's recommendations. All their children—five boys and two girls—were in the room, along with several grandchildren.

Jan explained the assessment process. Next, I shared my recommendations. "It's possible for Max to come back here if you convert the dining room into a temporary bedroom and hire caregivers to look after him," I said. "Hopefully, he'll get better, but if not, at least he'll be able to live at home. If I were living in this house, I would have probably made a bargain with God that I don't want to die any place other than this house."

A few people chuckled. It was a nervous laughter.

After a long pause, Doris spoke. "So, what kind of costs are we talking about?"

"Your husband is a bariatric patient," said Jan. "We will need to bring in two registered nurses and the cost will be somewhere between $15,000 and $20,000 a month."

Doris gasped.

This family was rich. How was money even an issue?

Doris looked down, shaking her head.

More silence. These aren't easy conversations to have.

The oldest son looked at me. "We need to think about this," he said.

"If you want to keep your dad at home, you know what needs to happen," I said. "If you want to place him in a nursing home, then somebody from the family needs to be there with him holding his hand. You need to be with him. He should not just be with strangers."

"Well, Rajiv is right," the oldest son said. "We will be there with Dad. He won't be alone..."

After what felt like an eternity, the son who had driven from Oregon spoke. "I totally disagree," he said. "We know that Dad wanted to come back home. Rajiv said he could make that happen. Why would we not want to do that?"

There was palpable tension in the air. It's a cliché, but you really could cut the air with a knife. Everyone was either looking down at the floor or nervously shifting around in their seat.

I let everyone marinate in the silence. I've learned to let these questions hang. Who is right? Who is wrong? There's no answer. The family has to work it out. Whatever they decide to do, I will support them.

Every single expensively clad person in that beautiful room on the coast was advocating from their own perspective. Now, take a moment to imagine Max Smith's perspective. You're lying there in the rehab center. You've told your family that you want to come home if you fall ill. That day is now here. What will your family do? They all want to do right by you. However, what's right by you may not be what they decide.

Finally, I stood up. "Why don't you think about it?" I suggested as I gathered my files. "Let me know your decision in the morning. Whatever you decide, we can make it happen. If you decide to put him in a facility, my recommendation would be to keep him in the rehab center as long as Medicare will pay for it. Any move you make will be hard on him."

The next morning came—and went. No one from the family called.

Two days later, the rehab center called to let me know that Max had died.

I was stunned.

This was a rich family, a family that would likely spare no expense to do complicated estate planning to protect their fortune from taxes, yet they were hesitating to spend a fraction of that to give Max the dignity of dying in the way he preferred.

While the family was hemming and hawing, Max died in a nursing home.

Money is no guarantee that your life won't end in an institution.

This is how families start falling apart.

In the end, living out your final days in the place you desire is not about money at all, even though everyone thinks it is. It's about having the right plan. Being able to continue to live at home even when your health fails takes a premeditated plan. We didn't have that plan for Bill, but we did by the time Vivian fell ill. Vivian did not have a lot of money, nor did Jamie and I at the time. What we did have was a plan. Everyone in the family was on board with that plan. They understood it and agreed with it.

If four-fifths of the world's population live without building nursing homes, we can do it here in the U.S.

The Problem with Not Wanting to Be a Burden

I hear many people say that they don't want to be a burden on their family as they age. Lots of people feel this way.

If a client says this to me and I have a good enough rapport with them, I will give them the unvarnished truth.

"Oh, you *will* be a burden on your kids," I will tell them. "It's just a matter of how much of a burden."

Make no mistake about it: SAYING that you don't want to be a burden, HOPING that you won't become a burden, and PRAYING that you won't become a burden means utterly nothing.

If you haven't done the right planning, the day that you fall ill will be the day you become a burden on your family. The only question is how much of a burden will you be? Anyone that you have nominated to be your agent in your Health Care Power of Attorney is now officially stuck in your life. The only question is, how well prepared will they be and how much time will they have to devote to you?

Why is that? I can show you how to come up with the money to be able to afford care at home to some extent by planning around Medicare, Medicaid, VA, and long-term care insurance to augment your own assets. I can help you create a plan to use your money to hire people to come to your home to provide care instead of sending you to a long-term care facility.

But ask yourself this: Who will be there to make sure that these people you have hired actually show up, don't take advantage of you, and don't leave you neglected? That is a role that someone will have to play. If you have children, it will likely be them.

So, if you want to stay at home, you are surely going to place some burdens on your children, but these burdens can be minimized. I can show you how your loved ones don't have to become your unpaid caregivers, but they will still have a role to play.

The Problem with Objections

During my years working with older adults, I've often heard people say that they want to age at home because living in a retirement community of some kind is unappealing. What are the most common objections?

The number one reason I hear is that living in a retirement community means being around old people, and they don't want that! Would you be surprised to learn that many of the people who have said this to me have been 85 or older? You can't make this up.

The next objection I hear from clients is that they have too much stuff in their home, and that downsizing to a smaller place is simply out of the question. When I hear that, I know that I'm probably dealing with a hoarder.

The third excuse I hear is a favorite among couples. One of the spouses believes that it is a good idea to move, but only after the other dies. As long as they are both living, they will manage things at home, they tell me. In most cases, it's the husband voicing the objection. Most men don't want to leave their homes, and many find a way not to. It's no accident that the population of most retirement communities is predominantly female.

There are as many excuses as there are people, but the real objection most likely has to do with fear of change. Any move is a change, and any change is difficult. We all have a deep affinity for our own homes, but that affinity can leave you with no other option than care in an institution when your health fails.

The Problem with Not Talking

All too often, housing issues are never discussed with family members beyond two general statements: "I want to die at home" and "I don't want to go to a nursing home." In my experience, this decision often means that people have to accept institutional care even when it might have been possible to avoid it.

Take the example of John O'Connor that I mentioned earlier in this chapter. It is my assumption that the O'Connors never actually sat down and discussed what John would have wanted when his condition got to a point where he could not independently make decisions. This likely led to the family making a decision that, given the complexity of caring for John at home and the burden it would put on Sandra Day O'Connor, it would be appropriate to move him to institutional care.

I wonder what John would have said to the question of him being moved to institutional care if he had the option to give his input when he was able to do so. It is very likely that he would have suggested to the family that it would be okay for the family to move him to an institutional care setting, which then would have been his choice.

What if he had said that he would have preferred to age at home? How would his preference have influenced the family's decision? We do know how his bout with Alzheimer's was handled. John O'Connor was diagnosed with Alzheimer's about two decades before he finally succumbed to it. Sandra Day O'Connor retired from the U.S. Supreme Court in 2006 to help her husband. Soon after the couple returned to Arizona, John O'Connor was placed in an institutional care setting, where he suffered from depression before appearing to finally accept the situation.[34] It is only conjecture, but I believe that if it were possible to have the discussion with John O'Connor about being placed in institutional care, it is quite likely that he might have expressed a preference to his family for aging at home. It is likely that only after his condition got to a point where he could not express his own feelings, or when his care needs started to negatively impact his wife, that the family decided to place him in an institutional setting.

The Problem with Waiting Too Long

Many people have it in their minds that they will move to a retirement community when their health starts to fail. This is an error in thinking. When you move as a result of your health, you are not moving to a retirement community, you are moving to an assisted living facility, a memory care unit, a nursing home, or a setting where others care for you—the very place you said you wanted to avoid. By the time you come to grips with the reality that living at home is no longer appropriate, you are usually too far gone to live in a retirement community. You are ready for the very place you were hoping to never end up: an institutional care setting. This will most likely be an assisted living facility, a nursing home, an adult family home, or a similar place where you know no one, and where the other residents are as miserable as you will be, all counting down to their sad and lonely end.

The Problem with Retirement Communities

All the problems I've discussed so far have two things in common: they involve resistance to change in some form; and they involve some level of denial about the possibility that failing health will create housing problems.

The next problem I want to address doesn't involve resistance or denial. This problem is something that happens to people who believe they're being proactive by moving into a retirement community. This problem involves the assumption that all retirement communities are the same.

Let's say you've been living in a retirement community for a decade. You develop dementia and start wandering the halls in the middle of the night. You're pounding on your neighbor's door at 2 a.m. After about the third episode (and after the neighbor reports you to management), the community asks you to leave because you have become a nuisance.

Here's another scenario. After 15 years in a retirement community, your money runs out. You figure that Medicaid will pick up the tab, and then you discover that the retirement community doesn't accept Medicaid. "You either have the cash or you move," they tell you.

In both cases, you thought you did the right thing by relocating to a retirement community, yet here you are, forced to move.

How does this happen?

The problem is in the assumptions. People assume that all retirement communities are the same. They aren't. Unless you have a written guarantee that you won't have to move—even if your health fails, and even if you run out of money—you're choosing the wrong community. The time to get this guarantee is before you move in, not when you're incapacitated or when your funds are gone. If the retirement community can't or won't give you this assurance in writing, it is the wrong retirement community for you.

Traditional Housing Planning Doesn't Exist

Ultimately, the biggest problem with the way Americans plan for housing in retirement is that we don't plan at all. The professionals we rely on to guide us—primarily doctors, financial planners, and lawyers—don't tell us we need to create a distinct plan for housing, so we don't. Even if we saw our parents or other relatives forced into institutional care after a health crisis, we remain convinced that somehow things will be different for us.

They won't.

If my work with clients over the years has taught me anything, it is that one of the biggest reasons people end up forced into institutional care after a health crisis is because they didn't know they needed to create a plan for housing that is integrated with the health, financial, legal, and family elements of their retirement plan. They didn't know it was possible.

If you are surprised after reading this chapter, I'm glad. That's my goal. We've covered issues that are almost never discussed during the retirement planning process as it's done today. You learned how a health crisis creates a housing crisis, why getting care at home is so difficult, and the problems with making housing decisions under pressure. You've learned why throwing money at your housing problem won't work, and why your pledge to not be a burden is meaningless if you don't have the right plan. You've learned why not talking about your housing preferences, voicing objections, and waiting too long to plan are almost certain to land you in an institutional setting as they create heavy burdens for your loved ones. You now know how your choice of retirement community can cause problems.

The bottom line is this: a defined process to plan for housing in a way that meets your goals for retirement (not forced into an institution, not broke, not a burden—even if your health fails) is not a part of the traditional retirement planning process. No one actively plans for housing and that's a big part of the problem.

Here's the good news! It *is* possible to create an integrated plan for housing in retirement, and in Part 2, I will show you how. For now, however, let's shift our attention to the legal industry for a look at how the traditional estate planning process contributes to retirement plan failure.

CHAPTER 4

THE PROBLEM WITH ESTATE PLANNING

Why is a Lawyer Criticizing Traditional Estate Planning?

Why is someone who creates legal documents for a living speaking out about the shortcomings of estate planning?

I formed my opinion after decades of watching people, including those with seemingly airtight estate planning documents, end up broke, a burden on their families, and forced into institutional care.

The same thing that happened to my in-laws was happening to the people who were coming to me for help. Like Bill and Vivian Wallace, my clients had done everything the legal profession told them to do to prepare for their retirement.

Yet they were still in trouble.

Why?

Law school taught me that elder law attorneys are well-equipped to answer one question:

Where will the money to pay for an older adult's long-term care come from?

This question is beyond the focus of traditional estate planning. In fact, the ability to answer this question is one thing that sets elder law attorneys apart from estate planning attorneys.

While law school taught me how to protect assets by helping an older adult qualify for VA or Medicaid benefits, it didn't answer the questions about Bill's situation that originally motivated me to go to law school. I was hoping that law school would show me how to have Bill's care costs covered at home and how to bring him out of the nursing home. I didn't learn that in law school, and that surprised me.

What I discovered is that law schools teach law. Law school taught me how to think. It taught me how to apply logic and case law to solve very specific problems for clients, and how to prepare certain types of documents. It didn't take me long to realize that while law school taught me how to think like a lawyer and create documents like a lawyer, it didn't teach me how to practice law. It didn't teach me how to apply the law within the context of my clients' lives. It didn't teach me how to look at their situations through a systematic lens, or how to assess the impact the legal solution I had crafted would have on other people in their lives.

Some attorneys are perfectly happy staying in the narrow lanes carved out by their law school training. I was not. I could see that the legal work I did for my clients was impacting the lives of their family members, and not always in a good way. For instance, the Powers of Attorney I drafted for my clients (exactly as I was taught to do in law school) often created burdens for the people identified as their agents. No one talked about this in law school, but I saw the effects in my office every day. On the contrary, in law school, they touted how a Power of Attorney helps people not become a burden on loved ones. This was not the reality I witnessed daily in my law practice.

The Problem of Incomplete Answers

Law school taught me that Medicaid is available to pay for care, even care at home in certain circumstances. I learned that older adults who have little or no money don't have much trouble qualifying for Medicaid. I learned that middle-class people can usually access Medicaid before they've spent all their resources if they know what to do. People who "know what to do" call someone like me—an elder law attorney who knows how to use legal planning techniques to help middle-class people qualify for Medicaid.

The problem is that many families don't ever find their way to an elder law attorney. The average family gets advice about Medicaid from a social worker in the nursing home or hospital setting. How much education does the average social worker have about the complex laws that govern Medicaid? The answer is very little.

Generally speaking, elder law attorneys help their clients answer one question—how to pay for care—while leaving many more questions unanswered. Questions like: Where will I go? Who will care for me? Will I become a burden? How can I live at home if that's where I want to be?

This was my question about Bill Wallace. My legal training hadn't given me a good answer. What it gave me was the skill set to qualify a client for public benefits like VA and Medicaid. My legal training did not prepare me to advise my clients on how the money from those programs would be used after the person qualified.

I was determined to find an answer. Clearly, no one I was in contact with in the legal circles seemed to be looking for this answer. I needed to find a way to make things better, and easier for all the Bills and Vivians of this world because I was seeing more and more of them in my elder law practice every day.

Bill and Vivian's situation had my brain functioning in problem-solving mode. I started thinking outside the legal box about the financial issues. I had spent about two decades in the insurance world. Might a solution be found there? Long-term care insurance was one way to address the issue, but it wasn't for everyone. And even for those who could afford it, no long-term care insurance could guarantee that they would avoid nursing home care. It was just a way to pay for the care. What if I offered a Medicaid-friendly annuity? Might that be one way to help middle-class families protect assets? What if I offered my clients both legal and financial solutions? Could that work?

I bounced the idea off attorneys in my network. Their reaction was swift—and negative. "You can't do that," one attorney told me. "That's a multidisciplinary practice of law. It's not allowed."

My questions didn't go away. They just increased.

Why weren't elder law attorneys doing more to alleviate the suffering of older adults and their families?

Why were elder law attorneys (with a few exceptions) so reluctant to address their clients' bigger problems?

Shouldn't it be our responsibility to help our clients find these answers?

Nobody seemed interested in looking at this.

The elder law attorney's job is to get people on Medicaid, but what people do with Medicaid is their business, I was told. We just assume they know what to do.

I saw that few of my colleagues had the appetite to go beyond the law to address what I knew was tremendous human suffering among their clients and their family caregivers, suffering I had witnessed in my own family.

The Problem with Traditional Estate Planning

Before I dive into what's wrong with traditional estate planning, let's look at what you get with a traditional estate plan. This is a complicated subject, so I will explain it briefly and in general terms.

A traditional estate plan consists of the following legal documents:

A Will. This document expresses your wishes as to how your property is to be distributed after your death. It also states who is to manage the property until its final distribution. If you die without a Will, there is no guarantee that your intended desires will be carried out. But if you die with a Will, chances are better that your wishes on how you want your assets distributed will be carried out, but not a guarantee. With a Will, there will be a Probate the estate will need to contend with if the assets exceed a minimum threshold.

A Trust. Trusts, like Wills, set out how your assets will be distributed upon your passing. Many people use Trusts to avoid Probate—in fact, this is the biggest reason why people choose to work with a Living Trust. Trusts are also established to provide other forms of legal protection for the Trustor's assets, to make sure those assets are distributed according to the wishes of the Trustor, and to save time, reduce paperwork and, in some cases, avoid or reduce inheritance or estate taxes. But, in the end, a Trust and Will both achieve the same goal, that is, to establish how assets are to be distributed upon the death of the owner of the assets.

A Power of Attorney. This is a legal authorization for a designated person to make decisions about another person's property, finances, or medical care. It allows the person you choose (the agent) to make decisions for you, or act on your behalf if you are unable to make decisions yourself. Note: A Power of Attorney is only valid while you are living; it has no validity once you die.

A Living Will. This document, also known as an Advance Directive, states your preferences for artificial means of life support if you are no longer able to make decisions for yourself because of illness or incapacity.

A POLST. Similar to a Living Will, the POLST (Physician Orders for Life-Sustaining Treatment) form documents your desire for extraordinary medical measures as discussed between you and your medical provider. A POLST form dictates (by way of a doctor's order) which types of care medical providers shall and shall not provide when responding to a patient's call.

Handling of Remains. This document details how you want your remains to be handled (e.g., cremation, burial, or something else) after you pass away.

If your situation warrants, you may require additional documents such as a Community Property Agreement, a Prenuptial Agreement, or others.

All of these documents are important. Everyone planning for retirement needs them.

The problem arises when we compare the goals of traditional legal documents to the goals you will have if you want a successful retirement.

Generally speaking, legal documents in an estate plan accomplish three things:

1. Define who gets what when you die (Wills & Trusts)
2. Define how you want to die (Living Wills)
3. Define who will manage your affairs when you can't manage them yourself before you die (Powers of Attorney)

I call it Die-Die-Die planning.

How does planning centered on your death help you during your life? If you don't want to...

- end up in a nursing home
- become a burden on loved ones or have your kids become your unpaid caregivers, or
- lose your assets to uncovered long-term care costs

… how will legal documents that define who gets what when you die, how you want to die, and who will manage your affairs before you die help you achieve these goals?

They won't. These are two ships passing in the night.

Traditional legal documents do little, if anything, to help you achieve these goals.

Don't get me wrong. I'm not minimizing the need for traditional planning. There's a place for Die-Die-Die planning, but it's not enough on its own.

In the rest of this chapter, I will explain the disconnect between the goals of traditional legal planning and the goals you have for your life so you can see how well-intentioned legal planning can turn your retirement into a disaster.

The Problem with Revocable Living Trusts

Clients with a net worth of $500,000 to about $2 million make up about 90 percent of my practice. When these people first call me about estate planning, they are usually looking for a way to transition assets after their death. If I do for them what I learned to do in law school, they will walk away from our work together with a Will or a Trust. Both legal tools answer this question: Who gets what from your estate when you die?

Choose a Will, and your heirs will have to go through Probate. Probate is considered to be an expensive and time-consuming process. Depending on where you live, someone will end up paying a lawyer between $2,500 to $10,000 or more to go through the process of transferring assets to your heirs. It usually takes between nine months and two years to complete the Probate process.

To spare your heirs the hassle and expense of Probate, a Revocable Living Trust will do the job. This minimizes the costs associated with transferring assets.

If you primarily have one goal—to transfer assets after your death without involving Probate—then choosing the right legal solution is a relatively simple matter.

However, if your estate is valued between $500,000 and $2 million, transferring assets after your death should not be your only goal. There is a bigger problem lurking in the shadows, whether you realize it or not: uncovered medical and long-term care expenses. If you're 65 or older, you have a 70 percent chance of having to deal with this.[35] If you are convinced that you're exempt, I have news for you: these expenses are the reason why so many Americans, even those with financial success, can and do die broke. Bill and Vivian were among this unfortunate group.

As I will discuss at length in Chapter 6, planning for your health care in retirement usually involves signing up for Medicare when you turn 65. This coverage is fine if you end up having a heart attack, a stroke, develop cancer, or come down with another acute illness. However, if you have a long-term care issue stemming from an illness, you're going to need services that Medicare doesn't cover. This includes things like having someone to cook for you, clean for you, get you out of bed, get you into the shower, and help with your medication. None of these expenses are covered in any meaningful way by Medicare.

How will you pay for these additional expenses? As you will see in Chapter 5, long-term care insurance is the funding source you will tap first. If you don't have long-term care insurance, paying out of pocket is the next option. If you don't have enough money to pay out of pocket, there's another option: Medicaid, a needs-based program available only if you meet strict income and asset requirements.

Will the Revocable Living Trust you created to avoid Probate also shelter your assets so you can qualify for Medicaid? With rare exceptions, the answer is no. Many people are surprised to learn that a Revocable Living Trust offers zero legal protection against long-term care costs.

If you have a Revocable Living Trust and you end up needing Medicaid to pay for long-term care, you will lose assets to uncovered long-term care costs because you didn't know that your legal planning should be focused on two goals, not one.

The Problem with Using Protected Assets

In 2003, not long after I started practicing law, two siblings came to me looking for help qualifying their elderly mother for Medicaid benefits to pay for nursing home care. The mother (I'll call her Eileen) was single and had an estate worth about $130,000. The son's goal was to find a way to protect some of Eileen's money, which would be gone in about two years at the rate they were paying out of pocket.

I did everything I was taught to do. We gifted money out of Eileen's name and applied for Medicaid. The children paid privately for Eileen's nursing home care until Medicaid started paying. Whatever is left at the end of the private pay period is the money you can protect. In Eileen's case, I ended up protecting about $80,000 of her estate.

I walked away feeling like a hero. Without me, all their money would have been gone. I had done right by the family. I was doing God's work.

About a year later, another person in the same nursing home sought my services for the same reasons. I went to the nursing home to meet this family, and began the process of helping them, as I had helped Eileen's family, preserve some of the hard-earned assets in their estate. As I was leaving, I remembered that Eileen was in the same facility, so I decided to stop and say hello. I retraced my steps to her room to see if she was still there.

Sure enough, Eileen was right where I had left her a year ago. Everything was the same, including her roommate. I struck up a conversation with Eileen and asked how she was. She was polite and generally very accommodating, though I don't think she remembered who I was. I asked her if she was happy. She gave a non-committal answer.

Clearly, nothing had changed in Eileen's life since the day I last saw her, even though the family had $80,000 that could have been used to improve her life. The family could have moved her to a private room. They could have hired a person to give her a shower once a day, instead of once each week as the facility did. They could have taken her out to have a meal or two from time to time.

Nothing had changed. I saw nothing that even remotely looked like an improvement in her life.

I left that encounter troubled. And then it dawned on me: It's no wonder people are critical of elder law attorneys, thinking that all we do is save Rolls-Royces and mansions. If all we do is protect money by placing additional burdens on public coffers, we deserve some of that criticism.

The reality was that yes, from an elder law perspective, I had done something good for Eileen. I helped her save $80,000 from being lost to nursing home costs. But for what? Was her quality of life any better? The answer was no, because she was still living the life of a Medicaid beneficiary in a nursing home. That $80,000 was sitting in a bank account, protected from the nursing home, yet not doing Eileen any good at all.

That's when I realized that elder law's focus on asset protection and not much more was fundamentally flawed. An elder law attorney should be protecting money to give clients on Medicaid a better life than they would have relying solely on Medicaid benefits. This means using the money saved to pay for the things that Medicaid won't cover, like a private room and caregivers to provide extras that the nursing home can't. The closest legal tool available to help preserve assets, the Special Needs Trust, did protect assets, but it was not enough.

Preserving quality of life during a long-term illness raises legal issues that can't be properly addressed unless you're focused on the right goals. If you're like many older adults whose legal planning has been focused on avoiding Probate, you may be setting yourself up for problems if you need long-term care in the future.

Let's take a look at how this can play out for married couples.

The Problem with Revocable Living Trusts

Jeb and Maria are a typical older couple. They have a house, two cars, and about $400,000 in other assets.

Jeb is diagnosed with Alzheimer's disease. Maria goes to Medicaid and says, "Rajiv told me that you can help people like me. You will help fund the care costs for my husband, either at home or in a long-term care facility."

Medicaid's response is this: "We can help you as soon as you can show us that Jeb only has $2,000 to his name."

Maria panics. She and Jeb have way more than $2,000. What should she do?

Some people in this situation will run out and start spending the money, oblivious to the fact that there are laws that protect spouses from financial ruin. Though the person who needs Medicaid, Jeb, can only have $2,000 in assets, the spouse, Maria, can have more. Many people don't know that until they consult with an elder law attorney.

Though the rules vary from state to state, Maria, who is living in Washington, is allowed to have one house of any value, one car of any value, and $60,000 in other assets. She can also have an unlimited amount of income. Once Jeb is qualified for Medicaid benefits, Maria could win the lotto and it wouldn't disqualify Jeb for Medicaid as long as he doesn't have $2,000 in assets to his name.

So, one solution is to move everything out of Jeb's name and put it in Maria's name to bring the husband's assets down to $2,000. However, that creates a problem. Together, Jeb and Maria have $400,000. The wife is allowed to have only $60,000. She has $340,000 too much. However, she can have unlimited income.

Fortunately, Maria has come to me for advice, so I take that extra $340,000 and go to an insurance company the day before I'm going to apply for Medicaid for Jeb. I tell the insurance company this: I'm going to give you $340,000 and I want you to return all this money in the form of a monthly income to Maria over the next five years. Over the next five years, Maria will get five equal payments of roughly $68,000 each. She will get her $340,000 back over the next five years, and Jeb will get Medicaid right now.

I didn't need any fancy Trusts or other legal documents to move assets out of Jeb's name and put them in Maria's name. All I needed was a Power of Attorney that authorized the agent, most likely Maria or someone else in the family, to move the money.

Now that Jeb is on Medicaid, I ask Maria to guarantee that she will not do anything as foolish as die before Jeb.

Of course, there can be no such guarantee.

Can you see where I'm going with this?

Even though it's more likely that Jeb will die before Maria, there is no guarantee. If Maria dies first, the typical estate plan says that everything the wife owns goes to the husband. Everything that we transferred to Maria's name to qualify Jeb for Medicaid ends up transferring back to Jeb. He gets the house, he gets the car, and he gets the $400,000.

Guess what? Jeb no longer has less than $2,000 to his name. He no longer qualifies for Medicaid.

For Jeb to qualify again, he will have to get back down to the $2,000 asset limit. What are his options now that he no longer has a spouse? Could he transfer that money to his children or to a Trust?

Not so fast.

Medicaid has different rules for transferring money to anyone other than a spouse. If you try to give money away to anyone but a spouse in an attempt to meet the $2,000 asset limit, Medicaid will penalize you. Thanks to Medicaid's five-year look-back period, any asset transfers you make to anyone other than your spouse during the five years preceding your Medicaid application will delay your eligibility to receive Medicaid benefits. This means that you will likely have to wait five years before Medicaid is going to cover your bills, unless you can find some other planning loophole.

Who pays for Jeb's nursing home in the meantime?

Jeb does.

Chances are good that Jeb will die broke in a nursing home, or at least lose most of his assets to uncovered care costs. A Revocable Living Trust does nothing to solve this problem.

The Problem with Living Wills

The typical Living Will form that they gave us in law school trained me to ask my clients five basic questions. If your body was shutting down on its own, but artificial means could keep you alive, would you want such measures? Do you want antibiotics? Do you want heroic measures? Do you want hydration? Do you want nutrition?

The Living Will makes clear a person's preference for medical intervention when all hope is lost.

There's just one problem.

Who decides when all hope is lost? What happens when not all family members agree on what to do?

Dissension in the family happens all the time. That's when your carefully crafted Living Will most often backfires.

Example 1: When Your Kids Can't Agree

Imagine yourself in the hospital. You're in a coma. A machine is keeping you alive. Your wife and your four adult children are standing around your bed. The doctor is there.

"I want to talk about your dad's Living Will," the doctor says. "Your dad doesn't want to be kept alive by artificial means if there's no hope of recovery. It is my professional medical opinion that your dad won't recover, so, based on your father's direction in his Living Will, it's time for you to make a decision about continuing life support."

This is the dreaded "pull the plug" conversation.

Your kids are standing there taking this all in.

Your oldest child looks at his siblings. "I think I agree with the doctor," he begins.

Your youngest interrupts. "I'm not sure," she says. "Why don't we give them another three or four days to see if anything changes? Maybe we should get a second opinion. I think we are being a bit too hasty. This is such a drastic decision. Once we pull the plug, there's no going back."

Will your Living Will break the stalemate? In a word, no. The typical Living Will gives absolutely no guidance about what to do if the family can't agree.

Example 2: Terri Schiavo

At its heart, the Terri Schiavo case was a family squabble that made international headlines.

Schiavo had been kept alive by a feeding tube after collapsing in 1990 from full cardiac arrest following an auto accident. Multiple doctors diagnosed her as being in a persistent vegetative state. Terri Schiavo was not in a coma, yet she could not eat or speak. Her eyes were open, and she would turn her head toward certain sounds.

She had no written Living Will when she collapsed. Michael Schiavo contended his wife once told him she would not want to be kept alive artificially with no hope of recovery. Court after court affirmed his right to let his wife die. Her parents disagreed and fought to keep her alive.

Because her wishes were unclear, Ms. Schiavo was kept alive for 15 additional years despite formidable legal attempts by her husband to allow her to die a natural death.

Example 3: When There's No Family

Mrs. Gray, an 83-year-old woman who lives alone, is brought to the emergency room by her neighbor. Mrs. Gray has been experiencing chest pains. She tells the ER physician that her heart stopped a couple of months ago while she was in the emergency room. She was revived and placed on a breathing machine for two weeks.

"I never want to go through that again," Mrs. Gray says adamantly. "If something happens to me while I'm in the emergency room, I don't want to be sent to a nursing home. I want to be allowed to die."

Mrs. Gray's paperwork for her Advance Directive is not in the emergency room, and her physician cannot be reached. She has no family. If Mrs. Gray suffers a cardiac arrest in the ER, is the ER physician required to comply with her stated wishes even though there are no written instructions?

The answer is yes, but it's not quite as simple as that because the ER doctor has to make a determination that she's mentally capable of making such a decision at the time.

That's one reason you shouldn't leave your wishes in the form of a verbal discussion with your doctor. If the doctor determines you don't have the mental capacity to make a decision, he or she is free to do whatever they think is in your best interest.

Even if you have a Living Will, the unfortunate reality is that doctors and other medical staff don't make checking the file their first priority before committing to an action. To complicate matters, Americans exacerbate the issue by believing that dying is somehow losing, that allowing someone to die is to not love them as much as someone who would have done everything in their power to make sure they didn't die. That failure extends even to health professionals.

Ultimately, a Living Will the way it is traditionally written doesn't guarantee that your family won't fight over what to do with you, or that your wishes will always be honored, even when the doctors agree that nothing more can be done for you. The good news is that adding the right language to your Living Will makes it possible to minimize and even eliminate these problems, shifting the power away from doctors and the courts to the family members you love and trust. I'll talk about how to do this in Chapter 12.

The Problem with Subsequent Relationships

When a person dies, leaving your assets to the spouse is what everyone expects to happen. It's the best way to provide for your loved one after you're gone. The assumption is that any assets remaining after your spouse dies will be distributed to heirs in the way that you and your spouse originally intended.

Is that assumption valid?

Let's say you die. What happens to your surviving spouse? Most people don't like to think about it, but surviving spouses, regardless of gender, are vulnerable to the advances of opportunistic people who want access to the surviving spouse's money.

This may seem like an overused movie plotline, but it happens every day. The need for human companionship doesn't go away.

I think about this myself. What are the chances that my wife, Jamie, might meet somebody else after I die? It all starts innocently enough. A caring neighbor drops by the house with a pie and says, "I'm so sorry for your loss. I'm here for you." The next week, he comes over with a bottle of wine. A month later it's a bottle of wine and a seven-course meal, and then the month after that, he's moving in.

Would I be thrilled about that? Probably not. Do I want my money to be there only for Jamie and our three children? Or am I okay with Jamie being able to run off with some other guy, changing her Will and leaving our three children out in the cold?

I've seen this happen to my clients more times than I can count. Many of my widowed clients will make an appointment to see me a few years after their spouse has died. Many of them have a new paramour in tow, and they are flush with the glow of love.

"I want to write my new Will," my client will say, looking adoringly at his new partner. "I want to make sure that [fill in the blank] is taken care of."

As a lawyer, I have an obligation to help this client with what he wants to do, even if I have concerns about the estate planning implications for the children from their previous marriage.

The happy couple smiles at me as they wait for my response. Depending on the degree of the public display of affection, my mind will start to wander.

What if your late wife could see you here in my office? Would you still be all lovey-dovey with this new person?

What if your late wife could hear you telling me that you want to make provisions for this new person and her family, a move that will impact the three children you had with her?

What would your late wife say if she knew that her share of the family assets—money that is now in your control—is going to be used to support another woman and her children, possibly shortchanging the children you had together in the process?

In law school, we talk about these situations conceptually in family law classes. We are taught that the solution to this issue is a Prenuptial Agreement.

These are great in theory, but they are awkward in practice.

There's nothing like a Prenup to kill the romance. Just imagine the conversation. "Honey, I love you and I want to marry you. Will you sign here first?"

Most people can't pull it off. Plus, Prenuptial Agreements only protect assets from a subsequent divorce.

This situation can happen in any family. The widow or widower's need for companionship is the root cause of this issue. The problem arises when this need for companionship is filled by a person who may take advantage of the surviving spouse when they are at their most vulnerable. The predator could pressure your spouse into listing them as the beneficiary or heir. They could remove other heirs, gain access to assets, and deplete funds that were intended for your spouse's needs.

One client, a man whose wife had died a few years earlier, remarried and his new wife took control of everything. The first wife and the husband's children were removed as heirs. Everything went to the new wife and her kids.

The problem with traditional estate planning documents is that they don't consider issues like these. They don't provide any legal protections. Given the reality of American society, they should.

When my grandmother passed away in India, my grandfather always had somebody he could talk to because there were at least a dozen people living under the same roof. Grandpa never lacked meaningful human companionship.

Jamie and I used to load up the kids in the car and drive to Spokane to spend the weekend with Vivian when she was dealing with Bill in the nursing home. On Sunday afternoon, she would come outside to see us off. She would stand in the driveway waving at us as we drove away. I remember watching her in the rearview mirror, a lone figure growing smaller and smaller by the second. Who would be there with her until we visited again? How would she cope? (Fortunately, her daughter, Jan, was close by, which made things better.)

This would never happen in India, I remember thinking. Vivian would never be living alone. She would be living with other family members. Thanks to that built-in companionship, she would never be alone.

Too many older adults end up alone after a spouse dies, leaving them vulnerable in ways we don't want to think about. It happened to a man named Dave. He and his wife, Matilda, had been married for 55 years. When Matilda was diagnosed with a rare form of cancer, Dave prayed for a miracle as he cared for her. That miracle never came. Within three months, Matilda was dead.

The funeral was a haze. Dave's four children and their families flew in from around the country to be there for him, but they couldn't stay long. After a week, they had all returned to their lives.

For Dave, there was no going back. There was nothing to go back to. Matilda had been his anchor, and now that she was gone, he was completely unmoored by grief.

The evenings were the worst. Before Matilda got sick, they would eat dinner, wash the dishes, and then enjoy a cup of tea on their spacious front porch. Rocking gently to and fro on the swing, they would discuss the events of the day. Desperate to preserve some connection to Matilda, Dave continued the evening ritual, but the nights were filled with a deafening silence that seemed to grow louder by the day.

A few months after Matilda's funeral, Dave was sitting on the front porch one evening when his neighbor, Fern, came up the sidewalk. Dave hadn't seen much of her since her husband had died a few years earlier, but now, here she was, on his front doorstep—with a peach pie in hand.

"Dave, I just wanted to check in and see how you're doing," Fern said. "I thought this might help a little." She handed him the pie.

Fern's attention was like a warm breeze that blew away the clouds of grief, if only for a moment.

"There are good days and there are bad days, but I'm doing okay," Dave said. Funny how he had never noticed Fern's beautiful smile before.

"Well, I just want you to know that if you ever need someone to listen, I'm here for you," she said. "I've been where you are, and I know how hard it can be."

Dave smiled and thanked her for her generosity. As he watched her walk away, he felt alive in a way he hadn't in a long time.

About a week later, Fern showed up at the porch again, this time with a bottle of wine and two glasses. "I was gifted this lovely bottle of Malbec and it just didn't feel right drinking it alone," she said. "Care to join me?"

Fern's attention was an intoxicant, and she gave it willingly. Wine on the front porch became dinner at her house, one night a week, then two, then three. Dave felt like himself again—only better.

After a few months of this whirlwind courtship, their conversations turned to the topic of a possible future together. Dave could see himself building a new life with Fern. He could see himself traveling with her, living with her, and loving her. He could see himself as a part of her everyday life, opening those stubborn jar lids that she couldn't, fixing her leaky faucets, and taking her car in for service.

But there was a whole lot more that Dave couldn't see. There was a whole lot more he didn't know.

What Dave didn't know was that Fern was broke. She didn't own her house. She was renting. Dave didn't know that she had blown her husband's life insurance payout on slot machines in Las Vegas. Dave couldn't see that she was deep in debt. Dave had no way of knowing that Fern was a drowning person in search of a financial life preserver, and that life preserver was him.

When Dave's kids got wind of the romance, they were concerned. "Dad, don't you think it's a little too soon?" his oldest daughter asked.

The words stung. How could his daughter be so callous? When Dave told Fern about his daughter's comments, Fern looked concerned. "She obviously doesn't care about your happiness, and neither do your other kids," Fern said.

Dave started spending even more time with Fern, while his contact with his children dwindled from once a month or so to almost never. Eventually, Dave and Fern got married. When Fern suggested that he rewrite his Will to leave everything to her and her children, Dave didn't flinch. When Fern suggested that he sell some of his rental properties and put the cash in Trust for her kids, Dave did it gladly.

When Dave's health problems began, his children discovered an awful truth. Fern had taken everything. By the time Dave needed long-term care, there was no money left to pay for it, and Fern was gone.

This sad story isn't an exception. It's the rule, and it plays out in a thousand different ways. When you need human companionship, but are left alone, it creates a vacuum that predators and bad actors are happy to fill.

What protection do your traditional estate planning documents give your widowed spouse from these bad actors?

Absolutely none.

The good news is that there is a way to protect yourself. I'll show you how in Chapter 12.

The Problem with the Power of Attorney

Many of the people who have been most interested in my approach to retirement planning are those who have had their lives turned upside down by elder care responsibilities, or they have seen the life of a loved one or friend turned upside down. They're interested because they get it. Maybe their parents didn't have a plan for old age. Maybe their parents had a plan but didn't share it with anyone. Maybe the failing health of their parents created a crisis for everyone else.

"I don't want to do this to my kids." I've heard these words from thousands of clients.

"I don't want to be a burden," they say.

In my opinion, that's the biggest lie you will ever tell your family.

When you get sick, someone's going to have to arrange for your bills to be paid, file your taxes, manage your money, take care of the dog, and call the plumber when the sink in one of your rental properties starts leaking.

The lawyer's answer is to prepare a Power of Attorney.

The Power of Attorney, which empowers your fiduciaries with legal authority to act on your behalf, doesn't relieve these burdens. In fact, it does the exact opposite. It practically guarantees that you will NOT be a burden to anyone OTHER than the person you choose to act as your agent. On the day that you fall ill, you will have saved the entire world from being burdened by your needs, except for the person whose name appears on that legal document.

This expectation that a Power of Attorney will relieve the burdens involved in looking after elderly loved ones is baked into American culture. Yet, every day I find myself sitting across the conference room table from the exhausted family members of my elderly clients. These family members were shouldering the very burdens that the Power of Attorney is supposed to prevent.

By now, you know that when I encounter a problem like this, I can't just let it be. So, when I encountered problems with the Power of Attorney, I had to investigate. It was like an elephant in the room, and I had to point it out. I had to ask the question that none of my fellow attorneys were asking:

How can legal work prevent anyone from being a burden?

The Problem with Assuming "They'll Figure It Out"

How will your agents know how to use the authority your legal documents give them?

"They'll figure it out," is the answer you're likely to hear if you pose this question to an attorney.

What does "figure it out" mean? What, exactly, needs to be figured out?

I'll answer that question in a moment. For now, know this: the process of "figuring things out" creates a burden for whoever is unlucky enough to be named as the agent on a Power of Attorney.

This is estate planning's dirty little secret.

Lawyers are trained to think that the Power of Attorney is "the" magic document that will whisk burdens away.

Not true.

A Power of Attorney, the way lawyers write it today, does two things: it grants authority, and it assigns responsibility. A Power of Attorney offers absolutely no direction about what you want your agent to do with the authority and responsibility the piece of paper grants them.

When an elderly relative counts on you to "figure it out," how does that look in real life?

Take a moment to insert yourself into the following scenario.

A few years ago, your elderly father downloaded a Power of Attorney form from the internet, filled it out, and named you as his agent. "I want to do the responsible thing," he told you at the time. "I don't want to be a burden."

Now, when you visit your father, you're finding stacks of unpaid bills. He's not taking his medication. He has become lost while driving. He was bilked in a tech scam. You worry about him constantly.

Finally, he is diagnosed with dementia. A friend suggests that you see an elder law attorney. Maybe Medicaid can help you protect his money from the nursing home, the friend says.

During your visit, the elder law attorney asks about the Power of Attorney. You give the document to him. The elder law attorney looks it over and confirms its validity. Your father's Power of Attorney gives you, the agent, the authority to manage your father's financial situation.

What exactly are you being asked to do?

It's not a short list of tasks. You now have the responsibility to pay your dad's bills, manage his investments, clean his house, figure out what to do with the three dogs, coordinate home repairs, sell the house, and figure out what to do with all the stuff your father had amassed over the years (a dumpster or two may be involved). And then there's the matter of his rental properties.

It's up to you to pick up the pieces in this high-stakes game. Take your father's tax return, for instance. How difficult was it for your father to do his taxes when he had his faculties? He knew where all his income was coming from. He knew where all the receipts were. He had a professional complete the tax return.

Where do you start?

You start by scrambling. You rifle through file cabinets and drawers. You try to log on to your dad's laptop, but you don't have his password. You try to find out who did his taxes. Trying to piece together another person's financial life is no easy task.

You spend every spare moment trying to sort this out. When you're not at work, you're working on Project Daddy. You're searching. You're waiting. You're holding your breath, hoping you find what you need.

At the same time, you're trying to figure out where Dad will live. The social worker at the hospital is pressuring you to put him into a nursing home. "He will be safest there," the social worker says.

Dad has other ideas. He doesn't want to go to a nursing home, and he screams at you every time you see him.

You and your father didn't talk about exactly how you would handle things for him.

And he said he didn't want to be a burden.

The lived experience of my clients was proof that legal documents don't eliminate burdens.

When you have a Power of Attorney written the standard way, you will be a burden. With the right changes to your Power of Attorney, you can minimize the burdens you place on your agents. I'll talk more about this in Chapter 12.

The Problem with Undefined Responsibility

When it comes to the assignment of elder care burdens, I can't help but compare the way things are done in America with the way they're handled in India.

Where I'm from, there's no question about who will assume the burden of an aging relative's care. It will be the oldest son. As my parents grew older, there was never any question that Jayant, my older brother, would be the one to make sure they had a place to live and that they were well cared for. In exchange, Jayant would be receiving the family home. In India, the responsibility is clearly defined. Everyone knows who will do what. There's compensation built in. While it's not a perfect system, it is, in my opinion, a better system than the one we have here in the U.S.

In America, we have rules. We have laws. We have lawyers. We have planning. We will do anything to avoid talking about the realities of aging. We have parents making declarations about not wanting to be a burden. We have the expectation that a legal document will remove the burdens for our family. Yet you are sentencing your agents to burdens they didn't expect when they have to "figure it out" because you didn't talk to them about your plans or preferences.

The Problem with Legal Documents

Lawyers have been drafting Powers of Attorney in one form or another for more than a century.

Why did it take a guy from India to see the inadequacy of these documents?

As I mentioned earlier in this section, I blame it on the legal education system, whose job it is to teach lawyers to understand the law—*not* how to practice it. This leaves lawyers in the uncharted territory of having to figure out how to practice law. Over millennia, certain practices have emerged, which have been embraced as the right way to practice law. Unfortunately, these practices are more legal industry-centric than they are consumer-centric.

Law school teaches that the best way to help those dealing with aging, long-term illness, disability, and frailty issues is to create legal documents. However, these legal documents can't answer questions that haven't been asked. So much is missed.

Even within the community of the National Academy of Elder Law Attorneys, where I've lectured on this topic dozens of times, little has changed. Very few attorneys are customizing Powers of Attorney to meet their clients' needs.

Imagine what would happen if attorneys said, "Let's look at when this document is going to be used and what decisions your agent will have to make. Does our document provide guidance on how to use the power the document bestows to the agent so they can make the right decisions that are in keeping with the principal's wishes? If not, how can we make the documents do just that, empower and guide the agent, not just empower them?"

Instead, lawyers focus on cranking out documents, convinced that their only job is to produce the standard Power of Attorney language, or to follow a process that has been codified in law, regardless of whether that process meets the known objectives of the client. What makes matters worse is that the estate planning area of law is just as adversarial in its approach as litigation or family law. Instead of making the resolution of family disagreements a collaborative process, the system invites litigation when family members disagree. On top of that, attorneys substitute their own judgments when advocating for a position, without really knowing what the client would have wanted because the attorney never got to know the client directly. This leads to disastrous results that are sometimes showcased in the media. Casey Kasem, Tim Conway, Mickey Rooney, Brooke Astor, and Britney Spears are just a few of the many recent examples.

Attorneys generally believe it's the family's responsibility to figure out what to do with the authority a Power of Attorney gives them. What makes this so tragic is that the family is counting on the attorney for guidance, which is mostly lacking. The older adult who has the Power of Attorney expects that this document will relieve burdens, when often the exact opposite result is achieved. The client looking to the attorney for guidance does what the attorney suggests, without realizing that they are sentencing their agent to hours upon hours of worry, aggravation, and hardship.

Everyone thinks they know what a Power of Attorney should do, yet I've had people come to me and say, "I don't need you to create my Health Care Power of Attorney. I already have one."

And then I find out that the document lacks any meaningful guidance for their agents to follow because it was prepared by an estate planning attorney, or it's one they got at their hospital or their church—a form that they simply fill out.

They don't realize that the document from the hospital or church may not give them the types of authority they'll need most, such as the authority to fire their doctor, the authority for their agent to get them released from the hospital against medical advice, the authority to gift assets, and more. These documents are incomplete at best, and if obtained from the medical community (hospital), they are likely designed more to protect the institution, not the person signing the document.

If you have goals for your future, such as not going broke, not being a burden to your family, or never living in a nursing home, you probably won't achieve them by relying on boilerplate documents provided by the estate planning industry or health care institutions. You may not even get them from your average elder law attorney, which makes selecting the attorney you work with such a challenge. Let me explain what I mean.

The Problem with Templates

You don't go to an attorney to pay for forms; you go to get advice that cannot be obtained online or from forms.

Yet, when you see an attorney, forms are often what you get. You go to a lawyer's office to get your legal affairs in order, and the lawyer does nothing more than have a paralegal add your name to templates.

Instead of paying your lawyer to simply customize boilerplate forms for you, you deserve something better. You should be paying for your lawyer to talk to you about things you may not be thinking about, especially things that may be impacted by your unique situation. You need your lawyer to teach you what you need to know so you can achieve your most important goals: not going broke, not becoming a burden, and not being forced into a facility.

Sadly, this doesn't happen. Even worse, we don't seem to mind. As a society, we have become quite comfortable with forms masquerading as peace of mind.

It's absolutely astounding to me how callously Powers of Attorney are often prepared. Very little thought is given to the structure of the document.

The typical Power of Attorney document reads like this:

"I, [fill in your name], nominate my [relationship], [name], followed by my [relationship], [name], to be my agents." And then there are a few pages of boilerplate powers that are added to the document. Occasionally, there may be a few variations made to the document, but not too often.

According to the traditional estate planning industry, you are done. You've planned for your incapacity. You have a Power of Attorney.

How does this play out in real life? Suspend your own reality for a moment as you insert yourself in the following story.

Your name is Donald. You're 85 years old, and you've been living on your own since your wife died five years ago. You have an adult son—we'll call him John—who lives with his family in the same city as you. You named John as your agent in your Power of Attorney documents, and he checks on you periodically, even though you tell him there's no need. When you look in the mirror every morning, you don't see an old person; you see a strong, healthy, and good-looking man who will be able to live independently for a long time to come. Old age, with its health problems and frailties, hasn't yet arrived for you.

When summer comes and you fall three times within the space of a few weeks, you're not concerned. As you see it, every tumble has a plausible explanation. An area rug was out of place. You reached for your cell phone and lost your balance. You slipped on wet concrete as you were washing your car. Each fall resulted in a trip to the emergency room, but you downplay the situation. As you see it, these falls are just coincidence, and have nothing to do with your age.

What you soon discover is that John doesn't share your opinion. His concern becomes apparent one day when he says he wants to come over to talk.

When John arrives, the expression on his face is a mixture of serious and uncomfortable as he joins you at the kitchen table.

"Dad, I don't know how to tell you this, but I don't think it's safe for you to keep living here," he says. "You've been in the emergency room three times in the past two weeks. I'm concerned. Maybe you should consider moving to the new assisted living center here in town. Have you ever thought about it?"

You chuckle. "I've thought about it," you reply. "I don't need it yet. Maybe next year."

This is your son, the person you named as your agent in your Power of Attorney. This is the person you chose to manage your affairs when you can no longer do so. This is the person you're trusting to "figure it out" when the time comes.

Well, your agent thinks the time has come. You don't.

To you, your falls were the result of simple clumsiness, not incapacity. Your agent sees your falls as evidence that you are unsafe at home and need to be protected.

This fundamental difference of opinion plays out day after day in millions of families in America. The older adult thinks things are just fine. The kids believe they have evidence that things aren't fine. This moment will arrive for most people, yet this topic is almost never discussed in a serious way, and the typical Power of Attorney document doesn't envision what will happen when this moment arrives.

What happens now?

You won't like it.

Here's how it usually unfolds:

Without telling you, John uses the authority you gave him through the Power of Attorney to go see your doctor.

"Doc, my dad has fallen three times in the last month, and he thinks everything is fine," John tells your doctor. "He won't listen to me. I don't know what to do."

Your doctor will listen to John's concerns and then suggest that he bring you in for an appointment.

By the way, most doctors will want nothing to do with these conversations. There is no reimbursement code to compensate an overworked primary care physician for an appointment with a concerned child of an elderly person. However, because you've been a patient for years, your doctor will agree to John's request.

When John tells you that he has made an appointment for you to see your doctor, you're enraged, but you agree to go.

At the appointment, the doctor asks you what's going on. "There is nothing wrong with me," you say. "So I fell a few times. Everyone does."

"Well, I have to disagree with you there," your doctor says, his face grim. "Falling isn't a normal part of aging. From the sound of it, you aren't able to live safely at home."

Then comes the kicker: "I'm a mandatory reporter, which means I have a duty to keep you safe or report this issue to Adult Protective Services," says the doctor. "Certainly, you don't want to be put out of your home against your wishes?"

His words land like a thud. You don't want to be forced to move, yet the thought of a state employee coming into your home to check on you is humiliating. That's not what you want.

John is standing near the door looking uneasy. His discomfort doesn't blunt your anger. "Well, son, it looks like you got your way. Looks like

I'll be leaving the home that I love and moving into that assisted living place. I hope you're happy."

This scenario happens all the time because no one plans for it, and the typical Power of Attorney doesn't address it. No one wins.

My question is this: If you had less than six months to live and qualified for hospice, when your child approached the doctor, the doctor's first response would be to call hospice and have them put together a plan to keep you safe at home. Why is that not being asked in every single situation where an older adult is having difficulty living independently at home?

Why is your Power of Attorney not telling your agent exactly what actions to take when this situation arises?

Wouldn't it be better if your Power of Attorney directed your agent to do more than just figure "it" out? What if your Power of Attorney helped your agent figure out a way for you to avoid institutional care? It can—and I'll show you how in Chapter 12.

The Problem with Losing Your Marbles

Let me give you another example of a provision that, in my opinion, should always exist as a stand-alone document in an estate plan, but almost never does. It's called a Mental Health Advance Directive.

To illustrate how this works, let's look at the case of Roger and Margaret, both in their 70s.

Roger spent many decades as an accountant. After he retired, he met with his buddies every morning for breakfast.

One morning after breakfast, he came home and informed Margaret about something he had just done. "Honey, I did something for the people at that breakfast place," he announced with a satisfied smile. "I bought all 28 of them watches for Christmas."

Margaret scowled. "You've never bought me a rose, you louse. What are you doing buying these people watches?" she says to herself.

But she lets it go, not wanting to pick a fight.

Next thing you know, every magazine printed in America starts appearing in the mailbox. Every person who approaches Roger on the street for a donation walks away with $5, $10, $20, or even $100.

One day, Margaret finds her husband hunched over the kitchen table. He's scribbling out a check.

"Who's the check for?" Margaret asks.

"The Nigerian king," Roger says matter-of-factly. "He is my cousin and I have an inheritance coming from there which I need to collect. I need to send $25,000 to cover taxes and other costs so they can release the millions that are rightfully mine."

Margaret has never heard her husband mention having cousins in Nigeria.

Now, imagine you're Margaret. How do you deal with this?

Do you take away the checkbook? Won't your enterprising but mentally compromised husband just march to the bank and get a money order? Taking away the checkbook is only a temporary fix.

If you're Margaret and you're named as the agent on Roger's Power of Attorney, would that give you the authority you need? The answer is no. A Power of Attorney gives you the ability to advocate on Roger's behalf so long as it doesn't go against his wishes. It does not give you the right to take away his rights or minimize his ability to act on his own behalf. When a person has mental health issues, as Roger clearly does, that involves taking away rights, which a Power of Attorney can't do. A Power of Attorney without a Mental Health Advance Directive provision is useless.

The only answer, in your case, is a guardianship process, which isn't fun for anyone. This process involves going to a court and saying: "Judge, someone has hijacked my husband's body, that's not my husband. You've got to take away his ability to write checks. He's squandering our retirement nest egg."

The judge will appoint an independent Guardian ad Litem to investigate the situation. This person will then give the court a report on the situation so the judge can make a decision. In the meantime, the judge says, "I want you to inform your husband about your concerns, and that needs to be in writing."

No matter how carefully you or your lawyer write the letter to avoid offending your husband, here's what your husband is going to read:

"Your wife thinks you're crazy. What do you think?"

Instantly, you're ready to battle. The cousin of a Nigerian king surely has enough wherewithal to know the gravity of his own situation!

On the day of the hearing, your husband is on his best behavior. He takes a shower, shaves, and puts on his best suit. Mind you, he has not taken a shower for the previous two weeks, despite your complaints about the odor in the house. You can see through his scam, but to the outside world, no one will know what has been going on.

Later that day, your husband stands in front of the judge. "I'm not the one who is crazy," your husband proclaims. "It's that old bat you need to put away. She's after my money. She is the one who is crazy."

Who will the judge believe? Typically, the judge will split the differ-ence, and your family will be at odds by the time it is all over. And before the judge issues an order, he or she will require you to undergo a mental health evaluation or look for confirmation from the appointed Guardian ad Litem that you have truly lost your marbles. No Guard-ian ad Litem will want to say that you do not have capacity without a psychiatric evaluation or confirmation from your medical providers, which means that there is yet more time that needs to be spent before this sordid affair can come to a conclusion.

Had Roger's planning included a Mental Health Advance Directive, much of this needless drama could have been avoided. A Mental Health Advance Directive gives an agent the authority to request a psychiatric evaluation at the first sign of mental health problems. This can often eliminate the need for a guardianship, and if a guardianship is still needed, it can be obtained much faster because the psychiatric evaluation is already complete. Without the report, or verification of Roger's incapacity from the appointed Guardian ad Litem, who will be hesitant to give a report without a psychiatric order, the court will not issue an order. I hope you get the point.

So, what's the problem? Traditional legal planning sees the scenario I shared as a legal issue, not a mental health issue. That's why you were sent to a judge. And few, if any, see it as a planning issue. With proper planning, however, most of the drama can be avoided, and much bet-ter results can be realized.

Most people have no idea that a Health Care Power of Attorney doesn't allow you to advocate for anything that might take away another per-son's rights.

People don't go from sane to insane overnight. It's a gradual process. One day you're fine; the next day you're a little less fine. Eventually, things you never dreamed of doing start sounding reasonable. You subscribe to magazines you never read. You start giving money to neighbors, strangers, televangelists, or anyone who asks for it. You become gullible, believing any story people tell you. One person I know, a man named Jed, encountered a homeless man on the street. "I'm a carpenter who specializes in home renovations," the homeless man told him. Two days later, the homeless man was living with Jed.

These are not normal behaviors.

But that's not the worst of it. Imagine one day your phone rings and it's your 90-year-old mother. She is angry.

"What's going on, Mom?" you ask.

"You won't believe it," she screams. "I had a small fender bender. It was nothing. Just a little scratch, but the cop took away my driver's license and said that I can only get it back if I go take a driver's test. This is wrong! This isn't supposed to happen in America, the land of the free! I've been driving longer than that cop has been alive. He should go..."

"Calm down, Mom, please," you say. "Don't worry about it. You'll go take the exam and you'll pass it. You've been driving your whole life. It will be a piece of cake."

Your mom waits two weeks, then you take her to the DMV for her driver's exam. She takes it—and fails.

She is told that she must wait a week to retake the exam.[36] She is livid. "This is bull!" she screams, pacing the floor like a caged animal. Her wings have been clipped, and she's not happy about it.

The next morning, without telling you, she walks next door and asks her neighbor to take her to the bank. Unaware of the situation, the neighbor happily agrees. At the bank, your mother withdraws $60,000, then walks next door to the car lot and buys a vehicle that she can't legally drive.

If you're the named agent, what do you do?

Your only answer is a guardianship. You have to go to a court and ask them to take away her rights, so she doesn't spend her way to broke oblivion. If you go this route, the court will take six to nine months to make a decision. Before they give you an order, the judge will tell you to take your mother for a psychiatric evaluation because he or she can't take away your mom's rights without knowing the psychological, pathological, or medical reasons why.

Nine months into the guardianship process and many thousands of dollars later, you are now despised by your mother for calling her sanity into question, and you're hating your mother for turning your life upside down. It is at this point that you will be given the order to take her in for a psychiatric evaluation. How cooperative do you think your mom will be?

She won't be cooperative at all. In fact, you will have to tell her a white lie to get her into the car. As you turn into the hospital parking lot, when she sees the hospital sign, you'll need to brace yourself for the abuse to come.

"You're not taking me to the loony bin," she screams, pummeling you with her handbag. "You just want my money! You just want me dead!"

Everything is infinitely more difficult when you're being beaten by a 90-year-old with a handbag on the way to the psychiatric hospital.

If you have a Mental Health Advance Directive, you—and your family members and fiduciaries—can bypass all this drama.

I'll talk more about Mental Health Advance Directives in Chapter 12.

Traditional Legal Planning Doesn't Go Far Enough

Every problem I've discussed in this chapter contributes to the epidemic of retirement plan failure in our nation. You're forced into a nursing home when you would rather live at home. You go broke paying for long-term care because the legal document that helped your heirs avoid Probate did nothing to protect your assets from long-term care costs. You end up burdening your family despite your investment in legal documents that promised to relieve those burdens—and then didn't. You leave your spouse vulnerable to the machinations of predators after you die. Your Living Will is silent on the subject of family disputes. You create massive headaches for your family as you insist you are fine, denying the obvious (to them) signs of decline.

I became a lawyer so I could understand these problems in our nation's legal system that landed my father-in-law, Bill Wallace, in a nursing home despite my family's desire to care for him at home. I became a lawyer in hopes of solving these problems from inside the legal system so I could help others avoid Bill's fate. What I didn't expect to find was this complete mismatch of goals—how Die-Die-Die legal planning does so little to help you reach your goals of not ending up in a facility, not going broke, and not being a burden.

Despite these realizations, as I worked with clients, I came to clearly understand that the cause of retirement plan failure wasn't just limited to the problems of legal documents. There was something more. Could a flaw in the way Americans were being advised to plan for their financial lives in retirement be making things worse? I had to find out, so that's what I investigated next.

CHAPTER 5

THE PROBLEM WITH FINANCIAL PLANNING

Why Is a Lawyer Talking about Financial Planning?

When you think of the term "retirement planning," what comes to mind?

For most Americans, financial planning is what comes to mind.

In America, retirement planning is synonymous with financial planning.

Don't believe me? Google the term "retirement planning" and see what comes up.

When I Googled the term recently, I got 594 million hits. Though I only looked at the first few pages, nearly every website in the search results was about how to invest and manage money, or how to invest in financial or insurance products.

I would even go as far as to say that the financial planning industry has hijacked the term "retirement planning." Thanks to clever and persistent marketing, nearly all Americans think that retirement planning is exclusively about saving and investing money for the future.

That's how the experts define it, too. Let's look at a few examples:

- Motley Fool: Retirement planning is a broad term that refers to learning about and choosing financial strategies that will enable you to be comfortable and secure in your retirement years. A good retirement plan, executed smartly, can provide you with enough money to cover all of your later-year living expenses.[37]
- Investopedia: Retirement planning refers to financial strategies of saving, investments, and ultimately distributing money meant to sustain oneself during retirement.[38]
- Merriam-Webster Dictionary: Retirement planning is a system for saving money for use during retirement.[39]

If retirement planning and financial planning are synonyms, what does the term "financial planning" really mean?

Financial planning, the way it's done today, answers three primary questions:

- Where is your money invested?
- How much risk can you tolerate?
- How are your assets allocated?

With this focus, financial planning *is* investment planning. It's all about buying the right products and getting the right rate of return on your investments.

Everything revolves around wealth. The financial planning industry's solution to helping you plan for retirement revolves around helping you accumulate wealth and buying products. That's how they make their money, and they do that without asking what I believe is the most important question of all:

What assurance do you have that on the day you fall ill, your children and your named agents will know what to do with your money or your products (e.g., a long-term care insurance policy) so your life turns out the way you want it to, not the way a hospital discharge planner thinks it should?

This question is never even asked, and this has led to a national epidemic of retirement plan failure.

In the end, what is clear to me is that it's not the size of your financial portfolio that matters most. What is even more important is the plan you've made in advance to use that money after you fall ill. You do that by having a plan that includes a very clear definition of what you will want your agents and your family to do when the time comes.

The problem is that most people don't do this in advance. They don't know they can, they don't know they should, and they don't know how. It's the black hole of financial planning.

There's a simple solution, however, and I'll teach you how to implement it in Chapter 11.

The Problem with Money

Money isn't the complete solution that so many people think it is.

The retirement planning industry is selling a dream. If you save enough money and do everything right, your retirement can be like what you see on the pages of glossy brochures selling investment products. You can travel the world, bike in Tuscany, paraglide in Antarctica, and take your grandkids on a safari.

Retirement is *your time*, the brochures say.

There's no doubt about it that money can fund your retirement dreams, no matter how big or small they are.

You may live your retirement dream for a while—maybe even a long while—but those years of adventure won't last forever. If you stay healthy, living your dreams is easy. The problems start when your health fails, and you are no longer able to live independently. That's when the retirement nightmare begins. Recall Susie?

If you think you'll be one of the lucky ones to die in your sleep, let me remind you that you're probably going to get sick first. In fact, 70 percent of people over 65 will need long-term care at some point in their lives.[40]

No one likes to think about this. And just about no one effectively plans around it.

Don't depend on money alone to give you the kind of retirement you hope for after your health fails. Money is just one of many factors in the retirement planning equation. Other factors, such as health, housing, legal, and family issues, are equally important, especially when you're sick—yet the traditional finance-centric approach doesn't address them.

Money alone is not enough to keep you out of the nursing home. Money alone is not enough to keep you from being a burden on your family. Money alone is not even enough to keep you from going broke.

Money is no guarantee.

Over the last 22 years, I've helped thousands of people create retirement plans. When these clients first come to me, they are almost always confident that they have done a good job planning for their retirement, usually meaning that they have made all the right financial moves. What they want from me are legal documents. They want a Die-Die-Die plan, although they may not realize that's what they are asking for. They view getting Die-Die-Die legal documents as the right thing to do because that is what their neighbor did, what the people whose advice they respect told them to do, or what their research told them they needed to do.

This kind of planning ignores the most important questions, those that will determine whether you end up broke, a burden, and forced into a nursing home.

If you are still working, the more important financial questions should be these:

- When should I retire?
- When should I start Social Security?
- How do I know I have enough money to retire with, even if I live to be over 100?
- Should I invest money into a long-term care insurance policy?
- Should I convert my money from IRAs to Roth IRAs?
- After I'm retired, how much money can I spend every month to maintain my quality of life without going broke?
- How will I know if I'm overspending?
- Do I have enough money to see my children benefit while I'm still living?
- How much money can I gift to my children?
- How much money can I give to charity?

If you are no longer working or you have already retired, the most important financial questions should be these:

- How do I know I have enough money to maintain my retirement, even if I live to be over 100?

- Should I invest money into a long-term care insurance policy?
- Should I convert my money from IRAs to Roth IRAs?
- How much money can I spend every month to maintain my quality of life without going broke?
- How will I know if I'm overspending?
- Do I have enough money to see my children benefit while I'm still living?
- How much money can I gift to my children?
- How much money can I give to charity?

These are important questions that are almost never asked. The issue is not simply spending money on cruises, bigger homes, or toys for yourself. The issue is leaving money to your children, but never seeing them benefit from your bequest. The issue is never seeing the plaque with your name on it hanging on the benefactors' wall of your favorite charity.

Would it not be better to see your kids pay off their home and enjoy the money now? Or see the charity use the money so you know how it is benefiting humanity, animals, or whatever cause you care about most?

To properly plan your retirement, you need to be thinking about more than just your investments.

The belief that money is the answer creates unique problems for people with mid-sized estates, those in the range of $1 million to $5 million. I've seen this time and time again with my clients. Though they have lived responsibly and accumulated a reasonable nest egg, they are terrified. They are afraid they will outlive their assets.

One aspect is living with the fear of overspending. Life can be miserable when you have millions in the bank, yet you're pinching every penny. Whatever dreams you had for your retirement—travel, new hobbies, adventures with grandkids—are put on hold and eventually abandoned as you hunker down out of fear of overspending.

This is one reason why people with mid-sized estates end up leaving large inheritances to their children, at the cost of seeing the money work for them while they are still alive. The kids may appreciate the inheritance, but it's a windfall created by people too fearful to spend the money for their own needs or enjoyment. That fear can create tremendous burdens for family members.

Another aspect is putting yourself at risk. Here's an example. One of my older clients had an estate worth about $5 million that included income-producing farms in the Midwest. His definition of success was based on his net worth at any given moment.

One day, when he arrived at my office, I noticed a large purple bruise on the side of his face.

"What happened?" I asked.

"I fell down," he replied.

"I think we need to hire somebody to help you," I said.

"I know, I know," he said. "I'll get around to it..."

That day never came, of course.

Do you know someone like that?

Are you that person?

If you are afraid to spend money on the help you need because you're convinced that you'll outlive your nest egg, you're creating burdens for your family, whether you realize it or not. If you have kids, they can see what's happening and they're worried about you. They would rather see you safe and enjoying your retirement. But since your definition of success is a bank balance of $XX.XX, and since you tell yourself that you can't spend money because you don't know whether you have enough, you end up spending nothing.

This is how people with mid-sized estates end up broke, a burden on their families, and forced into institutions.

The belief that money is the most important thing also causes problems for wealthy people, which I define as anyone with an estate valued at more than $5 million.

While people with smaller estates are worried about outliving their money, the wealthy are often overconfident. Many assume that money will solve every problem.

I have watched the following scenario unfold countless times. A wealthy older adult develops dementia. As his or her health declines, the family doesn't know how to proceed, so they do what the system tells them to do: move their loved one into a long-term care facility.

If you're thinking they just didn't have enough money, I have a question for you:

How big does a fortune have to be to keep you from being forced into institutional care?

Is $15 million enough? That's how much singer Glen Campbell was worth when he developed dementia and was moved to a nursing home.

Is $50 million enough? That's how much actor/comedian Tim Conway had when he developed dementia. He died in a nursing home with his wife and daughter fighting over which facility was more appropriate to care for him. Why was the question not the following: how many people need to be hired to allow Tim Conway to be able to live his life in his own home?

Is $80 million enough? That's how much American Top 40 host Casey Kasem had when he developed Lewy body dementia and ended up in not just one facility, but several, igniting a highly publicized family conflict along the way. Kasem's wife and children argued over his care, with the bedridden Kasem dragged from California through Oregon to die in a hospital in Gig Harbor, Washington.

Is $185 million enough? That was the value of Brooke Astor's estate as she spent some of her final days living in squalor.[41]

Is $500 million enough? That's how much heiress Huguette Clark was worth. When she died at age 104, she had been hidden away in a hospital room for 22 years.

These people were all rich. They lived in mansions and drove expensive cars; they had the best money could buy. But when they got old, frail, and demented, everything fell apart. Their families fought, and their privilege fell away. They ended up like everyone else, forced into institutions such as hospitals or nursing homes, even though they had more than enough money to have care delivered to them at home in private. They were unable to realize the most basic hopes we have in life about aging—to be able to take our last breath at home surrounded by loved ones.

I share these stories to burst the bubble on one common belief: if you have enough money, you can avoid the retirement nightmares. Many Americans—rich and not-so-rich—believe that enough money can keep you out of the nursing home, keep you from going broke, and keep you from becoming a burden. That's not true.

Let's bring it back to my in-laws. When I look at the situation Bill and Vivian Wallace faced through the lens of what I've learned over the last two decades, I see three truths about the role money plays in helping people avoid the retirement nightmare: being forced into institutional care, going broke, and becoming a burden on others.

1. Money isn't a panacea for older adults' most common fears. People of wealth might not need to worry about where the money will come from to pay for care, but they worry about everything else. They worry about diminishing mental and physical capacity as they age, losing control over their own destinies, being institutionalized, and becoming a burden on others. Money doesn't prevent these worries. It can't, and assuming it can is sheer arrogance.

2. Money is one factor in a plan to avoid the retirement nightmare, but it is certainly not the most important. Money on its own wouldn't have been enough to keep Bill out of the nursing home. If Bill and Vivian had amassed a large fortune and had developed a plan to use that fortune to keep them from ending up broke, a burden, and in the nursing home, Bill may have had a chance.

3. If you have the right plan, you need less money than you think to avoid the nursing home without going broke or becoming a burden on your family. That's why Vivian was able to draw her last breath at home. Vivian didn't have much money, but what she had was a family who was determined to keep her at home. We had a plan.

In the end, it is not the amount of money you have that will matter, but rather the plan you have put in place to make use of that money. It takes the right plan, and that's what I'll show you how to do in Part 2 of this book.

The Problem with Professional Advice

You look to a myriad number of professionals to help you plan. You rely on financial planners, accountants, insurance agents, lawyers, and other subject matter experts.

Everyone has an idea about how you should approach retirement planning. They will approach it from the perspective that enables them to make a living. Their goals are to make money.

The financial industry makes money by selling you products and investing your money.

Your goals are to not end up in a nursing home, to not die broke, and to not become a burden.

Ask yourself this question: out of all the financial planners, doctors, and lawyers you've worked with, which one has ever promised that if you work with them, you won't end up in a nursing home, die broke, or become a burden on your family?

I'm guessing your answer is zero.

You followed everyone's advice, but in the end, no one asked if you were confident that the planning they did for you would enable you to reach your goals of avoiding the nursing home, not going broke, and not being a burden.

Nobody asks these questions.

Why? Each professional is educated by their respective industry, and this creates a conflict.

Which industry will educate its practitioners on issues that don't create a revenue stream for the professionals in that industry? Only information that can bring money to the particular industry would be taught to professionals of that industry.

That's how you end up with a retirement plan riddled with the kind of gaps and holes that land you broke, a burden, and forced into a nursing home when your health fails.

How do you close those gaps and holes? Someone has to be looking at the big picture of your retirement plan. Who is helping you do that?

Is it your insurance agent? He gets paid if he sells you an insurance policy.

Is it your financial planner? She gets paid to manage your portfolio whether it grows or shrinks.

Is it your accountant? He gets paid for doing your taxes.

Who is looking at the big picture?

The tacit assumption in the retirement planning world is that your financial planner will be serving in this role. Financial planners often bill themselves as the quarterback of any retirement planning team. While this sounds good in theory, it fails in practice because your financial planner's scope is limited to investments, asset allocations, and account balances. No one is actively monitoring your plan to make sure it achieves your goal to avoid the nursing home, avoid going broke, and avoid burdening your family.

This is a classic case of "you don't know what you don't know." If you don't realize that your retirement planning efforts need a project manager to address this big picture—someone to coordinate your planning so you don't end up broke, a burden, and stuck in a nursing home— you will think you're just fine.

Not having a project manager looking out for the big picture isn't the only problem you'll run into when you work with professionals.

We are taught that the professionals know best. They're the experts, not us.

Yes, the professionals may have more education in the field, but it's your responsibility to be a smart buyer.

Caveat emptor—buyer beware—is especially important when you're creating a plan for retirement.

Do you know how to be a smart buyer? Do you know how to advocate for yourself?

When you meet with a financial advisor or insurance agent, explain your situation, then rely on them to tell you what to do, you're taking a big risk. They generally only address certain pieces of the puzzle—pieces that make them money, such as investment strategies, the sale of insurance and financial products, the preparation of tax returns, etc.

If you're counting on the professionals to help you come up with a complete answer, you're taking a big risk.

To close the loop, you must know what questions to ask. You have to know what you want to accomplish.

Do you know what questions to ask?

If not, Chapter 14 will show you.

The Problem with Long-Term Care Insurance

In Chapter 6, I talk about how most Americans think that planning for health in retirement involves signing up for Medicare.

Relying on Medicare to pay for everything when your health fails is a bad idea. Medicare is not a complete answer; it has gaping holes in coverage, especially when it comes to long-term care.

If you have a heart attack, cancer, stroke, diabetes, high cholesterol, or break a bone, the solution your doctor comes up with to address this is considered acute care. They can give you pills, they can operate on you, they can give you therapy, and they can put a cast on your broken bone. This is all covered by Medicare. If you have a condition where the medical community can profit from relieving your misery, that condition is covered by Medicare. However, if you have a condition for which there is no cure, you will have little to no coverage.

Let me give you an example.

Let's imagine you have a stroke. Your health insurance covers the immediate treatment needed to keep you alive.

Now your entire right side is paralyzed. There's nothing more the doctors can do, so they discharge you from the hospital to a rehab center. You make little progress there, so they send you home. You will need someone to cook for you, clean for you, get you out of bed, get you into the bathroom—all the things that are done by home care agencies and services that are provided in institutional care settings like nursing homes. None of these costs are covered in any meaningful way by our health insurance system, including Medicare.

The care you need could cost you anywhere from a few thousand dollars a month to more than $20,000 a month, *for every month you remain alive*. If you have a small to medium size estate, these uncovered long-term care costs are the single biggest threat to your financial well-being in retirement.

The problem with retirement planning the way it's done today is that very few people are ready for these expenses. Long-term care insurance seems like a good solution, but it's often inadequate.

Right now, fewer than 1 in 45 Americans[42] own a long-term care insurance policy, including less than 6 percent of adults over 50.[43] The raw figure of 7.5 million insured has not budged for several years.[44]

Many people with long-term care insurance run out of benefits before they run out of life. Research measuring the effectiveness of long-term care policies reveals that only about seven percent of long-term care policyholders have coverage that is considered "effective," meaning that the duration is long enough and the benefits provided are adequate.

And even those having a policy with a large enough benefit amount (let's say an unlimited amount of benefits—which a few of my clients do have) will not have their real problem solved. The real issue is not just being able to afford the care; the more pressing issue is affording it in a way that accomplishes your goals to avoid institutional care, avoid running out of money, and avoid burdening your family.

Let me explain.

About ten years ago, I was speaking to a group of insurance executives. During the presentation, I asked a question:

"Raise your hand if your company offers a long-term care insurance policy."

Most hands went up. In those days, just about every company was selling long-term care insurance.

"Keep your hand raised if the policy you sell includes a rider that guarantees that the holder of that policy won't end up in a nursing home if they fall ill."

Every hand went down. A few people even laughed.

No long-term care insurance policy includes a rider like that. Insurance companies know that long-term care insurance won't keep you out of the nursing home.

Long-term care policies are, at their core, about wealth preservation. Long-term care insurance is a risk transfer strategy. It's about money, not care, but most people don't realize that.

Here are five facts about long-term care insurance that everyone needs to know:

1. If your goal is to avoid being forced into a nursing home or other institutional care facility, long-term insurance can't solve that problem.

2. Policy details matter. Long-term care insurance is not always enough in terms of amount or duration. Most people don't find this out until they file a claim.

3. Getting long-term care insurance claims paid can require an unpleasant battle with the insurance company. Many providers are quick to deny claims.

4. You could buy a long-term care policy and not need to use it. You might be one of the 30 percent who dies peacefully in their sleep. Depending on the type of policy you buy, all your premiums could be down the drain.

5. You may not be able to afford long-term care insurance when the premiums go up over time, and find yourself dropping the policy. If that happens, you may have lost all the investment in the policy, which would be the same as if you were lucky enough never to need to use the policy.

Most people expect more from their long-term care insurance than it can deliver. I see this frequently in my work with clients. When I first start working with people who have long-term care insurance, they will often stop me when I tell them that our planning process includes a discussion about paying for long-term care. "We don't have to talk about that," they will say assuredly. "We have a long-term care insurance policy."

They have been served the Kool-Aid.

If you don't have long-term care insurance, why didn't you buy it?

Maybe you're skeptical. Many people are. You can pay hundreds of thousands of dollars in premiums and never use that policy. Or you can end up battling insurance companies to get them to pay. If you die without needing long-term care, doesn't all that money go into a black hole, never to be seen again?

That possibility paralyzes most of us.

Long-term care insurance is a complicated and confusing subject.

How do you know which type of policy to buy? There's more than one kind.

How much can you afford to spend on long-term care insurance?

If you're counting on the long-term care insurance sales rep to help you make these decisions, which most people do, you're making a big mistake.

Before I became a lawyer, I was an insurance agent, first with Metropolitan Life and then with Allstate. I used to sell long-term care insurance policies. I can tell you with total confidence that insurance agents are sincere when they say they want to serve you.

Insurance agents are trained to do just this: help you BUY a policy. Their answer to helping you deal with long-term care issues in life is limited to a long-term care insurance policy. They believe it's the be-all-and-end-all for all incapacity issues.

How do I know this? I was a training manager at Allstate. My job was to train insurance agents on how to sell life insurance, annuities, long-term care insurance, and financial products.

In training our agents, I taught them about the benefits of these products, but we never talked about the risks or the downsides. We never talked about the affordability issue. We didn't talk about the possibility that premiums would rise and you might not be able to afford to keep the policy. We never talked about the fact that if you can't afford the policy, you lose the coverage, along with every dollar you paid in premiums. We never talked about claims not being paid. In short, we never talked about anything that might jeopardize the sale.

The most important questions are rarely asked:

- Is long-term care insurance the right investment for you?
- How much long-term care insurance is enough?
- Will you have the financial bandwidth to afford steep premium increases when you're living on your retirement income?

If you expect your insurance agent to be the one to answer these questions, you're making a mistake. Your insurance agent is focused on making a living, which involves selling you that policy and collecting the commission. Your agent doesn't care whether you can afford the policy years from now.

In Chapter 11, I'll show you a better way to approach the decision to buy long-term care insurance.

The Problem with Paying for Care: Medicaid & VA Benefits

If you don't have money to pay for long-term care out of pocket and you don't have long-term care insurance, what's the alternative? For most people, it's Medicaid. For veterans, it may also be VA benefits.

How much education did you get from your financial advisor about how VA and Medicaid benefits might pay for long-term care?

I'm guessing you got nothing. Your financial advisor probably didn't even bring it up, even though VA and Medicaid have always covered long-term care.

How do you access Medicaid and VA benefits? The formula is simple: spend down your assets to almost nothing.

To see how this problem plays out for married people, let's return to the story of my in-laws, Bill and Vivian Wallace. The family did not know that Bill could qualify for VA benefits, so they only looked at Medicaid at the suggestion of a social worker at the nursing home.

At the time Bill became ill, they had their house paid for, a car, and roughly $400,000 in other assets. Vivian approached Medicaid in the state of Washington and essentially said, "I hear that Medicaid will offer me financial assistance so that I can care for my husband, Bill. Will you?"

And they replied, "Sure, we will. We'll pay for some or all of Bill's care as soon as you can show us that Bill has only $2,000 to his name."

Medicaid didn't tell Vivian that, because she and Bill were married, they had some options. Under Medicaid rules in the state of Washington, if you are married, your spouse can own a house of any value, one car of any value, and between about $60,000 to about $120,000 in other assets (these numbers change annually). You and your spouse can have a prepaid funeral plan and burial profits for all family members. Your spouse can have $1,500 cash value in a life insurance policy, all the personal property in the world, and an unlimited amount of income, and you can still qualify for benefits.

Vivian believed that she and Bill had to be broke in order for Bill to be covered by Medicaid benefits.

That was never the case, which is what was so tragic about her and Bill's situation.

If Vivian wanted to get the long-term care benefits covered by Medicaid, she would've had to transfer all the assets out of Bill's name and put them under her own. She could own a house. She could own a car.

This was Vivian's big hang-up: she had about $400,000 in assets, but she could only have between about $60,000 to $120,000 in other assets in order for Bill to qualify for Medicaid.[45] At the end of the day, she simply had too much money.

But even there, she had options. As I mentioned, she could have an unlimited income. She could've gone to an insurance company the night before she was going to apply for Medicaid benefits. She could have given her extra money to the insurance company and said, "Return this money to me in the form of a monthly income over the next five years." She would get the money back and would have Bill's expenses covered by Medicaid benefits.

That didn't happen.

If Vivian had understood how to access Medicaid benefits, perhaps Bill could have avoided dying in a nursing home.

As long as Medicaid is available, we owe it to ourselves to understand how to use it. It may not be the best solution for covering long-term care costs, but it is a solution.

Now let's look at how Medicaid works for single people.

In Washington State, the rules say a single person can have a house with equity of up to about $560,000.[46] If you're single, you can also have one automobile, a prepaid funeral plan, burial plots, the cash value of life insurance policies, and an unlimited amount of personal property.

Here's the unpleasant part. If you are single when you die after receiving Medicaid benefits, your estate will be subject to a Medicaid lien, which means your estate must reimburse your state's Medicaid program for whatever they paid out for your long-term care. Anything left after the state gets its cut will go to your heirs. In other words, the Will that you carefully crafted to leave everything to your kids will be rewritten by statute. Your hope to leave something to your kids is effectively erased.

It's not so easy for elder law attorneys to protect the assets of single people. The asset transfer rules that apply to married couples don't apply to single people.

People who don't understand how Medicaid works often try to skirt these restrictions by giving away assets to children or other family members. This always creates problems, thanks to Medicaid's infamous five-year look-back period which says that if you have given away any assets in the last five years you may not qualify for Medicaid benefits for a period of time.

If you are single and you wait until the last minute to conduct your planning, with a few exceptions, you may not be able to get the benefits without delays.

Early planning is the only option, but most people wait too long to get help from an elder law attorney.

The Problem with Paying for Care: Retirement Accounts

If Medicaid or VA benefits will be your payment sources for long-term care costs, certain planning must take place if you have a 401(k), IRA, or another retirement account.

If you want to apply for long-term care benefits under Medicaid, you can only have $2,000 to your name. Married people can transfer assets to a spouse. Single people can transfer money to a child, a Trust, or someone else.

What kind of taxes are incurred when you transfer a house to a spouse, a child, or a Trust? None. No money changed hands. It is a gift, a gratuitous transfer.

What kind of taxes do you pay when you transfer a car? None. No money changed hands.

What kind of taxes do you pay when you transfer a savings account with a balance of $400,000 to your spouse or your child or to a Trust? None.

What kind of taxes do you pay when you transfer $400,000 in a traditional IRA or 401(k) or another retirement account to a spouse or child?

This is a trick question.

Remember the deal you made with the IRA devil? When you put the money in, it was a pretax contribution. But when you take even a dollar out of that account, it's taxable income.

If you take $400,000 out of that IRA, you could be paying 32 percent in taxes to the federal government. The adjusted gross income for the highest marginal tax rate is about $540,000 for single people and about $648,000 for married couples (as of 2022).[47]

If there is any possibility that you may end up needing to look to VA or Medicaid to pay for long-term care, these retirement accounts can derail your plans.

Will your financial planner or accountant be able to help you deal with this problem? Will they suggest that you convert some of your retirement accounts to Roth IRAs?

You won't often get that counsel. Most financial planners and accountants are more focused on helping you *avoid* taxes, not inviting them.

In fact, the advice you get from financial planners that helps you achieve one goal for your life in retirement can cause major financial problems when your health fails. Here's a classic example.

The Problem with Guaranteed Income Solutions: Annuities

Let's say you took your financial planner's advice to take a large portion of your nest egg and buy an annuity to create a guaranteed stream of income in retirement. No longer worrying about crazy stock market swings is a good thing, right?

It is, as long as you don't get sick and need Medicaid or VA benefits to pay for long-term care. If you buy a guaranteed income annuity in early retirement and you later need to qualify for a means-tested benefit like Medicaid, this advice to buy an annuity and the guaranteed income it produces could cost you hundreds of thousands of dollars in lost benefits. I'm told by some insurance agents that some of the newer annuity policies give you the option to take your money out of the annuity account, but these withdrawals often create more problems than they solve, especially when it comes to taxes.

Most financial planners work hard to help clients to the best of their ability. The only problem is that most are only thinking about preparing you for one kind of retirement, the one where you're healthy and don't need long-term care. Most won't offer up any ways to deal with future long-term care costs beyond recommending a long-term care insurance policy. The financial industry is busy educating its sales force on the merits of an immediate annuity without necessarily discussing the potential downsides of it. If your financial planner understood the potential future negative impact of a guaranteed income annuity, he or she might not suggest it.

The Problem with Focusing on Minimizing Income Taxes

Another area where tax professionals and financial advisors some-times provide advice that is inappropriate in times of incapacity is when they dismiss the wisdom of converting qualified funds to Roth IRAs, or advocate for the funding of traditional retirement plans over Roth plans. I have met significant resistance at the hands of tax advisors and financial planners when I have advised clients to start converting the IRA to a Roth IRA, but the planners seem to find new religion when Medicaid and or VA planning calls for the distribution of any substantial sum from a qualified plan. What do you think are the tax consequences of withdrawing $300,000 from an IRA or 401(k) plan compared to the tax costs on a $30,000 withdrawal? It's not that financial planners are actively trying to sabotage retirement plans, it's that they are simply not focused on these situations you are likely to confront when your health fails during your retirement years.

I talk more about this challenge—and what to do about it—in Chapter 11.

The Problem with Medicaid Planning & the Ethics of Medicaid Planning

I've been on the radio for almost twenty years talking about how Medicaid works. Every other month or so, I'll get a call from someone quite irritated with me. The person usually says some variation of this:

"Why are you trying to convince everyone to go on Medicaid? Where's the money going to come from? America will go broke if everyone is on Medicaid."

Though I'm not an advocate of Medicaid for all, there is a grain of truth embedded in the caller's statement. It is true that our nation doesn't have enough money to fund Medicaid for everyone.

If our nation can't afford Medicaid for everyone, does it follow that no one should get Medicaid?

Some people believe it's wrong for middle-class people (or anyone, for that matter) to be accessing Medicaid to pay for long-term care. They believe that each person should take care of their own needs.

That's certainly one way to look at it. It's not the only way.

Let me repeat. I'm not advocating that everyone goes on Medicaid. This is a choice that you will have to make for yourself or a loved one when the time comes.

Consider this example: Let's say you're a veteran of the U.S. Armed Forces. You were sent off to fight to protect the freedoms we hold so dear. Now that you've done your patriotic duty, you come home, get a job, raise a family, and possibly save some money for retirement. After a lifetime of saving, you have a house that is paid for and a few hundred thousand dollars in the bank. You figure with your nest egg, plus Social Security and Medicare, you will be okay if you continue to live within your means.

And then the unthinkable happens: a dementia diagnosis. Your condition progresses quickly. You need care. You apply for Medicaid, and you're told that you have too much money. Anything more than $2,000 in assets is too rich, says the Medicaid system.

You spend your money down, then apply again. If you want to stay at home, Medicaid will provide care. In Washington, in most cases, Medicaid may provide up to six hours of care each day in the home. (There are exceptional circumstances where more care could be authorized.)

That's great, but you need more than six hours of care each day. If you go to a nursing home or care facility that accepts Medicaid, you can get 24/7 care.

Where would you prefer to be? The most likely answer to that question is at home. However, where do you get the most Medicaid benefits? In the nursing home.

You're moved into a semi-private room. Things start going wrong. You were told you would have one roommate, yet there are three others living in your room. One of your roommates is belligerent, up at all hours of the night. People are stealing things.

That's not all. Life in the nursing home is predictable. Each morning, a crew arrives at 7 a.m. to get you out of bed, get you dressed, move you to your wheelchair, and then move your wheelchair into the hallway.

Then a dining room crew will come to wheel you to the dining room to join five others sitting on one side of a horseshoe table. Sitting on the other side is a staff member charged with feeding you all.

After about an hour, no matter how much you've eaten (or not eaten), the crew cleans you up, and moves you into a common area to watch TV. From there, another crew will take you back to your room.

This happens again at lunchtime and again at dinnertime. When was the last time you have been to a nursing home and seen any of the residents enjoying the picturesque gardens featured in their brochures, spaces they spend thousands of dollars each month to maintain?

When I visited Bill Wallace in his nursing home during the summer months, the gardens in his facility were in prime condition, yet no one was ever out there. Every once in a while, I would see a resident in the garden with a family member, but most of the time, residents visited with their families in their rooms or in the common areas inside the facility.

When the weather was good, I wheeled Bill out to enjoy the space, and we were almost always alone. It broke my heart. After a few visits, it dawned on me why almost no one else used this space. It was a staffing issue. There were barely enough employees to see to the residents' most basic needs, let alone take them outside to enjoy some fresh air and sunshine.

This is the reality of life in an institution. What does this kind of care cost?

When Bill was in the nursing home, the cost was $5,500 per month. Today, that same room with the same care costs over $11,000 per month. You get a shower once a week. You get three institutional meals. If you're lucky, you get visits from your family. Not everyone is that lucky.

If your goal is to avoid this kind of institutional life, you are going to need money. Your private resources need to be protected to make that happen, because when added to Medicaid benefits, your money will last longer. Without that protection, you cannot blame anyone other than yourself. Medicaid funds and your own money can be used to hire help at home. Your loved ones need not be your only caregivers.

There is a famous quote from Judge Learned Hand, who wrote in a case: "There is no patriotic duty for any American to pay the highest possible amount of taxes. Indeed, it's quite the opposite. It is up to the people to take advantage of the rules that our government has created."

The same applies to people who want to access Medicaid. It is a choice you get to make using the laws the government passes.

There is no patriotic duty for any American who needs long-term care to voluntarily impoverish themselves when the law allows access to public benefits like Medicaid.

So, when somebody calls my radio show and starts spouting this morality, I listen, but I have no qualms about recommending that every person who needs Medicaid applies for it.

I just think about the veterans who put their lives at risk for our country and then come home to be treated like used car parts.

The Problem with the Safety Net

I'd like to say one more thing about Medicaid and its role in creating a safety net for American families.

When Medicaid was signed into law in 1965, it seemed like a landmark achievement for America. With the stroke of President Lyndon B. Johnson's pen, our nation seemed to be on the brink of solving an age-old problem: frail elderly people without family or resources now had a safety net. The Great Society would take care of its most vulnerable.

Medicaid, like most government programs, had earnest beginnings. It offered peace of mind to people looking after elderly loved ones from a distance, promising that those older adults would be cared for and not left to fade away in poorhouses, which had deservedly earned a bad rap for providing substandard care and being little more than prisons for the elderly.

Most people alive today don't realize just how bad life could be for frail older adults who had no money and no family to look after them. Most people alive today don't understand the history of old age in this country. For all but the very wealthy, old age frequently meant financial ruin and dependency.

Throughout the 19th and early 20th centuries, poorhouses were a reality for society's most vulnerable people. These locally run institutions filled a need at a time before Social Security, Medicare, and Medicaid became a reality. They also exposed the stigma and shame society placed on those who were unable to support themselves. Many older people ended life in indigence, including three U.S. presidents: Thomas Jefferson, James Monroe, and Ulysses S. Grant.[48]

Medicaid also gave hope to the elderly that they did not need to become a financial burden to their children. Social Security might be a smaller part of an older person's income these days, but it was a revolution when it went into effect in the 1930s. Thanks to monthly Social Security checks, older people now had a small income, so fewer died for want of food or basic necessities. Social Security was also partially responsible for the migration of millions of young families from cities to the suburbs. Adult children no longer needed to provide housing for their elderly parents because Mom and Dad had enough money to live on their own. Without Social Security, those parents would be living with their children or other members of the extended family.

For a very short time after the Medicare bill was signed into law, Medicare covered all health expenses, including long-term care. That didn't last long. The law hadn't even been on the books for a year when someone did the math and realized that covering long-term care expenses would quickly bankrupt the system. The law was changed to exclude long-term care from Medicare and point people to Medicaid for that coverage. Between Medicare and Medicaid, twin programs created on the same day, we have a more complete answer.

Now, nearly six decades later, has the safety net called Medicaid made things better for older adults?

In some ways, yes, but mostly no.

In the "system" that has grown up around Medicaid, care for the elderly continues to be delivered through an institutional care model, a model that has fallen out of favor with most older adults. In fact, if you ask the average retiree what he or she fears the most about getting older, you're likely to hear talk about the terror of falling ill and ending up in institutional care—and for good reason. Let me remind you of research I cited in earlier chapters: Seventy percent of all retirees will not be at home when they take their last breath.[49] Another study revealed that more than 60 percent of all Americans would rather die than end up in a nursing home.[50]

Don't get me wrong. It's great that older adults have access to Medicaid funds to help pay for long-term care. Earlier in my career as an elder law attorney, my practice was focused on helping families find and pay for long-term care for their elderly loved ones. In many cases, Medicaid was the best option.

However, after decades of this work, I see the flaws in the system.

First, Medicaid makes a promise it can't keep. The system holds out hope that it will take care of older Americans, but it does a pathetic job of it. It underpays. It has inadequate resources. The oversight is poor.

Second, Medicaid's design pushes people into institutional care. For decades, it has been easiest to get Medicaid to pay for care in a nursing home, not care at home. The result is the large-scale warehousing of our nation's frail elderly population.

Third, due to its bias toward institutional care, Medicaid effectively incentivizes families to walk away from what ultimately should be a family responsibility. Then, the bureaucratic labyrinth all but shuts families out.

I understand the thinking behind the creation of Medicaid. The government's message to families was this: You don't have to worry about your parents. The system will take care of them.

It sounds good, but the results have been disastrous. Within a few short decades, we've upended the cultural expectation that we will take care of each other. Believing that the government will take care of older adults makes it easier to walk away from our responsibilities.

To fully appreciate this monster we've created, look at it this way: The government has effectively replaced the family. The government tells the family that it will take care of their loved one by paying for care. That care is more readily available in institutional settings. The thought seems to be that families are not able to care for loved ones better than institutions are. This is patently false.

I'm not sure what Lyndon B. Johnson would say if he could see how the Medicaid system has evolved. I don't think he would be pleased.

The Problem of Managing Your Affairs

When you get sick, who will pay your bills? Who will file your taxes? Who will manage your investments? Who will feed your pets, mow the lawn, and reconcile your checking account?

Let me guess. You're expecting your family to do it.

But wait—you've also told your family that you don't want to be a burden.

What have you done to make sure you're not a burden?

Your finances will not magically manage themselves when a crisis arises. Your assets won't automatically be used in the way you prefer.

If you were incapacitated today, how easy would it be for your agents to manage your financial affairs?

How easy would it be for your agents to access account information, receipts, and records? Where is all this information? What planning have you done around that?

What about when you die? How difficult will it be for your family to handle your final affairs?

If you haven't thought about these things, I can promise you one thing: You are guaranteed to be a burden on your named agents and your loved ones.

Spending time hunting down passwords and making trades isn't the half of it.

On the day when you can no longer make your own decisions, someone else will be making those decisions for you, most likely the agent named in your Power of Attorney.

Will that someone else know how to use your money to give you the life that you want—and not the life a discharge planner or a social worker thinks is best for you?

That's the real question.

Where do you want to be cared for? If your family is told that you need round-the-clock care, instead of paying the nursing home anywhere from a few thousand dollars to upwards of $20,000 each month, why couldn't they just hire two or three people to come to the house and take care of you full time?

That's what happens in the majority of the world.

The reason why your kids put you in a nursing home is simple—they don't know what else to do. They don't know how to take care of you while also managing their own busy lives, so they do what the social worker or discharge planner says.

Have you talked to your family about this?

Probably not, or at least not in a manner that is effective. Most of us just brush it under the rug.

You tell your family that you don't want to go to a nursing home, but when the time comes, you expect your family to figure it out without giving them any tools or resources to work with.

And then you're surprised when everything blows up in your face.

In Part 2 of this book, I'll explain how to avoid this.

The Story of Mrs. Jones

One morning about fifteen years ago, the phone rang. It was a woman who said she listened to me on the radio every week.

"I need help right now," said Mrs. Jones, her voice wavering. "My husband is in a nursing home, and I don't know what to do."

"Where do you live?" I asked.

"I live on the Olympic Peninsula."

If you're not from the Seattle area, the Olympic Peninsula is a beautiful and remote stretch of land in western Washington that lies across Puget Sound from Seattle. It is bounded on the west by the Pacific Ocean, the north by the Strait of Juan de Fuca, and the east by the Hood Canal. Many areas are accessible only by ferryboat.

We arranged for a meeting at Mrs. Jones's home. I did a lot of house calls in the early days of my law practice.

On the day of our meeting, I drove to her oceanfront home, catching a ferryboat for the final leg of the journey. When I arrived at the address, I turned into a long private driveway. At the end was an 80 ft. yacht moored at a pier in front of a palatial home. An army of groundskeepers was tending to the property.

I looked around. Why wasn't this woman's husband getting the care he needed in this beautiful setting? I wondered. Why couldn't the care be brought to him right here, just like the care was being brought to this woman's home, her yard, and her boat?

I remember thinking, "Mrs. Jones, this isn't the nursing home's husband, this is your husband, and you need to take responsibility for making sure he gets the best care. If you're paying $18,000 a month to the nursing home, then we need to be looking at how we can spend that $18,000 a month on care that comes here to this lovely place with this beautiful view."

It may seem like I was angry with Mrs. Jones, but my irritation was mostly aimed at a system that favors institutional care over everything else, a system that tells a woman that moving her husband to a place of care is better than bringing the care to him.

This is what happens when you have a lot of money but no idea how to use it.

Mr. Jones's retirement plan failed because he ended up in a nursing home. He had enough money to stay home, but his family, despite their ample financial resources, didn't realize that keeping him at home was even an option. Mrs. Jones didn't know she could.

Remember Max Smith, the man who died in the rehab center while his family hemmed and hawed about where he should go next? Max's family knew they could bring him home, yet they balked.

Do you remember how they reacted when I told them that it would cost around $20,000 a month for two people to provide care for Max at home?

They froze.

This was a family who had enough money to take care of Max forever, yet $20,000 a month seemed like too much to spend. I can only speculate why. Maybe Doris was raised in the Depression era or by people who grew up believing that they never had enough money.

Over the years, I have seen hundreds of well-off clients in this same situation. They all needed care. They all had boatloads of money. They all ended up in long-term care facilities despite having enough money to age at home because the people charged with making the decision about care didn't want to part with the money.

It's tragic, and this tragedy happens every day.

Traditional Financial Planning Doesn't Think Big Enough

We think retirement planning is all about the money.

It's not.

In this chapter, you've seen why this belief is so persistent—and so damaging. You have seen the danger of believing that money is the answer to every problem in retirement. You've seen how the profit motive, especially for financial professionals, makes getting objective professional advice so difficult. You've seen how the assumption that long-term care insurance will keep you out of the nursing home leads to a false sense of security. You've seen how the planning you do to create guaranteed income streams can cause problems if you need to access public benefits to pay for long-term care in the future.

Please don't misunderstand me. Money is important. You need money. You need to accumulate it. You need to manage it. You need to protect it.

What you also need—and almost certainly don't have—is a plan to use your money to help you achieve your goals of not ending up in a nursing home, not going broke, and not being a burden.

You can't create a solution until you know what the problem is. And the problem with the financial professionals helping you plan for your retirement is that they're defining your problem from their own perspective. Like lawyers, financial planners each want to do their little part without regard to the big picture. This results in what I call a Swiss cheese retirement plan, a plan riddled with gaps and holes.

In Part 2, I'll show you how to bridge the gaps and fill the holes in your retirement plan. But first, let's take a look at what I consider to be the root cause of retirement plan failure.

CHAPTER 6

THE PROBLEM WITH HEALTH

Introduction

What is your most important asset as you enter retirement?

Is it your home? Is it your financial portfolio? Is it your long-term care policy? Is it your close-knit family?

No, no, no, and no.

Your most important asset in retirement will prove to be your health.

Your ability to live your retirement dreams is 100 percent dependent on your health status. Without your health, you won't be sipping wine in Napa, biking in Tuscany, parasailing in the Mediterranean, or playing pickup basketball with your grandkids.

The greatest wealth is health, as the saying goes.

As you've already seen, your retirement plan fails when one of these three things happens:

1. You're forced to move into institutional care
2. You lose money paying for unexpected long-term care costs
3. You become a burden on your family

Nearly every case of retirement plan failure began when the older adult's health failed.

Why Is a Lawyer Talking about Health?

In case you're wondering, I'm not a doctor. I don't pretend to be one.

So, why am I talking about health?

Failing health isn't a legal problem. However, failing health causes legal problems. Likewise, failing health causes financial problems, and failing health causes housing problems.

As I looked into the many cases where retirement plans failed, they always started with an illness of some kind. Ask yourself this question: Who do you *not* find in a nursing home?

Healthy people.

Failing health is the root cause of retirement plan failure.

Failing health is the falling domino that sets into motion the cascade of housing, financial, legal, and family problems that leave older adults broke, a burden on others, and stuck in a nursing home.

My reason for talking about health is simple. I want to help you minimize your risk of retirement plan failure, which means prolonging your independence for as long as possible.

As long as you are healthy and can live independently, you don't have to worry about going to a nursing home. That's why I'm talking about health.

The Problem with How We Plan for Health

How does the average American plan to address the health needs that may arise during their retirement years?

Traditional planning involves getting the right insurance. You enroll in Medicare when you turn 65, and maybe buy a supplemental insurance plan. You expect this insurance to cover all your health care-related expenses.

This is the mainstream approach. This is how Bill and Vivian Wallace planned. It's how our parents planned. It's what we are all told to do. The traditional way to plan for your health in retirement is to make sure you have insurance so you can access care after you fall ill.

We all feel safe and secure, certain that America's vaunted safety net is protecting our health.

Except, simply having a good insurance plan to cover health care costs isn't the answer, especially if we hope to avoid institutional care.

The problem with focusing on enrolling in Medicare and investing in a supplemental insurance plan, and then identifying the physician who will become your primary care physician is that it is all about accessing medical care *after* you fall ill. And after you fall ill, you are already halfway to a care facility, a burden, and losing money to uncovered medical and care costs.

A better focus would be to learn to use the health care system NOT to fall ill in the first place. Healthy people don't end up in care facilities; sick people do. The longer you are healthy, the longer you are not in a care facility, a burden, or losing assets.

Sadly, far too little is done to see that you don't fall ill in the first place.

See the point?

This is the hole you must fill if you want to avoid ending up in institutional care against your wishes.

The Problem with America's Health Care System

At a social event not that long ago, I met a person who had sought me out, most likely because she had heard me on my radio show. A mutual acquaintance made the introduction.

When I asked her what she did for a living, she told me that she was the administrator of one of the largest hospital chains in the state of Washington.

"That's interesting," I said. "I've been sending letters to your leadership team trying to get them to add a geriatric medicine department. Why don't hospitals offer geriatric medicine?"

She looked me in the eye. "I'll be blunt," she said. "It doesn't make money."

"What do you mean it doesn't make money? Your biggest repeat customers are geriatric patients."

"That's true," she said, "but they're all on Medicare. Medicare doesn't make us money. It is surgeries and procedures that are the profitable part of a hospital system. In fact, we usually lose money on Medicare patients. Geriatrics is about how to use medicine to keep people out of the health care system. My leadership team has no interest in offering a service that will stand in the way of our profitability."

As much as I wish I could say this was the first time I heard an executive at a health care-related corporation tell me that geriatrics is a money-losing proposition, sadly, it wasn't. I've heard this many times before. Hospitals make money treating people once they get sick, not by offering ways to keep them healthy and out of the "system."

As I see it, this is the root cause of the problem with health care in retirement. This is the head of the snake. Our system is set up to deliver care *after* you fall ill. This model is a setup for failure as you age, espe-cially if your goal is to avoid being forced into a nursing home.

I'm grateful for the things America's health care system does well. When it comes to addressing our needs after we have an illness, there's no better place to be than America. If you're going to fall ill, America is the greatest place to do it. Our nation has cutting-edge solutions to stitch, patch, and dose you back to health, especially if you know where to look. When it comes to preventing illness, how-ever, America's health care system leaves much to be desired.

Even the worst insurance companies will pay benefits when you fall sick, but even the best insurance companies aren't all that interested in preventing illness.

Why?

The fee-for-service model is part of the problem.

The more tests ordered, the more procedures one undergoes, the more bionic knees and hips implanted, the more the medical community stands to profit. By the "medical community," I mean doctors, hospi-tals, pharmaceutical companies, prosthetic device manufacturers, and others providing solutions to older adults with failing health.

There is little incentive for these providers to see you stay healthy. They make no money unless you're ill. Which hospital will be profit-able when you do not use hospital services? Which pharmaceutical manufacturer will make money unless you buy pills? Which medical practice will make money if you don't show up to the clinic?

Insurance companies bear the brunt of our health care bills, which gives them an incentive to keep you from frequenting medical provid-ers. Even so, there seems to be little appetite to see them cover preven-tative care efforts beyond certain non-traditional medical providers.

The government has only recently started to take steps to advocate for laws that make wellness checks (as distinct from your annual physicals) mandatory and without cost to the consumer. The wellness check varies so much in quality that few take advantage of this opportunity.

In Chapter 9, I'll show you how to work both within and outside of the insurance system to preserve your health.

The Problem with Lifestyle Choices

This next problem involves the way we choose to live. Many Americans procrastinate—we delay taking action until the last possible moment. Why do now what you can put off until tomorrow?

For example, we all know that exercise is good for us, yet many people don't start taking exercise seriously until after they've had a heart attack. That's when they take up jogging, weightlifting, and everything they should have been doing all along.

We know how important it is to eat a healthy diet. We know that being overweight has a great impact on our ability to function and live independently as we age. Yet, there we are in the drive-through lane, binging Netflix on TV while we eat junk, vowing to turn things around tomorrow.

Some say that baseball is America's pastime and football is America's sport, but I believe that procrastination is America's true passion. In my opinion, this is one of the most important root causes of retirement plan failure that is actually within our power to control. We neglect our health for decades, put off planning for the day when we might not be able to live at home without going broke or sentencing our family to life as our unpaid caregivers, and then we wonder what went wrong when our money runs out and we become a burden to those we love. We then become part of the 70 percent of Americans who will take our last breath in a hospital, hospice center, or long-term care facility instead of at home.

The Problem with Choosing a Health Care Provider

Decisions about lifestyle aren't the only choices we have to make. Choosing a doctor is equally important. You may even have a doctor you've been working with for years, perhaps even decades.

Your primary care physician is likely a board-certified internist or family medicine physician, both specialties that focus on the adult population. Your doctor is familiar with you and your health history. He or she is likely the quarterback of your medical team, supported by various specialists you may see for specific issues.

If you have a great relationship with your primary care doctor and you've been seeing him or her for years, your plan is most likely to stick with the same doctor after you're retired.

Why change?

That may not be the best move to make.

Though most of us know that older adults end up with certain kinds of conditions not often seen in younger people, few of us give much thought to changing our health care provider as we age.

Think about it. It's not like our culture doesn't already offer specialized medical care based on the unique needs of people in certain age groups.

If you've had children, I'm reasonably confident that you didn't take them to your regular internal medicine doctor or family medicine physician. You took them to a pediatrician, because you recognized that the physiology of children under the age of 18 is different than that of the rest of the population. Treatments and medications that are good for adults may not be appropriate for children.

The same applies to older adults. The physiology of people over the age of 70 is different than that of the rest of the population.[51] Medication that worked well for you at 30, 40, or 50, may not work so well when you're 70, 80, or 90. Problems with medication could be the reason why you start exhibiting signs of dementia without having dementia.[52]

Age isn't the only issue. When you look at children across the board, they are all very similar. They are growing and developing. They are curious and eager to learn. As we move into our later years, however, these similarities decrease. One 65-year-old might have significant memory loss and be living in a nursing home. Another 65-year-old might still be healthy, working, and living an active life. A one-size-fits-all approach to health care for older adults doesn't take these differences into account.

How many times have you heard your health insurance company, your health insurance agent, or even your doctor tell you that if you're over the age of 70, you should be working with a physician who specializes in the care of older adults?

I know the answer to that question. It's precious little beyond an admonishment to lose weight, exercise, and eat better.

If you want to avoid the nursing home, working with a doctor who specializes in the care of older adults can make a real difference. A research study led by physician Chad Boult from the University of Minnesota backs this up.[53]

Dr. Boult focused a part of this study on 568 retirees, all over the age of 70. This group included individuals who, in his opinion, faced a high probability of experiencing a decline in their health in the near term. He divided this group into two segments. One group was directed to continue seeing their regular doctors, which included internal medicine, family medicine doctors, and general practice physicians. The other group was assigned to see a team of specialists.

Eighteen months after the study began, Dr. Boult looked at the results. Ten percent of the people in both groups had died. The people who were seeing specialists weren't living longer.

Then Dr. Boult noticed something else. People who were seeing specialists were 50 percent less likely to be dealing with depression. They were 40 percent less likely to need home health and homecare services. They suffered 33 percent less chronic illness and disability.

Let me repeat: those in the group who saw the team of specialists were 40 percent less likely to need home health and homecare compared to the group who was seeing internal medicine physicians or family medicine practitioners.

What does life look like when you don't need home care or home health? Nowhere close to a nursing home; that is what life looks like.

The "specialists" in the study who were able to generate the impressive results were board-certified geriatricians, otherwise known as geriatric care physicians.

If you've never heard of this specialty, you're not alone.

Have you informed your insurance company that you will only pay them your hard-earned money by way of insurance premiums if they can offer a board-certified geriatrician for you to choose as your primary care provider?

Probably not. That's not how most of us buy insurance.

In Chapter 9, I'll talk more about how to find and work with a health care provider who specializes in geriatrics.

The Problem with Choosing Insurance

If you're 65 or older and making health insurance decisions, it's easy to get lost in the jargon. Medicare Advantage, Original Medicare, Medicare Supplemental Coverage, Donut Hole, etc. ... it's enough to make your head spin.

This complexity makes insurance decisions difficult. Most of us dread having to mess around with insurance. So, we take the easy way out. We look for an insurance company with a familiar name. We review the costs, focusing primarily on the numbers. As long as the price is equal to or lower than what we are currently paying, we buy the policy. And then we cross our fingers, hoping we will be spared any unpleasant surprises during the next twelve months.

Once we've signed up for the policy, the insurance company sends us a big, thick book that we crack open, hoping to find a doctor close to us. Many of us assume every doctor in that book is the same.

After we make the decision to see one of these doctors on the list, most of us never give it another thought.

When Medicare open enrollment comes around every fall, most of us stick with the policy we have. Most of us never change insurance companies after the initial purchase. We're intimidated by the complexity.

That's where the problem starts. We choose insurance based on the cost and the name of the plan rather than how the plan gives us access to the right doctor.

When we do this, we're overlooking the power of health care to help prolong our independence.

In Chapter 9, I'll explain how to choose an insurance company that can help you stay healthy.

The Problem with Advocacy

If you develop a health problem as you age, chances are that at some point in the process you will be relying on the support of others—most likely family—as you interact with the health care system. You will be relying on others to make decisions about your care. You will be relying on others to make sure you get good care. You will be relying on others to make decisions that will benefit you in the end—such as where you will live and how you will get the care you need.

That's the interesting thing about late-stage retirement, the part where you get sick. Everything ends up being done by others.

Will those others know what to do? Will they know how to do it?

For most people, the answer is no.

To illustrate this problem, I will share a situation from my own life.

For years, my parents had spent six months with me in the U.S. and six months at home in India. In 2014, when my parents were visiting, I came home from work one day and discovered that my mom had been complaining about not feeling well.

This wasn't the first time I'd heard her talk about this. We had traveled a lot that year, including a trip to Las Vegas. During that trip, I found myself urging Mom to walk faster. She couldn't.

Now, Mom said she was having chest pains. My wife, Jamie, took Mom to see a cardiologist. The doctor ordered an EKG, and the results came back abnormal.

"Take her home," the doctor told Jamie. "I've ordered a stress test and they will call you when they're ready for you to bring her back for the test."

Jamie was incredulous. "She doesn't feel well," Jamie said. "You're going to let her leave?"

Later that evening when I came home from work, Dad was tending to Mom, who was resting in bed. Something seemed off. Her skin was an ashy white color. "I don't feel well," she whispered.

We took Mom to the emergency room. The doctors there took her complaints seriously. After a few tests, they confirmed what Jamie and I had suspected: Mom was having a heart attack. The doctor who saw Mom in the morning sent her home in the middle of this heart attack!

After going through several diagnostic tests in the emergency room, Mom was transferred to a larger hospital where she received a stent to clear the blockage. She also needed open-heart surgery to fix a problem with a valve.

This is a radical form of surgery—mitral valve replacement surgery. The doctors cut you open, saw your sternum so they can reach your heart, take out the heart and stop it while machines keep your blood circulating. Surgeons cut the heart open, take out the bad valve, replace it with a good one, and then reverse the process.

Before this procedure, I spoke to the surgeon, Dr. John Luber. After telling me that he frequently listened to my *AgingOptions* radio show, Dr. Luber was reassuring. "The mitral valve replacement procedure is going to be invasive, but it's not risky," he said. "We do three or four of these a week. It will be okay."

After the surgery was finished, I managed to find Mom in the recovery room. I wasn't supposed to be there, but I needed to see her. A machine was keeping her alive. A nurse shooed me away, but I was able to come back and see her once her condition stabilized.

Following these surgeries, they get you up and walking in just a few days. Though it was hard for Mom to get started, she was able to take one step, then two, then five, then ten. I was there with her the whole time.

A few weeks later, she was moved from the recovery floor to the general floor, then to a private room. After a week in the private room, a social worker came to see us.

"Your mom is making great progress," she said with a smile. "Which rehab center do you want to send her to?"

This is the moment when the needle scratches across the record.

The question arrived like clockwork, exactly as I describe when I'm talking to people at seminars, listeners on the radio, and viewers on my TV show.

"She's not going to a rehab center," I said. "She's going home."

The social worker looked at me like I was insane. "Oh no, you couldn't do that," she said.

You can't make this stuff up. These were the actual words from this social worker's mouth. It was like I was inside a case study that I talk about in my own seminar.

"Why can't I take her home?" I asked, knowing what the answer would be.

"You don't know what you're getting into," the social worker said.

I laughed. "My mother just came out of anesthesia and she's plucking things out of the air," I said. "She's talking to relatives who've long been dead. English is not her first language and so she speaks in Hindi. Which rehab center can I send her to where I will not need to be her shadow so she can get through the day, as I have had to be in the hospital? She's not going to a rehab center. She's going home with me."

What this well-meaning social worker didn't realize was that the person she was talking to had spent the last 15 or so years telling people to just say no to the rehab center.

So, when I said, "I'm going to take her home," her response was a stunned "Wow. This is beyond me. I'll send somebody else to talk to you."

An hour or so later, the supervisor of the discharge planning department stopped in. "It's time to choose a rehab center for your mom," she said.

I shook my head. "I'm taking her home," I said.

Eventually, the doctor who conducted the surgery walked in. "Dr. Luber," I said, "you know my story. If my mother goes to a rehab center, I will be the biggest hypocrite in town. For years, I have been shouting my lungs out that if you know how to plan your affairs, the nursing home will never be your only option, no matter how dire the situation is. Exceptions exist, but as a rule, one should be able to access rehab at home. My mother is not going to a rehab center. You've got to help me out."

"If I can get her rehab in the hospital, would you be okay with that?" Dr. Luber asked.

My first thought was no, but when he explained the concept of inpatient rehab in the same hospital, I was more receptive. There were just 24 beds for the sickest of the sick, and they were only available at a moment's notice. "I'll put in for one of those beds," Dr. Luber promised. "When they call you, be ready to leave in about 10 minutes. They could call you today. They could call you tomorrow. Those beds don't stay open."

"Why didn't the discharge social worker offer this to me?" I asked.

"It's not an option we give very many people because it's for the sickest of the sick."

I was able to get Mom moved to inpatient rehab. I remained with her as I had done from the day she was admitted. The staff there did everything right. Eventually, Mom made a full recovery and came home.

Let's take a closer look at what happened. Mom was able to avoid an outside rehab center (a nursing home by a different name) only because I, the family member who was making decisions on her behalf, knew what to do to keep her out of the nursing home. I knew what to ask for. I knew what to demand. I knew what Mom wanted and I fought to get it for her, even when the social worker was pressuring me to transition Mom to a rehab center.

How would this have ended had I not pushed back against the system? You know the answer.

How will your children or named agents know to push back when a well-meaning social worker wants to send you to a nursing home? Unless they were educated about this issue well ahead of time, they won't.

Without that education, most people don't know that they're allowed to say no to rehab, and if they do, they don't know how to say no. The average family caregiver will do exactly what the social worker says to do.

If it's you in the hospital, and your spouse or child talking to the discharge planner, will your family member go along with what the discharge planners tell them without question?

The answer is probably yes.

Do the family members who are supposed to be your advocates in the hospital know what your preferences are? Do they know how to get what you want?

I'm guessing the answer is yes to your preferences, but no to how they are to advocate effectively for your preferences in the heat of the moment.

My mom's story doesn't end here, so let me continue.

In the summer of 2019, my parents came to visit me like they always do. They went back to India in January 2020, just as COVID was emerging.

Shortly after they returned to India, my brother, Jayant, called to tell me he thought Mom and Dad were ill. They were having difficulty breathing, were extremely tired, and had all the signs of COVID—without a diagnosis. He got them medical care and they soon were well enough to return home to their village. In January 2021, my brother called again. "Dad is retaining water," Jayant said. "His whole body is swollen, and he won't listen to anyone. I'm going to go there and see what I can do."

Jayant took Dad to a doctor in Delhi who diagnosed him with congestive heart failure. The doctors gave Dad diuretics. Eventually, he was well enough to return home.

Then, Mom started hallucinating. She would call me telling me she was concerned about the people in the house. There were no people there. My dad did what he could to help my mother, but to no avail. Then, in one of our phone calls, I asked him, "Why don't you go stay with my cousin in a nearby town? You shouldn't be going through this alone."

Dad refused, so Jayant went to the village, picked my parents up, and took them to my cousin's house. While they were there, Mom fell and broke her femur.

By that point, things weren't looking so good in India. COVID was everywhere and people were scared. Mom needed surgery on her hip, but the local doctors refused to do it because of her past heart problems. Jayant hired an ambulance to transport mom to Delhi, admitted her to the hospital, and made plans for her surgery and post-op recovery. Just when all the plans were finalized, and as Jayant tested positive for COVID, the hospital in Delhi was turned into a COVID hospital, and Mom's surgery was postponed.

In the meantime, Mom's hallucinations were getting worse. During a phone call, she told me she had been kidnapped and was being held in a church, and that she was afraid for her life.

That was the last real conversation I had with her. I was crying silently. I could not travel because India had closed its borders. I could not see her before she died on May 28, 2021. She did not die of COVID, but rather, because COVID made getting the care she needed impossible. The saving grace: she died at home with my brother, who had recovered enough to bring them back to his home. She did not die in an institution. This was the only comfort I could take in the sordid mess she dealt with at the end of her life.

I knew that if Mom had been here with me in the Seattle area, she wouldn't have died. That's the blessing of living in America. The curse of living in America is that if you don't know how to advocate for yourself, you risk being eaten up and spit out by a callous system that values revenue above all things.

Here's the moral of the story: If you're an older adult and you don't have an advocate who knows how to navigate the health care system, you're likely to end up in an institution.

Our system is stuck on autopilot, and we have normalized what every older person dreads the most—what every older person resists.

We have normalized institutional care.

In the process, we have institutionalized a dysfunctional system that leads to nightmares, not just for the older adult who is stripped of all dignity and control, but for the family members who will be left to clean up the mess.

Traditional Health Planning Isn't Proactive Enough

As I investigated how planning for health in retirement can either help or hinder your ability to stay out of the nursing home, not lose money to long-term care costs, and not become a burden, several realities became clear.

The way Americans plan for health during retirement isn't working. Signing up for Medicare when you're 65 isn't enough. Going to the doctor when you get sick isn't enough. You've seen how this reactive approach to managing your health overlooks the simple fact that healthy people don't end up in nursing homes. You've seen how, whether you like it or not, lifestyle choices matter—a lot. You've seen that working with the same doctor when you're 70 that you did when you were 40 isn't necessarily the best idea. You've also seen how the insurance system limits access to preventive care due to the health care industry's fee-for-service model.

How do you get what you need from a system that is more about "sick care" than "health care?" I'll answer that question in detail in Chapter 9.

If you are serious about not ending up in the nursing home, not going broke, and not becoming a burden as you age, you must start by addressing the root cause. Good health is your most important asset.

CHAPTER 7

THE PROBLEM WITH FAMILY

Why Is a Lawyer Talking about Family?

As an elder law attorney, nearly all of the work I do with my clients is facilitated by members of their families. Family members are often the people who call me about their elderly loved ones. Family members bring their loved ones to meetings. Family members are the ones who provide care. The family is the elder care shock absorber. They're the ones deciding what to do, and they're the ones carrying it out. Family members are the ones named to carry out responsibilities when a person falls ill. Family members will serve as agents, trustees, executors, and more.

Even if you don't have actual blood relatives, there will be people filling the roles that family members typically play. It could be anyone—a friend, a neighbor, an attorney, a professional fiduciary, or someone else. These people become your family.

You can't talk about aging without talking about family.

Why, then, are so few families talking honestly about the realities of aging?

The Problem with Assumptions

In our sickness-phobic and death-averse culture, no one wants to talk about the unpleasant parts of growing old.

Most people just assume that family members will be there for them when the time comes. That's what family does, right? We make these assumptions, yet most of us don't talk about what we want for ourselves or what we want family members to do when they have to step in on our behalf.

Can you see the problem? When you create a plan for retirement, most of that plan will be implemented by someone other than you if you become incapacitated. This person is usually a spouse, a son or a daughter, a friend, an extended family member, or some other person.

Every chapter in this book involves a family component. In the chapters covering financial planning, you saw the burdens family members assume when it's time to manage your affairs. In the chapters covering legal planning, you learned how traditional Power of Attorney documents don't give your agents—usually family members—any directions about what to do with the powers those documents give them. In the chapters on housing, you learned how your housing choices determine the involvement your family will need to have. And in the chapters on health, you learned how your lifestyle choices can create the health crisis that sets the elder care machine in motion.

Family members are a factor in every aspect of your life in retirement, including where you live, the care you receive, how your affairs are managed, and the quality of life you will live.

Family members are the project managers of your life when you're incapacitated.

Yet, we don't talk about it. We simply assume.

If you have talked about it, maybe your conversation was limited to something like this:

"Promise me you won't put me in a nursing home."

"If I'm in a coma, promise me you'll pull the plug."

Most conversations don't go beyond that. There's little discussion of the "what," and even less discussion of the "how."

If you assume that your kids are your "Plan A" for your old age, but you never talk to them about it, you're almost guaranteeing that your life will turn out in a way you don't want it to. If you assume that they will take you in, be the agent for your Powers of Attorney, or be your caretakers, you're headed for trouble.

That's a big reason why so many of us land in nursing homes. Our families just don't know what to do when we get sick.

They just aren't prepared, so they do what the "system" tells them to do.

That's how you end up broke, a burden, and stuck in a nursing home.

The Problem with Filial Responsibility

What duties do children have to their parents? There have been more than a few stories about filial laws in the news, including a story about a Montana man's mom who received care from a nursing home. When his mother, Dena Mae Jarrell, entered the home, Jerry Jarrell, acting under Power of Attorney, signed the admissions forms on his mother's behalf. When his mother died, the nursing home sued Jerry Jarrell, alleging that as his mother's attorney, he was liable for the debt under Montana's filial support statute.

Financial obligations under family law are largely the responsibility of the states rather than the federal government. Filial support laws are state laws imposing a duty upon adult children for the support of their impoverished parents. Twenty-nine states have filial support laws that make adult children with the means to pay for care responsible for necessities like food, clothing, housing, and medical attention for their parents. The laws are modeled after the Elizabethan Poor Laws of 1601 that made blood relatives the primary source of support for family members, including the elderly. Those laws had been enforced until the New Deal and the advent of Social Security, and later Medicaid. In all but two of those 29 states, filial law was rarely addressed in the courts. And that's how things stood until Medicaid started having financial problems and some states began to reassess filial law to help cut their own costs.

As a result, nursing homes that have cared for elderly individuals who don't have the means to pay for care have begun turning to the children of those individuals using these filial laws. In 2012, a Pennsylvania appeals court found a son liable for his mother's nearly $100,000 nursing home bill when his mother received care and then left the States for Greece, leaving her bill unpaid. Rather than seeking payment from Medicaid, the nursing home went to the son for payment. The result was that nursing homes in other states began to look to this case as precedent.

Let's get back to the story of Jerry Jarrell. The nursing home sued him, saying that he had a duty to pay his mother's debts. Jarrell filed a motion claiming he was acting only on behalf of his mother and was not personally liable for his mother's debt. He also argued that Montana's filial support statutes did not permit nursing homes to force relatives to guarantee payment as a condition of admission. Montana's Eleventh Judicial Court granted Jarrell's motion for summary judgment finding that Montana's specific prohibitions against soliciting third parties for payment trumped the more general language of the filial support law.

But that doesn't stop nursing homes from trying.

The Problem with Who Does What

I had a case involving a single mom with four daughters. They were a loving family who cared about each other.

One of the daughters (let's call her Emily) had lived with Mom for years. Emily looked after Mom. She got groceries, cooked, managed her mom's health care, and took her to doctor appointments. The sisters all trusted Emily. They were grateful for her willingness to provide such loving care.

When the family showed up at my office, Mom's mental capacity had diminished to the point where the family was ready to place her in a nursing home. They wanted Medicaid to help pay for this long-term care while protecting Mom's assets to the greatest degree possible.

In cases like this, the state always has the right to look at financial transactions over the previous five years. Before we submit the application, we always go over at least one year of bank statements so we can answer questions if needed.

We started the application, the family signed the fee agreement, and everyone went back home. As my staff reviewed the bank statements, they noticed dozens and dozens of electronic withdrawals that weren't noted on the mother's check register.

I called Emily and asked for an explanation. She promised to send me all the details.

No response.

I called her again. "Can you get me this information?" I asked. "I need it to finish the Medicaid application."

Again, Emily agreed to send me the details, but she didn't follow through.

I kept calling. She stopped responding.

I needed to get this resolved, so I called the mom. In her diminished state, she was unable to help, so I started calling the sisters. "I need this information and Emily is not cooperating," I told each one.

They all promised to get back to me.

I pushed back. "No, I just want to see all of you together in my office so we can go over these bank accounts and figure out what's going on with these withdrawals," I said.

What I didn't mention was that my staff had continued to dig into the bank records and had discovered hundreds more withdrawals over the first few years alone. The withdrawals weren't large—under $100, in most cases—but they were happening every day, often from more than one ATM per day. If the withdrawals continued at this pace during the entire five-year period, the total could be more than $400,000.

This could put Mom's Medicaid application in jeopardy.

Finally, all the sisters came in and we went through the records. Emily was extremely uncomfortable answering questions about the withdrawals.

Where did the money go?

Eventually, the truth came out. Emily had a gambling problem. No one else in the family knew about it.

Now, we had a real problem. Emily's actions had thrown a major monkey wrench in Mom's Medicaid application. You've already heard me talk about the five-year look-back period. In Mom's case, we can't say that Mom has gifted any money, because she hasn't, yet we must account for the money that Emily took.

We had two options, and both were bad. If we told the state that Emily had been using her mom's Power of Attorney to steal money, the case would have been referred to the Attorney General's office, and Emily might end up in jail.

If we declared these withdrawals as a gift, Mom wouldn't get any Medicaid benefits for the next five years.

It was a difficult situation.

The sisters were angry when they discovered what Emily had done, but they ultimately decided against sending Emily to jail.

This case points to two problems with the way our society handles family involvement during the retirement years.

The first involves a mindset. Emily had been serving as her mother's unpaid caregiver for years. The family members were all fine with this, and it's no surprise. In the U.S., many of us are quite comfortable relying on the unpaid labor of others to provide care for elderly loved ones. It's expected. It's what you do for family. The underlying mindset is this:

Shame on you if you pay for a service you could do yourself.

Where I grew up, it's different. There is no shame in paying people to perform tasks you could do for yourself. When I was a youngster living in India, I saw my family pay for outside help with all sorts of household and caregiving tasks.

Second, Emily had been able to steal money because there had been no transparency in her actions. The sisters had no idea that they could demand an accounting from Emily. There was no mechanism in place.

The Problem with Who Gets What

There was a Wall Street Journal article several years ago that said about 70 percent of estates won't leave all their assets to family members. Some of those assets will be lost through family fights.

We never think that conflicts are going to happen in our families, but there's a good chance that there will be disagreement between the children when they have to deal with your end-of-life issues.

Not long after I started practicing elder law, I got a call from a young Japanese man. I'll call him Lee. He was calling about his mother, Esther, who was completing rehab in a nursing home very close to my office. She didn't have any estate planning documents in place and wanted to get things done. Lee asked me to visit Esther in the nursing home and I agreed.

I found Esther in the dining room. She was very nervous. She didn't like lawyers, but she knew she needed to get her affairs in order.

Esther told me her story. She had three children. Her son, eking out a living on a low-paying warehouse job, had moved into her house just before her medical event. Esther's daughters, on the other hand, were both very successful. Esther and her husband had done a lot to give these daughters a good start in life. They had paid for their education, helped them both pay for their weddings, bought them each a home, and helped them set up their households. Esther was very proud of the fact she had given her daughters such a good start in life, but she was concerned about how her daughters might treat Lee after her death.

Esther knew exactly what she wanted me to do for her. "I want to make sure my home goes to my son, not my daughters," she whispered. "Can you help me do that?"

I assured her that I could. A properly written Will would do the trick.

When I got back to the office, I started the case. About two days later, I stopped into the nursing home to collect some missing information. Esther wasn't in her room, so I tracked her down. I found her in the beauty shop getting her nails done. She was happy to see me.

"Oh Rajiv, I've been sleeping like a baby," she smiled. "I have been at such peace knowing that everything will be okay."

"Of course, it will be," I said. "I'm glad that you called."

We chatted for a bit, and then I left. What I had only suspected before was now perfectly clear. Esther believed that her daughters were going to try to take the house from her son after Esther died.

The next day, I got a call from the nursing home. Esther had slipped into a coma.

I went back to the nursing home with the Will. I sat by her bed and waited for hours. She never woke up. She died the next day, without signing the Will.

A few days later, I called Lee and his sisters and invited them to my office. "I'm your mom's lawyer and we need to go through the Probate process," I said. "Come to my office and I will read you the Will your mom had prepared right before she died."

On the day of the meeting, Lee, his sisters, and their husbands all filed into my office. I was expecting a fight, so I decided to open the conversation with a Chinese proverb.

"Before I read the Will, let me share a story with you," I said. "This story will put your mom's Will in context, and then you can decide what you want to do."

It was a beautiful summer day. A monkey was sitting on top of a tree trying to soak up the sun and catch a nap. Below him, two cats were hissing and fighting, making sleep impossible.

The monkey climbed down to the cats. "Why are you fighting on this perfect day?" the monkey asked.

"There's no food to eat," said the first cat. "We found this piece of bread. We tore it into two so we could share it, but the other cat's piece is bigger than mine. I want my half."

The monkey looked at the cat with the bigger piece and said, "Here, let me see that bread."

The cat handed over his piece. The monkey took a big bite out of it and gave it back to the cat.

The second cat looked at the piece and said, "Not fair! My piece is smaller than his. I should get more."

"Sure thing," said the monkey. He turned to the first cat, asked to see his piece of the bread, and then took another big bite.

The monkey did this until all the bread was gone. The cats ended up with nothing.

"The moral of this story is that your mom's Will may not be how each of you wants it to be, but if you don't agree on a solution, the monkey will end up with the bread," I said. "It is my strong suggestion that you try to settle this."

I proceeded to read the Will. Esther was leaving her home to her son. The house was worth $350,000 at the time. Everything else was to be split equally between the son and the daughters. But, because the Will had not been signed, it had no legal force. It was just moral persuasion for the children to honor their dead mother's known wishes.

Four days later, I got a notice from an attorney on behalf of one of the daughters, followed by another notice from another attorney representing the other daughter. The legal battle was on. I don't do litigation work, so I referred Lee out to another attorney. I don't know what the outcome was, but my guess is that Lee didn't get the house.

Though this case is about what happens when you don't get your legal planning done in time, I include it in this chapter about family because it's a striking illustration of the rifts you can create when you delay planning. Despite your best intentions, the things you want to happen often don't happen. Some families, like Esther's, never recover.

The Problem with Who Decides What

If you experience a health crisis in your later years and you've been married more than once, conflict between your current spouse and your children from a previous marriage can cause no end of problems.

In Chapter 5, I talked about how American Top 40 host Casey Kasem's $80 million fortune wasn't enough to keep him from dying in an institution. It wasn't enough to overcome deep-seated family divisions, either. At the end of his life, Kasem was involved in a bitter legal battle as his wife, Jean, and his children from his first marriage argued about what kind of care he should receive after he was diagnosed with Lewy body dementia.[54]

In 2013, as Kasem's health worsened, his wife prevented any contact with him, particularly by his children from his first marriage. The older Kasem children sought conservatorship over their father's care,[55] but the court denied their petition.[56]

Jean removed Kasem from his Santa Monica, California, nursing home on May 7, 2014. On May 12, Kerri Kasem was granted temporary conservatorship over her father, despite her stepmother's objection.[57]

The court ordered an investigation into Casey Kasem's whereabouts after his wife's attorney told the court that Casey was "no longer in the United States." He was found soon afterward in Washington State.[58]

On June 6, 2014, Kasem was reported to be in critical but stable condition in a hospital in Washington State, receiving antibiotics for bedsores and treatment for high blood pressure. It was revealed he had been bedridden for some time.[59] A judge ordered separate visitation times for Kasem's wife and his children from his first marriage.[60] Judge Daniel S. Murphy ruled that Kasem had to be hydrated, fed, and medicated as a court-appointed lawyer reported on his health status. Jean Kasem claimed he had been given no food, water, or medication the previous weekend. Kerri Kasem's lawyer stated that she had him removed from artificial food and water on the orders of a doctor and in accordance with a directive her father signed in 2007, saying he would not want to be kept alive if it "would result in a mere biological existence, devoid of cognitive function, with no reasonable hope for normal functioning."[61] Murphy reversed his order the following Monday after it became known that Kasem's body was no longer responding to the artificial nutrition, allowing the family to place Kasem on "end-of-life" measures over the objections of Jean Kasem.[62]

On June 15, 2014, Kasem died at St. Anthony's Hospital in Gig Harbor, Washington, at the age of 82.

In November 2015, three of Kasem's children and his brother sued his widow for wrongful death. The lawsuit charges Jean Kasem with elder abuse and inflicting emotional distress on the children by restricting access before his death.[63] The suits were settled in 2019.

This situation made headlines as it was unfolding. I remember hearing about it on the news.

I have little firsthand knowledge of this situation, but I can see both sides of the story. Jean was married to Casey Kasem for 33 years. I can see why Jean would feel like she had the right to make decisions about his care. I can also understand why the children from Kasem's first marriage were so upset. I talked to Kerri Kasem about the situation, and I understand why she and her family felt as they did, and why they did what they did. I know Kerri to be a fearless advocate for what she believes in, and she truly believed that Jean did the family wrong. My conjecture, based on my decades of experience working with families in similar situations, was that Casey Kasem didn't sit down with his family and explain how he wanted things to be when his health failed. Like so many Americans, he assumed that his family would just figure it out. The trouble was, there were two families who had different ideas about what "it" was, not to mention how "it" should be figured out.

Traditional Planning Overlooks Family

You've heard me say it before, and I'll say it again. Aging is a family affair. Once your health starts to fail, your family, whoever that is, will become more and more involved in your life. Despite this reality, traditional retirement planning advice—with its focus on money and legal documents—is completely silent on the topic.

There's an assumption that family will somehow be there to pick up the pieces for you, even when you've never talked about these things in advance. You've seen how these assumptions can leave families in shambles. You've seen what can happen when family members believe caregiving should be a free service. You've seen what can happen when older adults don't share their plans or preferences with their families, or they share them too late. You've seen what can happen when warring factions can't agree on anything, much less what needs to be done.

Every element of retirement planning I've talked about so far in Part 1 has a family component. Your family will be involved when your health fails. Your family will be involved when your health issues make it impossible for you to live safely at home. Your family will be involved in the management of your financial affairs, including how your funds will be spent (or not spent) to pay for your care. Your family will be involved in the management of your legal affairs, including all the decision-making authority that Powers of Attorney give them. Your family might even be asked to pull the plug.

If you planned for retirement in the traditional way, your family will be scrambling to pick up the pieces as they guess about your preferences and put their lives on hold to manage yours. When that happens, get ready. Odds are good that you'll be part of the 70 percent who land in a nursing home, end up broke, or become a burden on the people they love the most.

If that's not how you want your life to go, I have a better way. Just turn the page to get started.

PART 2

A BETTER WAY TO PLAN

CHAPTER 8

INTRODUCTION TO
LIFE PLANNING

As you have seen, traditional retirement planning is about having a financial plan, an estate plan, access to medical care, and all sorts of time to *live*. Traditional retirement planning is about funding and then experiencing the adventures we have been planning all along, things like travel, leisure, time with friends and family, new hobbies, and fun things that require time and money. After all, it is finally our time to do what we want to do, not what others want us to do.

To assemble the components of a traditional retirement plan, most of us have worked with many professionals along the way, including financial planners, insurance agents, lawyers, accountants, realtors, mortgage brokers, and perhaps others. We have done many kinds of planning, but none of it was coordinated. It was bumble bee planning, which involved going from one professional to another, from one topic to the next. Though there was no mechanism to coordinate the work that was done by different professionals, our plan somehow seemed to come together.

Once retired, we expect to live out our dreams—dreams that don't include falling ill and ending up in a nursing home. It's not on our bucket list to be a burden to others, or to go broke paying for unexpected care costs. No, that was never in the cards, even though 70 percent of retirees meet with one, two, or all three of these realities, for all the reasons I've explained in the previous chapters. There was no master plan in place that would ensure that your dreams would come true—and that the nightmares wouldn't.

You have seen that, for most people, their most deeply held goals for retirement are to avoid the nursing home, avoid losing money to uncovered long-term care costs, and avoid being a burden on loved ones.

If your biggest fear is that you won't accomplish those goals, you are by no means alone.

In Part 1 of this book, you learned why that happens.

Were you surprised? Most people are.

It can be a shock to discover that the people you've been working with to plan your retirement haven't been focused on the goals you hold most dear. They've been focused on providing you with the guidance their profession thinks to be important for retirees and soon-to-be retirees; the goals they have been trained to help you achieve. Following the advice of the many different professionals, or the advice we are aware of if we try and put the plan together without the help of professionals, here is what the planning amounts to:

Health care planning involves signing up for Medicare, and investing in a supplemental insurance plan. This will ensure that if you fall ill, you will have access to health care services that we know we will need in our later years. And you pick a doctor from the big book that the insurance company makes available to you. The doctor reminds you to make an appointment to see him or her if you develop a health problem.

Your financial planner tells you to accumulate money and buy insurance and financial products.

Your lawyer does "Die-Die-Die" planning by creating legal documents that define who gets what when you die, how you want to die, and who will manage your affairs until you die should you become incapacitated.

Each professional has your best interest at heart. Each professional wants to help you succeed in retirement following their guidance.

But answer this: Which professional has promised you that their plan is the one that will help you achieve your goals of not ending up in a nursing home, not going broke, and not becoming a burden?

Every professional is doing exactly what they were trained to do, but that training does not involve helping you achieve your goals of having a path to avoid nursing homes, not become a burden, or not lose money to uncovered care costs (outside of the purchase of a long-term care insurance policy).

If you're in your 60s or older and you fell ill today, what would happen? Where would you end up after being discharged from the hospital? Would it be possible for you to come back home without becoming a burden on your family or running out of money?

If you cannot answer this question with a confident YES, please keep reading. Part 2 of this book is where I explain how to achieve these goals.

I will show you how to plan for health, housing, financial, legal, and family issues in a way that will help you avoid the nursing home, avoid going broke, and avoid burdening your family.

I call it a *LifePlan*.

A *LifePlan* is a master plan for retirement that coordinates health, housing, finances, legal, and family issues so you can avoid the nursing home, avoid going broke, and avoid being a burden. No other retirement planning system coordinates planning efforts in support of these goals.

In the chapters to come, I will show you how to create a *LifePlan*. You will learn when to start working on it, what to include, and how to connect each element of planning so you can achieve your goals.

My goal is to empower you to take control of your retirement planning process. Following the guidance in this book, you will step into the role of architect and project manager of your *LifePlan* for retirement. You will learn how to create a plan that meets your goals for every stage of retirement, including the years when you are healthy, and the years when you are not.

In the process, you will overcome blind reliance on so-called experts to tell you what you need. You will learn how to require the professionals you choose to work with to deliver what *you* want, not the solutions they want you to adopt because that is how they are trained to think and plan.

I will show you how to take your rightful place as the quarterback of your own retirement plan. That's what the rest of this book is about.

Looking Upstream for Answers

How did *LifePlanning* come to be?

You've heard me talk about my "Groundhog Day" elder law practice. I went into the practice of law because I saw my father-in-law's planning fail him in every way, even though he had followed the advice and counsel of many different professionals. My practice was set up to help people who were facing incapacity, as my father-in-law was. During the first few years of my practice, day after day, I saw people in the same situation. The faces, the names, and the account balances were different, but the suffering was always the same.

After a few years in the trenches, I started noticing patterns. I began to track my cases in a journal.

I started wondering.

What was the root cause of this retirement plan failure? What could these people have done ten years earlier to avoid the crisis that landed them in my office today? What could Bill and Vivian have done differently? If I could have intervened earlier, could I have helped them avoid the crisis? What would I have told them to do differently?

This became my obsession.

Here is how the concept of *LifePlanning* evolved. Once I started obsessing about wanting to do more than what law school had taught me to do for my clients when they came looking for estate planning, I needed to develop a playbook. The playbook would have to evaluate how my clients were approaching each aspect of their retired life, not just legal planning. And I would try and give them a glimpse of how that planning could backfire, along with ways for them to change the approach so they may be able to avoid the outcomes experienced by Bill and Vivian, and countless other clients I was helping after they got into trouble. That soon became known as an assessment letter, something no law school taught me, but that I learned from the school of hard knocks.

I wrote my first assessment letter in the early 2000s. It took me about a year of reflecting on Bill and Vivian's situation (Vivian was living with us at that time) and analyzing dozens of cases where people had hired me after a person ended up in a care facility before I started feeling a sense of confidence in my analysis of why dreams turn into nightmares. The first assessment letter I wrote was thirteen pages long, and it explained what legal planning the client needed to do to avoid being forced into a nursing home. Over the years, I added to this letter, and it included more than just legal advice. It delivered advice about other aspects of retired life that the client would eventually have to deal with. A few years later, I came up with the process that a client could follow to develop a coordinated plan for health, housing, financial, and legal issues that I knew the client would be dealing with in retirement. It took a few more years to develop the system that I now call *LifePlanning*, which evolved into its current form by the early 2010s. It was truly an evolutionary process.

If I had to summarize my approach in just a few words, it would be this:

LifePlanning is upstream retirement planning.

Let's say you schedule a consult with me today. Your family brings you in because you had a stroke, and you can't return home. Your family needs to figure out where you will live and how they will pay for your care. If I could have met you ten years ago, knowing that you and I would be sitting here trying to pick up the pieces after your stroke, what guidance would I have given you so that when you came to me today, you wouldn't be facing a one-way trip to the nursing home? How could I help you focus your planning efforts so you avoid institutional care, avoid going broke, and avoid being a burden? If I could have advised you ten years before your stroke, you would have done things differently, and your outcomes would have been very different as well.

Being born in India was an advantage for me as I developed the *LifePlanning* process. Being born in India allowed me to question the givens of the American system. If the Third World did a better job with the aging process, why couldn't the richest country in the world also do better?

LifePlanning is a hybrid approach to planning that blends the best parts of America's system with the best of how aging is handled in other parts of the world. It offers an unobstructed path to reach the three goals that matter most: avoiding institutional care, protecting assets from uncovered long-term care costs, and not being a burden on others.

LifePlanning: The Master Plan for Retirement

Recognizing how retirement dreams turn into retirement nightmares, the *LifePlanning* process delivers a comprehensive and coordinated plan for health care, housing, financial, and legal issues in retirement that helps you achieve these goals. Each client's journey is a bit different, but the key elements are almost always the same.

By following the guidance in the chapters to come, you can develop your very own comprehensive *LifePlan* long before catastrophe strikes.

I will show you how to:

- Have confidence in your plan for retirement by learning how to bridge the gaps in traditional retirement planning that I covered in the previous chapters.

- Use your health insurance to focus on preventative care so you can prolong your years of healthy independence, possibly eliminating the need for expensive long-term care.

- Find a housing option that lets you live a happy life while you are healthy and gives you assurance that you will be able to access care without moving should you face incapacity in later years.

- Protect your assets from being lost to uncovered medical and care costs, or to other outside forces, when you are no longer in control of your decisions, regardless of the size of your financial portfolio.

- Continue to enjoy a good quality of life without going broke or creating burdens for the people you love.

- Integrate your planning efforts between professionals to avoid unintended conflicts.

- Set up guidance for your loved ones to follow when it's time for them to step into your life, so you can have predictability of outcome without becoming a burden.

- Achieve the confidence to hold every professional you hire accountable to a higher and more personal standard that will help you achieve your goals.

Let's begin your *LifePlanning*.

CHAPTER 9

A BETTER WAY TO PLAN FOR HEALTH

Foundational Insight

Traditional health planning in retirement generally involves enrolling in Medicare and buying a supplemental plan so you can access medical care if you get sick.

LifePlanning is staying healthier longer.

Introduction

What is the single most important thing you can do to avoid the nursing home?

The answer is simple: avoid falling ill.

How do you do that? You accomplish that by learning how to use the health care system to stay healthier longer and prevent illnesses, not just how to access care if you fall ill. In other words, you focus on prevention.

In Part 1, you learned a surprising truth about planning for health in retirement. Enrolling in Medicare, seeing your doctor a few times a year, and getting care when you get sick isn't enough.

Good health is your most valuable asset in retirement, and you must do all you can to protect it. In order to avoid getting sick, you must approach the preservation of your health as an integral part of your retirement plan.

The ideas in this chapter came to me over time as I worked with clients in my elder law practice. Many of these clients were coming to me in crisis. Their health problems were creating the cascade of housing, financial, legal, and family problems that you've read about in previous chapters.

As you already know, I'm a voracious reader and researcher. You could also call me a voracious reflector. I would see clients during the day, and reflect on their situations later at night. I would research their unique issues after working hours.

I was seeing people get sick before their retirement. Many more were getting sick soon after retiring. It was sad to watch, but it was also very frustrating. If I could have worked with these people ten years earlier, maybe some of these sad situations could have been prevented.

This thinking, this reflecting, this reading, and this research are what came together to create what I now call the Health Pillar of the *Life-Planning* process.

Some of my ideas came from my own perspective as a person born in India who now lives in the U.S. Some ideas came from my friends who were physicians who took the time to explain the basics of preventive care. One of those doctors talked about these issues on his radio show, which aired right before mine on Saturday mornings in Seattle. Other ideas were little more than the focused application of conventional wisdom.

During my nightly reading, I started looking into how insurance plans both help and hinder older adults who are looking to prevent illness, not just treat it once it happens. I discovered new ways to use insurance that can help more of us stay healthier longer. My experience working for insurance companies was helpful because I had some familiarity with how these policies were written and how they worked.

As a lawyer, I tell my clients this: if you are concerned about living a good life and hope to avoid a nursing home, start with health care. Don't fall ill.

How do you do that? The prescription is simple. Eat right, exercise, socialize, and have the right people on your medical team.

Eat Right

I have often joked with my wife that if you are looking for the devil on earth, you'll find him in our kitchens, hidden away in foods we don't need and can easily do without.

Eating right is vital for everyone at every age, but it is especially important when you're over 50. However, most of us don't eat all that well. Government statistics show that obesity among older adults is on the rise.[64]

Eating right means making healthy choices with your food. There are many trendy fads in the world of eating, but there are few that are consistently recommended and evidence-based. Though I won't be recommending any specific diets, I can recommend some basic habits, such as eating lots of fruits and vegetables, eating the needed amount of nutrients, such as the correct ratio of protein-rich foods proportionate to your weight, decreasing caloric intake, and paying attention to portion sizes.

If you're not sure how much or what to eat, there's a great online resource called My Plate which uses illustrations to help individuals make healthy dietary choices.[65] The Older Adults section points out the strong correlation between eating well and being able to manage existing health issues such as heart disease, stroke, type 2 diabetes, bone loss, some forms of cancer, and anemia. Eating healthy has been proven to reduce chemicals associated with inflammation, improve sleep and mood, boost energy levels, improve memory, and lower the risk of Alzheimer's disease.

As you grow older, some foods may be better for you than others according to the National Institute of Health (NIH). Many of the medicines older adults use for heart problems can affect how foods taste. Some foods can reduce the effectiveness of drugs. Grapefruit is one of those foods. It can reduce the effectiveness of blood thinners, blood pressure, and allergy and cholesterol medications, just to name a few.[66]

Keep a Food Journal

A study published in the American Journal of Preventive Medicine found that the most powerful predictor of weight loss in study participants was how many days per week they kept a food journal.[67] Individuals who kept records of their food intake six days a week lost twice as much weight as those who kept track one day a week or less. Researchers in that study determined that the increased awareness participants had for just where their calories were coming from was the most powerful motivator for losing weight, second only to being held accountable. Writing down what you eat and drink increases your awareness when it comes to your nutritional habits.[68]

Find a Nutritionist

In the end, I will acknowledge, left to our own devices, changing eating habits is not easy. So, get help. Along with keeping a food journal, I recommend that you see a nutritionist, someone who can guide you as you keep your food journal and recommend good eating habits to practice. If proper diet can help keep high blood pressure, high cholesterol, and other chronic ailments away, why shouldn't a nutritionist be as important, if not more so, than a primary care provider who will diagnose the ailment only after the damage has been done? A nutritionist can provide you with the most comprehensive and up-to-date information on eating well. Your nutritionist can also act as your coach. Many insurance plans cover visits to nutritionists. Call your insurance company to find out if your plan does. If not, consider switching to a plan that does.

Finally, along with keeping a food journal and seeing a nutritionist, find someone who will keep you accountable, whether it be a family member, a friend, or a group. Face-to-face and online support groups can provide a stepped-up level of accountability for those who need a higher level of support. One of the benefits of using apps for tracking calories is that they usually include communities of like-minded people.

If you do nothing more than take these steps listed above and stick to them, your health will undoubtedly improve over the coming months and years. Remember to talk with your primary care physician before making the move to healthier eating habits and lifestyle. The longer you can maintain your health, the less money you will need to spend on expensive long-term care.

Exercise

As important as healthy eating is to successful aging, it is not as effective by itself as it is when paired with good exercise habits. Experts say that older adults need to be educated on the importance of maintaining regular exercise in addition to healthy eating.[69]

Exercise is not just about getting fit to look better (although it helps with that, too). Exercise is also about maintaining your ability to function independently. The loss of that ability is one of the main reasons people end up institutionalized.

What we know from study after study is that exercise isn't just a way to build muscle or lose weight. Exercise also maintains the integrity of your bones, and improves balance, mobility, and coordination. In addition, strength training can also reduce the signs and symptoms of arthritis[70] and improve mental abilities.[71]

Exercise can improve energy and self-confidence. It can lessen anxiety and depression. Physical activity can help you maintain a healthy body weight, which in turn relieves stress on weight-bearing joints, improves blood pressure, and lowers blood sugar and blood fat levels. Research has also shown that regular exercise helps to prevent blood clots, which is a particular benefit to people with heart- or blood-related diseases.

An active lifestyle also improves sleep, which plays a critical role in immune function and is one of the strongest anti-inflammatory tools to help reduce disease. Exercise can benefit you greatly as you age by strengthening your muscles, which will help you improve your balance and ultimately reduce your risk of falling. Lastly, regardless of age, regular exercise can also lead to greater intellectual vigor, specifically improvements in executive functions.

This is important because executive functions, which are responsible for emotional and cognitive control, tend to fade as we age.

How is your daily exercise lately? Would you consider yourself sedentary, active, or fit? Sedentary means you don't move much. Likely you get around the house, but not much more than that. Being active means that you are regularly moving around the house and the yard, but you do not engage in vigorous activity on any regular basis. And fit means that you make it your business to get your heart rate up, perspire, and proactively pursue physical fitness, since exercise plays such a large role in helping you prolong your healthy years.

If your physical condition is such that you cannot walk, consider a water exercise. If you identified as active, your goal should be adding a routine to get your heart rate up and perspire a bit. If you find that to be difficult, see if your health insurance policy includes gym privileges. If it does not, look for a policy during the next open enrollment period that does, and then use those benefits to create a healthier future for yourself. Going to a gym will allow you the opportunity to work with a personal trainer.

Research shows that when you make yourself accountable to someone for personal behavior, you will be more likely to follow through on your commitments. Be sure to consult with your physician about what exercise would be appropriate for you at any point in the process of aging, and as you start to feel your muscles getting weaker or your bones getting more brittle. Often, the response is to not do as much anymore, or to be fearful about doing more.

Exercise also benefits the brain. Exercise protects our learning and memory centers in the brain from neurodegeneration and increases synaptic plasticity (the ability of synapses to strengthen over time).[72]

Few older adults in the United States achieve even the minimum recommended amount of physical activity (150 to 300 minutes of moderate exercise, or 75 to 150 minutes of intensive exercise, per week).[73] According to the National Institutes of Health, only about 30 percent of people ages 45 to 64 say they engage in regular exercise. That number falls to 25 percent for those between the ages of 64 and 74, and only 11 percent for those over the age of 85.[74]

Where do you start? If you haven't exercised in a while, starting a new exercise routine can be intimidating, especially at the gym where you see others running on the treadmill for hours or lifting heavy weights. Remember, don't try to do too much too quickly. There are studies that show that doing something as simple as setting an alarm for every half hour and moving around just a bit actually helps to improve muscles, balance, and circulation. So again, look for simple ways that you can slowly and safely improve your exercise routine. I suggest that you start with little habits and work your way to building a larger system of exercise.

We'll begin with something very simple: sitting and standing.

Don't Just Sit There!

Some medical experts have started referring to long periods of inactivity such as sitting and its consequences as "sitting disease." Several studies associate time spent sitting with mortality for men and women.[75]

It's not just that sitting for long periods of time is unhealthy and even deadly for you, it's that even when adults meet physical activity guidelines, sitting compromises metabolic health and increases the risk of disability for individuals over the age of 60. One study comparing two 65-year-old women found that the difference in one additional hour of sitting amounted to a 50 percent increase in the likelihood of becoming disabled.[76]

The good news is that to counteract the problems associated with sitting disease, you don't really have to do much. Some experts say that being more active may simply mean moving more during the day. This could be as simple as standing on an hourly basis or walking while on the phone or chatting to co-workers.[77]

Take the First Steps

Now that you know that a sedentary lifestyle is an unhealthy lifestyle, you are ready to take active measures toward exercising on a regular basis. When you decide to pursue a more active lifestyle, you might face intimidating questions: What kind of activity is best for me? How often should I be exercising? How much is enough? The simplest place to start is right outside your house.

Walking 30 minutes a day is the easiest way to get your foot in the door (or out the door) when it comes to fitness. Walking 7,000 to 10,000 steps a day is another way you can measure your activity.

The great thing about walking is that you can do it anywhere: on your neighborhood sidewalks, in the mall, or on the treadmill at the gym. The key is to stay consistent. If you have trouble staying accountable, you can buy an activity tracker. There are plenty of these on the market such as those from Apple, Nike, Jawbone, Garmin, Fitbit, and Body-Media. Activity trackers combine a wearable device—usually a bracelet or watch—with a website or smartphone app. They track not just when you're active but also when you're not active, as well as sleep patterns. One study found that even sedentary people who wore an activity tracker increased their activity levels.[78]

Surrounding yourself with a supportive group of people is another way to help you stay accountable. This could include friends or family, or you could even look online for forums of people who have similar fitness goals and are at fitness levels close to your own. I've found that when you choose someone with similar fitness levels and fitness goals as a workout partner, you tend to stay more accountable to that person because you are going through a similar experience.

Incorporating movement into your lifestyle doesn't have to be difficult. Consult your doctor. Set small, attainable goals. Once those are met, create bigger ones. Start slow ... but start!

Regular physical activity contributes to healthy aging and the ability to lead an independent lifestyle for a longer time. It may also save you money if your better health outcomes lead to lower amounts of medications. Likewise, ignoring your health will lead to a higher chance of you needing medical attention.

Don't forget to check your health insurance plan to see what exercise programs it covers. Your plan may cover a gym membership, personal training, group fitness classes, or the Silver Sneakers program offered by YMCAs across the country. Look for those in your insurance plan to maximize the health care system for your benefit.

Here's another thought: If you live in a place where exercising outdoors can be a challenge at times, the use of a sauna can have many of the same benefits as regular exercise. The University of Eastern Finland commissioned a study to test the benefits of using a sauna. The findings show that those who sat in a 174-degree (F) sauna for an average of 14 minutes five to seven times each week had significantly reduced incidence of cardiovascular issues (e.g., heart attacks, strokes, blood pressure, cholesterol, etc.), and also reduced their risk of dementia by 66 percent.[79]

About Discipline

We all know that we need to move more. So why don't we?

One reason is a lack of discipline. We all struggle with this. I know I have at times.

It's easy to let outside activities dictate our lives. We are not in charge of our lives when we fail to exercise. Treat time like your most important currency. You only have so much of it before you will run out.

We all have 24 hours in a day. What we do with that time is up to us, but only if we are disciplined about it. Here is what you want to cram in your 24 hours to have good health:

1. Sleep (8 hours at night + about 1 hour of naptime)
2. One hour of exercise
3. Two hours of socializing

That leaves you with 12 hours for other activities. If you are working, ration the amount of time for work—say 10 hours. You still have 2 hours left over.

Habits will go a long way. It is okay for you to deviate from time to time, but not as a rule. Start slow ... but start!

If you are creative, you might combine your exercise with other normal daily activities. Maybe your exercise could come in the form of walking to the store three days a week. You will be surprised how wonderful it is to breathe fresh air when you walk. This is smelling the roses.

The point of exercise is to build muscle and raise your heart rate. Your heart is a muscle. Exercise it, and it stays stronger. Let it slow down and not too many good things happen.

Socialize

You might be surprised that I included socializing as a recommendation in the health section of this book. I included it for one very specific reason. Many studies have come out over the last decade or two that have strongly recommended socializing as a foundation for preserving mental health.

AARP states on its website: "Many scientists now believe that social interaction is key to maintaining good mental health and warding off diseases like dementia and Alzheimer's. Recent studies document the positive effects of social interaction."[80]

The article goes on to say, "Close relationships and large social networks have a beneficial impact on memory and cognitive function as people age." Socializing, along with challenging your brain with mental activities, such as taking up new hobbies and reading, are integral to staving off memory loss, one of the symptoms associated with Alzheimer's disease.

Dementia-related diseases can last years, even decades, and currently, there are no cures. Socializing has been found to be one way to slow this degenerative process.

Connection Slows Cognitive Decline

As we age, the effects of social isolation and loneliness increase, and this is experienced by as many as 40 percent of aging adults. Why is this such a problem? Research indicates that loneliness often equals depression and accelerates cognitive decline, which is your ability to remember. Cognitive decline is among the leading reasons people enter institutional care. Anything we can do to lower the risk will be of benefit to that end.

During my research on this subject, I discovered a published article that talked about a study comparing the brains of a Hispanic man and a Caucasian man, both of whom died from complications of Alzheimer's disease. Researchers dissected the brains thinking that their brains would be equally affected. They discovered that the brain of the Hispanic man was far more affected by the disease, yet he had been functioning at a much higher level than the Caucasian man. The reason was connection, researchers concluded. The Hispanic man was living in a joint family system where he had plenty of social contact with other people. The Caucasian man was living in a nuclear family system with little mental stimulation.

Then there are other studies on this topic. Arguably, the leading study on this topic is the Nun Alzheimer's study. The Nun Study on Aging and Alzheimer's Disease is a continuing longitudinal study, begun in 1986, to examine the onset of Alzheimer's disease.[81] This study looked at a group of nuns who donated their brains to be examined. The results showed that many of the nuns had Alzheimer's disease, yet these nuns showed no signs of the disease while they were alive.

How could the nuns have had Alzheimer's disease but not show the signs? There are many reasons that are cited as contributing to this unbelievable phenomenon. When I read the study, what jumps out at me is that the nuns whose brains were studied never stopped leading a life of purpose. To their dying days, they were out there helping the poor and those in need. This is not the pattern you find with most who succumb to the ravages of Alzheimer's. Staying meaningfully engaged with life, holding oneself accountable to the needs of others is more than merely being social. It is having a purpose in life. I believe it is that purpose that allows nuns to have Alzheimer's yet not be sidelined by it.

I find support for this way of thinking in the lives of many of my clients and many public figures. Ronald Reagan is a great example. He had Alzheimer's while he was in office, but he continued a very active life. He may have slowed a bit, but it did not sideline him.

The more I studied, the more I saw that there is a clear connection between Alzheimer's disease and the lack of social contact. My own experience working with older adults bears this out. Socialization, having a purpose to wake up to every day, and remaining meaningfully engaged in life is just as important as having a good diet and regular exercise. It will do more than you think to preserve your health, keeping you out of the nursing home.

Dementia Prevention

The second, and in my opinion, the more important aspect of dementia care, is engaging in a way to prevent it from becoming reality in your life. The prevailing view on this issue seems to be to address it after a diagnosis, because there seems to be little anyone can do about it. But, by definition, prevention is taking action when you are healthy and not ill, not after you begin showing signs of an ailment.

To that end, understand that although presently, there is not enough work that is being done on the prevention and cure of dementia, this does not mean that there is *no* work being done. The leading study on this issue is a research study that was published in 2014 by UCLA, where they reviewed ten individuals with mild to severe cognitive impairment and developed protocols designed to reverse the condition in the patients.[82] They succeeded doing so in 90 percent of the cases. The one instance where they were unable to reverse the condition was because the dementia had become too advanced. Given the small sample size in the initial study, the study was then repeated with a larger group, and yielded similar results.

Although the bulk of the research into dementia-related issues is focused on slowing the progression of the illness, there are some exceptions to this reality. These exceptions adopt the findings of the UCLA study with the aim of helping people stave off the negative effects of dementia. The three exceptions in the Puget Sound area of Washington State are Dr. Mary Kay Ross (https://brainhealthandresearch.com/), Dr. Jerry Mixon (https://www.longevitymedicalclinic.com/), and Dr. Jonathan V. Wright (https://tahomaclinic.com/). All three doctors are working on preventative care for dementia. You may have similar medical providers in your area, but don't expect to find them easily. You will need to search for them.

Dr. Ross was the chief clinical officer for the UCLA study and the one most qualified to understand how the study worked. Her clinic helps people understand how to deal with the day-to-day challenges of a loved one with dementia.

Dr. Mixon's Longevity Medical Clinic had taken an early lead in addressing dementia issues from a preventative point of view. After visiting UCLA and studying their methods, Dr. Mixon has been offering these protocols to patients who are either dealing with dementia or are at a higher risk of the illness.

Dr. Wright, at the Tahoma Clinic, is also offering the program, which is based on the UCLA study and its health professional training program. The goal is to get ahead of the illness and prevent dementia, or at a minimum, prolong cognitively healthy years.

Rethinking the Alzheimer's Diagnosis

What would you say if I told you that some people with pathological evidence of Alzheimer's disease show no symptoms of the disease? An article that appeared on *CNN* a few years ago explains this fascinating proposition.[83]

If you are up on the latest research about Alzheimer's disease, you have probably heard that there are specific signs in the brain that indicate the presence of the disease. Doctors look for telltale evidence in the form of deposits called plaques, and nerve clusters called tangles, that, when discovered, should mean cognitive decline is imminent, if not already present. But what if someone has all the pathological markers of Alzheimer's disease but few, if any, of the symptoms? Does that person have the disease or not?

According to the article, many neurologists are starting to ask that question, and it's causing some to rethink what "having Alzheimer's disease" actually means. The *CNN* article was written as an opinion piece by New York physician and neurologist Gayatri Devi. She describes a 64-year-old patient, a high-powered attorney, who had started experiencing some memory loss. Even though he appeared fine on initial examination, Dr. Devi gave him a thorough neurocognitive evaluation which revealed some auditory memory problems. "Because he was still functioning extremely well, I diagnosed him as having cognitive impairment," Dr. Devi wrote, "and put him on medications to help his memory."

Over the next three years, this man's memory test scores continued to show some decline, and he wanted to know what was happening in his brain. Finally, a more detailed analysis revealed the presence of tell-tale plaques and tangles. This patient now had biological evidence of Alzheimer's disease. Nevertheless, he was still functioning well at his law firm. "Few people suspected problems," the doctor wrote. "Even I, his neurologist, with 25 years of experience in cognitive neurology, could not tell from repeated conversations with him over three years that he had any real memory issues.

So, what was my verdict? Did he or didn't he have Alzheimer's disease? My answer has gotten more complicated over the years."

Apparently, evidence of this anomaly—what the article called "this disconnect between pathology and clinical symptoms"—is creating confusion for patients and physicians alike. A July 2019 study published in *JAMA Neurology* examined more than 5,000 American adults between the ages of 60 and 89, and found "significantly more people with biologically defined Alzheimer's ... than there were people with clinical Alzheimer's disease, exhibiting symptoms."[84] In fact, the older the patient, the greater the disconnect. "Among 85-year-olds," wrote Dr. Devi, "for every three people with the pathology, only one person had symptoms. In other words, most men and women with biologically defined Alzheimer's had no symptoms." As many as 40 percent of adults 80-plus have plaques in the brain, yet are without symptoms, states the article.

With so many people showing the pathology of Alzheimer's disease without the outward symptoms, the definition of the disease is shifting. "It is becoming clear that the association between such pathology and symptoms varies from person to person," wrote Dr. Devi. "Many factors affect the progression to Alzheimer's, in addition to genetics, including cognitive and physiological factors, and the areas of the brain that are affected. These factors are so influential that even in identical twins, symptom onset of Alzheimer's disease can vary by as many as 18 years."[85] For some reason, patients like Dr. Devi's 67-year-old attorney appear to have healthy brains that can resist the typical progression of Alzheimer's disease.

For many of these patients who are functioning well despite biological markers of Alzheimer's, the biggest problem can be psychological. The disease carries with it a commonly-held belief that the prognosis is inevitably grim. Dr. Devi worried that her patient, once he learned that he was—medically speaking—an Alzheimer's sufferer, would stop trying to live his active life and instead buy into the "nightmarish predictions" concerning his future. "I needed him to understand that an individualized approach is key to diagnosing, treating, and living fully with Alzheimer's disease," said the doctor. Because every brain is unique, "some people [stay] stable for years, even without treatment. Yet … with Alzheimer's disease the overwhelming belief is that everyone ends up in a wheelchair, unable to recognize family and themselves. While this is true in some, it is not the case for all."

In her article, Dr. Devi advocated for what she calls a "better definition of different types of Alzheimer's" so that researchers can do a better job of developing different drugs to treat different types of patients. She also said the "scientific narrative" which recognizes the nuances of Alzheimer's disease needs to align with the "societal narrative" that the illness is always a grim death sentence. "Bridging this divide is crucial for destigmatizing the disease and for providing the type of tailored treatment that will bring success in treating those with clinical symptoms of the illness," she wrote. Meanwhile, patients like Dr. Devi's now-67-year-old attorney, who, in many ways, is functioning normally, will have to deal with continual worry and doubt (what she calls "The

Doubting Disease") as he wrestles with the implications of "his own private Alzheimer's disease."

I applaud Dr. Devi's approach and agree that it is time for us as a society to rethink what "having Alzheimer's disease" truly means.

Creating a Sense of Purpose

Meaningful interactions benefit our hearts, our minds, and our souls. How do you create a sense of purpose in life? How do you stay meaningfully engaged? You do so by staying involved in life. You do it by cultivating high-quality relationships and vibrant, active social groups. The benefits include enhanced mental health that helps with a positive outlook on life, a sense of belonging when doing something meaningful with others, and better self-esteem that comes from contributing to others outside of yourself.

For example, being engaged in religious or charitable organizations, civic groups, or other circles whose purpose has an impact on how you find meaning. Any of these will have positive impacts on your health, and are a good way to expand the age range of your circle of friends. Who do you interact with regularly? Could you benefit by expanding your number of friends or the meaningfulness of your interactions?

When you're finding ways to connect with others, keep age in mind. It is important to also recognize that we often make friends within our age group, but this group shrinks as we age, so it is vital to make friends with folks 5, 10, 15-plus years younger.

It can be quite depressing when your circle of friends shrinks. I've heard my 92-year-old father talk about this. "Everybody's cutting in front of me in the line to the next world," he has said more than once. That's why it's so important to make friends with people of all ages.

Things to Do

Here are a few recommendations to remain social and keep your brain active:

- Join a retirement group. Many employers offer formal groups to keep their retired employees connected. There are retiree groups for doctors, military, teachers, and many other professions. Check with your former employer to see if they offer a group that might work for you.

- Volunteer. Many organizations benefit immensely from people no longer interested in full-time work. You can volunteer in your career field or try something different. The list of organizations that accept volunteers is long. National parks, disaster relief programs, and local libraries are just a few of the organizations that are always looking for help. The Corporation for National & Community Service is a good place to start looking.

- Find purpose by doing what you've always wanted to do. Your retirement may be able to provide you with opportunities you missed out on in your previous career. Those opportunities may include travel, meeting lots of people, and doing something you find valuable.

- Start a new business or work a part-time job. A part-time job may not provide enough revenue to support you, but it might provide enough income to fund travel, meals in restaurants, and other entertainment that you might not be able to afford otherwise. Driving for Uber and Lyft are great options for part-time work. I took an Uber ride in Hawaii not long ago and my driver was a 70-year-old retired nurse.

- Take classes. Challenge yourself to learn something new. This is one of the best ways to keep your brain active. If your education was interrupted by a stint in the service, an addition to the family, or the need to earn a paycheck, attending school now can help you achieve an unfulfilled dream. You might also earn more income in the process.

- Read. Thanks to technology that delivers reading material in e-book and audio formats, it's easier than ever to get your book fix. Reading stimulates your mind, and there is another important bonus: it provides all sorts of conversation topics when you're connecting with others. Book clubs are a great way to combine your love for reading with the socialization opportunities you need to stay healthy. Create your own book club or find one at your local library, senior center, or online.

- Embrace new technology. All too often I see retirees get set in their ways and avoid new things, such as streaming services, smart gadgets around the home, and the like. Embracing new technology can be fun and keep you mentally young.

- Engage with family. This is one aspect of my Indian heritage I can truly say is different in my world today. I grew up in a system where one could easily take their parents' and grandparents' presence in their life for granted. You learned as much from your grandparents as you did from your parents. Here, I see the role of grandparents marginalized. Sometimes, it is because grandparents do not wish to become the free babysitting service their children will abuse; in other cases, I see the children keeping the grandchildren from their grandparents because of personal differences. What a shame that the grandchildren lose out on being able to broaden the source of their learning by not having regular contact with grandparents. Though it brings a level of complexity in one's life to be living with the presence of a different generation, it also brings with it the opportunity not to have to look outside the natural family network for a purpose in life, or a way to be meaningfully engaged with life.

The good news is that there are many avenues to live a life where you stay meaningfully engaged, challenged, and with purpose. These steps can help you avoid dementia or deal with it more effectively if it happens to you.

Gather the Right Medical Team

As you learned in Chapter 6, one of the biggest health-related reasons that retirement plans fail is because, as a rule, our current health care system is focused on one and only one aspect of health: fixing you after you fall apart. This does not mean that there is no work being done on helping people stay healthier longer, but it is not something that one can expect to receive without a degree of effort. And that is where knowledge comes into play—how to use the health care system to stay healthier longer!

Using the health care system to prolong your healthy years starts with gathering the right medical team.

Work with the Right Professionals

How did you find your primary care physician? Most of us have one, but you probably found your doctor based on who was on your insurance company's list at the time you needed a doctor, rather than by making a deliberate search. Most of us, therefore, have internists or family physicians as our primary care physicians, not a physician who specializes in the care of older adults. This is likely because we don't view ourselves as being old enough to need that type of specialty care.

The story of a couple celebrating their 40th anniversary in their favorite restaurant makes this point very clearly. They order their favorite wine, and after a glass or two are feeling quite relaxed. The husband looks at the wife and acknowledges how lucky he is to be married to such a perfect and beautiful wife and mother of their children. He casually looks around, taking in the surroundings, and sees an older couple to his left. He smiles and nudges his wife.

"Honey, look over my shoulder at the older couple sitting there," he whispers. "That is exactly what we will look like ten years from now."

His wife looks at the couple and then back at her husband.

"You realize you are looking at a mirror, don't you?"

Where do the years go? How irrationally we act to keep reality at bay. Yet there is one thing I know for sure—most people who have reached retirement resist the urge to see themselves as "old."

What if I told you that working with a geriatrician can lower your risk of needing home care or home health services—and by extension, your risk of needing to access care in a nursing home—by 40 percent? Would I have your attention? Well, that is not just a hope, it is a fact that I discovered early in my research about our health care system, and a fact that was cited by Dr. Atul Gawande in his popular book, *Being Mortal*.

Dr. Gawande wrote:

"Several years ago, researchers at the University of Minnesota identified 568 men and women over the age of seventy who were living independently but were at high risk of becoming disabled because of chronic health problems, recent illness, or cognitive changes. With their permission, the researchers randomly assigned half of them to see a team of geriatric nurses and doctors—a team dedicated to the art and science of managing old age. The others were asked to see their usual physician, who was notified of their high-risk status. Within eighteen months, 10 percent of the patients in both groups had died. But the patients who had seen a geriatrics team were a quarter less likely to become disabled and half as likely to develop depression. They were 40 percent less likely to require home health services."[86]

Mr. Gawande was citing research from Dr. Chad Boult, a physician whose work I have already mentioned in this book.

Who wouldn't want those outcomes? If a pediatrician is a good choice for a child under age 18, a geriatrician is an equally good choice for those over 70.

One of the most important things you can do to gather the right medical team within the insurance system is to choose a geriatrician.

Geriatrics is a very unique, personalized approach to medicine. As we get older, we can develop more and more medical conditions. Oftentimes, those conditions can't be cured, but we can manage them well so that we can have a good quality of life as we get older.

Geriatricians are well suited to help people achieve that goal. It's very important to see a geriatrician early if possible, so you can get established with them and develop a relationship with them. You want to select someone who has specialized knowledge to keep you healthy as you age, to keep you out of the hospital, and out of the emergency department.

Finding a geriatrician may be difficult. You won't find one on every corner. In a 2012 "man on the street" survey of 82 people in Baltimore's Inner Harbor area, only 10 percent of the respondents knew what a geriatrician was.[87] That's not surprising since there are only approximately 8,200 full-time practicing geriatricians nationwide.[88] Based on those numbers, only 5.1 million of the 41.4 million Americans over the age of 65 have access to a geriatrician.[89] The authors of the Baltimore study speculated that there is so little recognition of the specialty because people who need a geriatrician do so for something totally unavoidable (namely they continue to live) and from which they cannot recover.[90]

And the reality is that there is not much of a demand for them either. Without a demand by consumers, a geriatrician is paid and treated the same as an internal medicine doctor by the providers—the same pay and same hours, despite a specialty in hand. Without the public making a huge demand for geriatricians, there will not be an incentive to provide geriatricians as a specialist, all to the detriment of retirees.

Geriatric physicians have completed a residency in either Internal Medicine or Family Medicine, but in addition, have undergone one to three years in additional study of the medical, social, and psychological issues of individuals 65 and over. Rather than concentrating on just the treatment of physical problems, a geriatrician addresses issues such as memory loss, arthritis, osteoporosis, and mobility issues, and recognizes how those health conditions impact patients on a social and emotional level. They are also trained to work with other specialists in the geriatric field such as social workers, home care agencies, pharmacists, physical therapists, and within long-term care settings such as nursing homes.

This multi-dimensional training results in a more holistic approach to care for medically complex patients. For instance, some tests and procedures that make sense for younger members of society not only don't make sense any longer, but actually pose a risk to the elderly.

In his book *What Your Doctor Won't Tell You About Getting Older*, geriatrician Dr. Mark Lachs wrote the following: "In the same way that seemingly small errors or oversights in pediatric health care such as poor nutrition or missed vaccinations can produce preventable but lifelong misery, the improper care and feeding of baby boomers can lead to "later life" disabilities that could spell the difference between living independently and having a nursing home as your last address."[91]

A study from Brown University Alpert Medical School found that physicians routinely prescribed drugs to elderly patients that were specifically advised against for older patients because of severe side effects or the tendency of the drugs to stay in their systems for longer than prescribed.[92]

In the study, researchers found that one out of five seniors were prescribed medications from a list of 110 drugs to avoid prescribing to the elderly. About five percent of the seniors had been prescribed at least two medications from the list. The study looked at six million men and women who were enrolled in Medicare Advantage plans. You can check your own list of medications against the list of Beers Criteria at https://www.guidelinecentral.com/guideline/340784/.

Dr. William Hazzard, a retired geriatrician from the University of Washington, defines a geriatric patient as anyone age 75 or older.[93] But to me, to wait until age 75 to start looking for a geriatrician is usually foolhardy. There are simply not enough geriatricians to go around.[94] Given that most people have an internist as their primary care physician, and that every geriatrician is an internist, but not every internist is a geriatrician, leads to one simple conclusion: having a geriatrician as your primary care physician is wise at any age beyond 65. Since you may well find yourself being put on a waiting list to be able to see a geriatrician, the sooner you start your search, the better.

By no means do I suggest people have to change physicians, but if you are not totally enamored with your current physician or don't have a compelling reason to stay with them, consider exploring the benefits of making a change to a geriatric physician before shutting the door.

Geriatric Care Options

When you start looking for a geriatrician, you have four options: geriatric care clinics, board-certified geriatricians, physicians advertising as geriatric care services, and other medical providers.

Geriatric Care Clinics

A geriatric care clinic is, in my opinion, your best option when choosing geriatric care. While standalone geriatricians are subject to restrictions imposed by Medicare, geriatric care clinics are not. They have entire teams of health care providers and staff who specialize and focus on geriatric care.

These clinics offer a robust range of services focused on maintaining your health and recovery from illness episodes. Examples of these services often include:

- Transportation to and from clinics
- Care/coach manager for each patient, short wait times, and significantly longer time with the doctor
- 24-hour access to a doctor (or a nurse)
- Team approach
- Excellent coordination of additional social services

If this is the option you choose, find a true geriatric clinic by looking for those open only to Medicare patients and staffed with geriatric care-focused professionals.

Board-Certified Geriatricians

Working with a physician who is board-certified as a geriatrician is another excellent option. When you're in the process of selecting your doctor, look for someone who is board-certified in geriatrics, is accepting new patients, accepts your insurance plan, and is younger than you.

Finding a geriatrician can be difficult. Don't be discouraged if it takes you some time to find one.

Where should you look? There are many resources designed specifically to help you find geriatricians in your area, including:

- Your insurance company's website
- Medicare (https://www.medicare.gov/)
- The practitioner search function on American Board of Internal Medicine (https://www.abim.org/) or American Board of Family Medicine (https://www.theabfm.org/)
- The American Geriatrics Society (https://www.americangeriatrics.org/)
- Healthgrades (https://www.healthgrades.com/)
- Vitals (https://www.vitals.com/)
- The AgingOptions Resource Guide (https://agingoptions.com/)

Once you have a few names on your list, look them up on https://www.healthgrades.com/ or https://www.vitals.com/. I found out about the geriatric physician that I'm going to sign up for when I get to 65 by looking at my insurance company's list.

After you have found a geriatrician, it's important to remember that all physicians must deal with the restrictions set forth by insurance companies. Though geriatricians have the specialized knowledge to better help you, they are expected to see patients in high volume, the same as any physician in the insurance-run world, which only allows them a small amount of time with each patient. Most have to carry a huge patient load and must see between 30 to 40 patients a day. The average face-to-face time a physician spends with a client is 18.7 minutes or less.[95] This makes it very difficult even for a board-certified geriatrician to give the client adequate time to truly help engage in preventative care, leaving a vacuum for private pay physicians to fill.

While a board-certified geriatrician still has to deal with these limits, they are more able to offer you specialized care focused on specific health issues affecting patients aged 65 and older.

Physicians with Geriatric Specialty

Depending on your location, you may find that there aren't many geriatricians available in your area. If this is the case, consider finding a physician who advertises as a geriatric care physician while not board-certified. These physicians may have received additional training in geriatrics, or may be self-taught on geriatric issues. If they advertise themselves as geriatricians, I would hope that they are dedicated to helping serve the older adult population. This would make them more desirable, in my opinion, than an internal medicine or family practice physician.

Other Providers

If you're still unable to find a good geriatric care physician, we suggest you find an advanced nurse practitioner (ARNP) or a physician's assistant (PA) who has an education and background in geriatric care, and who is working under a physician with a similar background. Though not a physician, many such practitioners have the training to be able to help you with geriatric issues, working under the supervision of a physician.

The bottom line is to do your due diligence. Call prospective providers and ask to schedule a short interview so you can meet with them and find out if they are a good fit.

How to Gather Your Team

If you're getting a little nervous and wondering how you will find the support needed to help you eat right, exercise, socialize, and find the right medical team, I want to let you in on a little secret. There are two ways to do this. One is to go through your insurance plan; the other is to use providers outside the insurance system. Here's how it works.

1. Inside the Insurance System

If you're over 65, you most likely have Medicare, in addition to supplemental insurance if you choose to purchase it. While going into detail about Medicare is outside the scope of this book, I want you to know that your insurance coverage is the gateway to nearly every action I suggest related to eating right, exercising, socializing, and gathering the right medical team. If you choose the wrong insurance policy, you'll have trouble accessing the services you want.

The way you select your insurance policy will go a long way toward making sure you have the support of a coterie of professionals who will help you in your quest to preserve your health. That means looking at more than just the cost of the monthly premium when it comes time to choose your coverage. Don't expect every insurance plan to offer access to the same level of benefits or the same types of providers. Select your insurance so it gives you access to the providers and the services you want. If you don't, getting what you need will be much more difficult.

Choose the Right Insurance

I'm often asked how to choose the right insurance company. What follows is a quick primer on this issue, but I always recommend working with an insurance agent to get more personalized input about your own situation.

Begin with the understanding that when you look for health insurance, your choices will fall into two general categories:

1. A Traditional Medicare and a Medigap plan, or

2. A Medicare Advantage plan.

Traditional Medicare, often called Original Medicare, is a benefit program regulated by the federal government. The program offers a standard benefits package that covers medically necessary health care services. Traditional Medicare does not offer coverage for prescription drugs. In traditional Medicare, you may have to buy a Medigap plan as well as a separate Part D prescription drug plan.

Medicare Advantage Plans are very similar to the group health insurance plans that you might have had during your working years. Medicare Advantage Plans have networks, and you pay for medical services as you go along. Medicare Advantage is technically still a part of Medicare, but it is not as heavily regulated by the federal government. The government sets rules and guidelines, but private insurance companies sell and administer the plans. In theory, the market is supposed to keep the companies in line and do right by the consumers. Medicare Advantage plans can be confusing to compare because every company is trying to differentiate itself, and there is no regulation that requires these competing companies to all offer a similar set of benefits, as traditional Medicare plans do.

Which one is for you? How should you decide?

As I see it, nearly all insurance companies in America do a pretty good job of allowing you access to world-class acute care (i.e., care that helps you survive an illness or cure a medical malady). As you saw in Chapter 6, what our system does not do well is preventative care.

You will be much better off if you change your focus from merely looking for a company that you think will do a better job helping you cope with an illness after the fact, and focus instead on a company that offers preventative care.

How will you recognize an insurance plan that offers good preventative benefits in addition to excellent acute care coverage? Look for a plan that offers as many of the following features and benefits as possible.

- Access to a large pool of board-certified geriatric care physicians
- Assurance that they will not drop your choice of physicians and medical providers in the middle of the policy term
- Ability to see any doctor of your choice without having to get a primary care physician's referral
- Access to naturopaths who tend to focus a bit more on preventative care and natural medicine
- Access to a large pool of nutritionists
- Access to a gym membership
- A plan with no deductible (or a very small one) and no co-payments
- A plan with no requirement for you to fill out claim forms
- Access to your local university-connected research hospitals, which will give you access to cutting-edge medical care in such settings
- No issue about in-network or out-of-network care. You should be covered nationwide the same as where you live.

Don't forget that you need to choose a plan that will give you access to a board-certified geriatric team. You must insist, no matter what anyone says to you, that you need to see a geriatric care physician as your primary care physician if you are over age 70.

My Recommendation

In my opinion, most who can afford the coverage would be better off choosing a Traditional Medicare plan with a Medigap policy. In 2022, a good Medigap plan costs around $200/month, in addition to the Medicare premium deducted from your social security check each month.

If the thought of paying monthly premiums doesn't sit well with you, then you can opt for a Medicare Advantage plan, but consider choosing one that offers a zero premium. With a Medicare Advantage plan, you won't be able to see any doctor of your choosing; you will have to pick one from their network. You will have deductibles and co-payments, as well as an out-of-pocket cap of about $7,500 or so. The upside of the Medicare Advantage plan is that for every year you do not need heavy-duty care, you will save about $2,400. During the years when you do need lots of expensive care, your out-of-pocket limit won't exceed about $7,500 per year.

For most of my clients, I will suggest the Traditional Medicare route with a Medigap plan, together with a prescription drug plan, as this will allow the broadest coverage available. Know in advance that these policies won't include dental, vision, or hearing coverage, for which you could obtain coverage from outside the Medicare plan if you so desire. Though some Medicare Advantage plans offer dental, vision, and hearing benefits, the coverage is usually sparse. If you decide to choose a Medicare Advantage plan, know that in most states, Washington included, if you want to switch from a Medicare Advantage plan to a Traditional Medicare plan, you may be denied because companies can ask for medical underwriting. So, don't think that you can switch to a Traditional Plan from a Medicare Advantage plan when your health starts to fail you.

2. Outside the Insurance System

If your retirement income allows it, you can purchase health care services directly from providers who don't participate in the insurance system.

Why would you want to consider an option where you would not be able to use insurance coverage? Insurance-covered medical care is heavily managed and tends to prevent qualified physicians from having the freedom to focus on preventative care. These restrictions usually prevent doctors from being able to administer or suggest treatments they believe are required simply because the patient's insurance doesn't cover it. The shortcomings of insurance-covered medicine are no secret. The insurance-covered system is highly restrictive and leads to a frustrated health care community.

Consider the limitations of working with an insurance-covered physician. The average U.S. primary care physician carries 2,300 cases in the traditional medical system. To be able to properly treat the average caseload, a physician needs to spend 10.6 hours per working day to deliver the recommended care for patients with chronic conditions, plus 7.4 hours per day to provide evidence-based preventive care.[96] This adds up to an 18-hour day.

Under this model of care, unless you are ill or have a specific complaint, once a year your insurance covers a visit with your physician to review your health. During that visit, you receive a few standard tests. Unless those tests reveal that you are symptomatic of a particular ailment, there is no follow-up until the next year, during which time your body may well start sending signals about impending health issues. Because a whole year must go by between appointments, this process does not provide the continuous monitoring necessary to avert a catastrophe. This is not *preventative*, but rather *reactionary* medicine.

To fill this gap, there is an industry outside the insurance system that caters to those willing to invest in their own health. These providers can offer things insurance won't cover, such as immediate access, wellness services, tests to detect genetic problems, or screenings for factors that might put you at risk.

Outside the insurance world, there are four types of care: convenience care, preventative care clinics, concierge care, and wellness science.

Convenience Care

One of the frustrations of working within the insurance-covered health care system is that accessing care quickly is more of a dream than reality. If you wanted to see a doctor because you have the flu, or you had an accident, you would likely be waiting weeks to access your primary care physician. That is why in recent times, there has been a plethora of urgent care clinics that have mushroomed all over the country. These clinics allow you to access care as quickly as you would in an emergency care setting, without the cost. Well, some physicians have managed to break into the demand for quick and ready access by offering just that—prompt access to care by charging a nominal amount of money each month for such care. If you look hard enough, you will find medical chains offering this feature for an additional monthly fee. The fee ranges from $50 per month to $200 per month or more. What does this fee give you? Access to prompt care. The care is still provided by the same physicians who you would see after waiting a while. So, don't look for specialized care or specialized knowledge in these clinics, just convenience, even though many will likely want to dub themselves as "concierge care physicians," a term that seems to find ready acceptance by the public.

Concierge Physicians

A concierge physician is a primary care physician who handles a very small number of patients who pay large fees for exclusive access. Some concierge physicians work with just one patient.

On average, if you are willing to commit between $75,000 to $300,000 or more per year, a concierge physician can give you access to a level of medical care that simply doesn't exist in the insurance-funded world.

Some concierge physicians will make themselves available 24/7/365 to address the needs of their patients. If you're one of their patients, they will help you avoid emergency room visits, or, if that's not possible, they will meet you in the emergency room to be your advocate and to make sure you are treated promptly and appropriately. They will travel with you and be at the ready whenever the need arises.

Be careful here. The term "concierge" has been hijacked by hospitals and medical chains who have figured out a way to get around restrictions imposed by Medicare. Hospitals know that if they accept Medicare, they can't accept any other form of payment—except for services Medicare doesn't cover. As a result, many hospitals are now offering these non-covered Medicare services and calling them "concierge services," not specialized care.

If you can afford it, convenience care and concierge physicians are both great options for primary care outside the insurance system. There's just one catch: don't expect preventative care from a convenience care clinic or a concierge physician. For that, you will need to work with a clinic that specializes in preventative medicine.

Preventative Care

Clinics that fall into the preventative care category don't generally offer instant access to care. Instead, their focus is on prescribing preventative care to foster long-term wellness. This type of clinic won't diagnose or treat your illness; they will help you prevent it. This type of practice is often called Functional Medicine.

One of the major advantages of preventative care clinics is that they develop custom guidance to address your specific health needs that include diet, supplements, exercise, and other lifestyle issues which can keep you healthy and prevent disease.

Another major benefit of preventative care is that it focuses on looking for issues before they become problems by diagnosing them early, sparing you the cost and complications that come with these diseases. Since preventative health care clinics aren't governed by insurance system dictates that require seeing a certain number of patients each day, preventive clinics serve a smaller number of clients. As a result, they can focus on each patient to a degree that mainstream clinics cannot. The routine exams and health screenings these clinics provide are both more frequent and more thorough.

Here's an example from my own life.

Dr. Jerry Mixon, the founder of Longevity Health Clinic in the Seattle area, had a show on the local radio station that aired right before mine on Saturday mornings. I listened to this show for years. During each episode, Dr. Mixon took calls from listeners who wanted to know how to deal with the effects of aging. So, after my 50th birthday, when I started to notice that I was getting tired earlier than usual—by 4 p.m. on most days—I decided to give his office a call.

I completed a questionnaire, the staff ran all sorts of blood tests, and then they made an appointment for me to come in and discuss the results of the blood tests with Dr. Joe Kennedy, one of the physicians on staff and a man I knew from the school my sons attended.

On appointment day, a nurse ushered me to the exam room. Dr. Kennedy strode in with my chart in hand.

"Great to see you, Rajiv," he said, extending his hand. "What brings you here today?"

"I'm getting tired earlier than usual," I said. "I want to know if there's anything I can do about it."

He looked down at my chart. "Rajiv, that tiredness you're experiencing should be easy to fix," he said. "You're low on Vitamin B and Vitamin D. That's easy to fix. With a targeted supplement regimen, I promise you'll feel better."

Then, he flipped to a different page on my chart and gave me a concerned look. "I've told you the good news, but, unfortunately, there's a bit of bad news, too. You have a bigger problem. According to your blood tests, you could be at risk of a stroke."

"A stroke? What are you talking about?"

"It's all in your blood levels," he said. "I don't know anything about your medical history, but I'm willing to bet that if I had met you 15 years ago, your blood levels would have been much more normal. If you were living in India, I would probably be looking at a very different blood chemistry report."

I had always considered myself a healthy person, but this got my attention.

"But you're not in India," he continued. "You're living here, in America, and like most of us, you're working insanely hard, and you don't give yourself a break. I can see it in your blood levels."

He showed me the report, which detailed my results in dozens of blood tests. He pointed to one. "If you exceed this threshold, you could end up with a TIA—a transient ischemic attack—the kind of stroke where you don't even realize you had one. Or you could end up with a hemorrhagic stroke that kills you. Or you could end up somewhere in the middle with a stroke that disables you. If we watch your blood chemistry carefully, my job will be to make sure you never exceed that threshold."

I listened carefully, but I would be lying if I said I wasn't a little skeptical. Dr. Kennedy was selling pills, and I wanted to feel better, so I ordered the supplements. Next, I took the report to Dr. Fang, my primary care doctor.

"How come you don't talk to me about this?" I asked as I handed her the report. "I'm at risk for a stroke. Why didn't I hear this first from you?"

Dr. Fang flipped through the document, then handed it back. "You must be going to a private doctor," she said. "A regular doctor wouldn't be doing this blood work. Are you going to a private doctor?"

"What difference does it make?" I replied. "He's a doctor. You're a doctor…"

"You don't understand," she interrupted. "It's not that I don't want to run these tests, it's that your insurance company won't pay for them. No insurance company will. They won't allow me to run any of these tests until you are symptomatic. Once you're showing symptoms, I can run whatever tests I need to run."

"Can you run them going forward?"

She nodded. "With blood work like that, I can."

How do you hold your doctor accountable when their hands are tied by insurance company rules? You do it by investing in a panel of blood tests from a private physician or a Functional Medical doctor every other year or so, and then you take those results to your primary care doctor. This will mean paying for an exam and blood work with your own money, but if you're serious about preserving your health in your retirement years, this out-of-pocket expense will be a small price to pay.

Preventative health care clinics are surprisingly affordable to those who consider themselves middle-class. At the time I'm writing this (2022), access to preventative care typically costs between $3,000 and $7,000 per year in the Seattle area. It may cost more or less where you live.

You may be surprised to learn that the major drawback of this type of care is availability. There is a growing demand for preventative care, and it can be hard to find a clinic. If you're interested in exploring this option, the Institute for Functional Medicine is a good place to start. Locate a practitioner near you at https://www.ifm.org/find-a-practitioner. The AgingOptions Resource Guide (https://agingoptions.com/) can also connect you to preventive clinics in your area.

Wellness Science Organizations

For those who still find concierge medicine or private pay preventative care clinics too expensive or impractical, new organizations called wellness science organizations are popping up to fill the gap. These companies offer virtual care and coordinate their work with local labs and providers.

With such an organization, you will be linked to a wellness coach, often a dietitian who will be your day-to-day contact. This coach is backed by virtual physicians who read your charts and map out a strategy on how to keep you healthy. This knowledge is then relayed by the coach, who will discuss health in a more comprehensive way, and will motivate you and hold you accountable. Wellness science organizations are growing in popularity and are a valuable resource when it comes to understanding how health-related changes will affect you. They can also help you understand the science behind them. InsideTracker, a preventative care service with a virtual component, is one of the latest services to emerge in this space. They offer testing services that analyze your blood, DNA, lifestyle, and nutrition habits, and then offer personalized advice for actions you can take to stay healthy.

A Closing Thought

With good health, you have a better opportunity to avoid dealing with a long-term illness that can drain resources, leave you a burden on your loved ones, and force you into an institutional care setting. If you stay healthy, you can avoid these outcomes.

Every day that you wake up and say, "I know I should exercise, I know I should eat better, I know I need to socialize more," but continue to put it off, shortens the number of days you will remain independent.

Who is going to make you eat right, exercise, and socialize?

Who will make you gather the right medical team?

It has to be you. Nobody else can make you do that.

Write this down and tape it to your refrigerator or your bathroom mirror:

I eat right, exercise, and socialize.

I have the right professionals on my medical team.

I do this because I don't want to end up in a nursing home, becoming a burden on my children, or running out of money while I'm living.

Don't wait another day to make this your top priority. Do it now.

OUR DAILY PLEDGE

WE MUST:

- ❖ EAT RIGHT
    - ❖ EXERCISE
        - ❖ SOCIALIZE

BECAUSE WE DO NOT WANT TO END UP:

- ❖ IN A NURSING HOME
    - ❖ BECOMING A BURDEN
        - ❖ RUNNING OUT OF MONEY

_____   _____

Your name   Spouse's name

CHAPTER 10

A BETTER WAY TO PLAN
FOR HOUSING

Foundational Insight

Traditional retirement planning is hoping to live out your old age at home.

LifePlanning is knowing you can age at home because there is a plan to make this hope come true.

Introduction

When an older adult gets sick, one question is asked more than any other once their health condition stabilizes:

Where will they live?

This was the question that almost every client in the early years of my elder law practice was struggling to answer.

What if I could do more than just help these families react to their elderly loved ones' housing crises?

What if I could prevent these crises?

My advice on planning for housing in retirement hasn't been without controversy. There are some who believe that my goal is to keep people away from care facilities and retirement communities. They claim that I want everyone to age at home. That's not the case. I just want you to have the opportunity to grow old in the place of your choice, not the place a doctor or discharge planner thinks you should be. I want you to retain agency over the decision.

Fortunately, with the right planning, done well in advance of your health crisis, you can access care in the home of your choosing without becoming an undue burden on your loved ones or running out of money.

A New Take on Housing

When I first started wondering if a different approach to planning might help older people avoid the housing dilemma, almost no attorneys in NAELA were talking about housing. I had the good fortune to hear a presentation from an attorney in South Carolina who talked about housing issues, and he pointed me to research on the subject.

I started researching the topic of housing in my spare time. I browsed many studies coming out of well-respected universities such as Yale, Brown, Stanford, and more. I read reports from the AARP that explained the state of housing for seniors in America. I perused Alzheimer's Association reports that talked about how many older adults with the disease would like to be able to live out their life at home—and all the reasons they can't.

What I read in these studies and what played out in real life had little in common. I watched the housing drama unfold in my office every day as I helped family caregivers, often adult children, find and pay for long-term care for their elderly parents. The experience of moving a parent into long-term care was almost never pleasant at the start. The parent didn't want to go, so the family had to leave them at the care facility. The family was told to stay away for a week, two weeks, or even as long as a month until the older adult became accustomed to the new environment. This practice reminded me of breaking in a horse. Eventually, the elders adjusted to their new home, but the whole thing, especially the abandonment part, never sat well with me.

There had to be a better solution to this problem, but it seemed to me that the adult children I saw in my office were headed to a similar end. They were following the same conventional retirement advice that had led their parents into crisis. It was like they were all on a conveyer belt moving silently toward life in a nursing home, financial ruin, and family burdens—yet they couldn't see it.

I could see it clearly, because the conveyor belt passed directly through my office. The very same people who had sought my help to deal with their elderly parents would likely be facing their own housing crisis in ten, fifteen, or twenty years.

So, I started wondering. If a person wants to stay at home all the way to the end, what would it take to make it happen? Is it even possible?

And then it occurred to me that the problem is that we are making these decisions at the last minute, without any degree of effective pre-planning in place. Sure, people have thought about the possibility of ending up in institutional care, and many have a strong desire to avoid this fate, but almost never is there any meaningful planning around the issue.

When we are in the planning stages for our retirement years, most of us do not expect to find ourselves in a situation where we are unable to care for ourselves. We don't think we are going to need such an intervention. And when we watch our friends, neighbors, and family members get stuck in care facilities, we become resigned that there is little that can be done about the issue, other than hope that it does not happen to us. In other words, most of us go through life hoping (or assuming) that we will simply peacefully die in our sleep.

Unfortunately, it doesn't happen that way for most of us.

During my years as an elder law attorney, I have seen more than my share of older adults scrambling to make last-minute arrangements because they didn't have a plan for where they would live after a health crisis or how they might pay for the care they need. These people— and often, their family caregivers—would land in my office desperate for help.

In many cases, I would recommend that these people work with a geriatric care manager and a housing expert to find a suitable place to live. The care manager would see if there was anything that could be done to keep the person at home, and if that was not an option, a housing expert would help the family find the right place.

Most of the time, when a person could not live at home, it was because the house was not age-friendly, the children lived far away from the incapacitated parent, or there was simply not enough money to pay the care costs that Medicaid would leave uncovered. I talked about many of these situations back in Chapter 3.

It occurred to me that if people would look at these issues ahead of time and know what it takes to age in place, they could make better decisions. It seemed to me that if we had thought through the possibility of incapacity and built a plan around dealing with it ten years before falling ill—if we did the planning upstream long before the health crisis—we could avoid the crisis altogether. People wouldn't be forced to move into a facility. They could age at home if they wanted to because they would have a plan to do it.

Unfortunately, that's not the society we live in. Few people take the long-term view on anything. Businesses focus on profits quarter to quarter, individuals live paycheck to paycheck, and year by year. We operate on near-term goals and short-term realities. When we are in the planning process for our retirement years, we are usually healthy; yet, unless we can picture ourselves as older and incapacitated, how can we truly plan? Most of us picture ourselves as older and still healthy, not older and incapacitated. If we remove those blinders, we will have a better chance of creating a realistic plan for housing—and a better chance of avoiding a one-way trip to the nursing home.

It appeared to me that while having a long-range perspective was a new idea here in the U.S., it is not at all a new way of thinking in India or, I suspect, in a majority of the Third World. Where I was born, long-term thinking is the norm, not the exception. And the results show the benefits of such thinking.

As a result, long-term planning has become the foundation upon which I help my clients build their housing plans.

Instead of helping people at the point of crisis, I wanted to push the planning upstream a decade or more—before people got sick. What if I could help people address this housing issue *before* they retired or within the first few years of retirement?

There was no playbook for that.

So, I created one.

What are we trying to accomplish by being more deliberate about our plan for housing in retirement? You know the answer by now, but I want to state the goals for housing explicitly because they are such an important part of the big picture.

The goal is for you to avoid a forced relocation to an institutional care setting after your health fails. If you need care, you have a plan that brings the care to you wherever you are living. You won't need to be institutionalized to receive care. You will be able to accomplish all of this without going broke or recruiting your loved ones into service as your unpaid caregivers.

This is how you plan for a successful retirement.

Home Defined

Now that you understand what we're trying to accomplish by planning for housing in retirement, let's look at what it means to have a home.

"Home" means different things to different people. An interaction with Vivian drove this point home.

One day I came home from work and saw Vivian sitting up in her bed listening to one of my kids play piano. Vivian's eyes were filled with tears.

I went over to her and took her hand. "A penny for your thoughts," I said.

She shook her head. "It's nothing."

"What is it, Momma?" I said. "What are you thinking?"

"I won't be able to see this much longer," she whispered. "It won't be much longer that I'll be able to do all this. Maybe I shouldn't be here."

"What do you mean maybe you shouldn't be here?"

She looked down. "It's too much for the children," she said.

In my mind's eye, I could see my family in India, all of us living together in a giant compound full of chaos and racket, but most importantly, full of love. Vivian had lived with us for years and she was still concerned about being a burden.

"Okay, let's pack your bags," I said with a smile. "Where do you want to go? Where else can you go and still see your grandchild play the piano, an instrument you taught him how to play? Where will you be more at home? Wherever that is, let's go. If you don't go, I don't want to hear you say anything more about being a burden."

Vivian was nearing the end. She knew it and I knew it. Most people in the Third World observe birth and death in the same household in short spans of time. In America, it's different. We are living a sanitized existence. Death happens somewhere else, far from our everyday experience.

I was glad Vivian was going through the emotions. I knew that she was recognizing that she was not long for this world. I knew she was gearing up for the moment of transition, a pivotal moment in any life, yet a frightening one even for the most well-prepared.

It was also clear to me that the place Vivian was most comfortable was home. It didn't matter whether it was with Jamie and me in Federal Way, or with another of her children. Home is where we find the most meaning as we approach the end of life. It's where we make the transition to whatever comes next, which is one of the most important moments in life.

What is home for a person in retirement? For many of us, the answer is the place we've been all along. Home is the place we've been living for the last ten, twenty, or [fill in the blank] years. Home is where you don't bump into furniture when you walk to the bathroom in the middle of the night. You know what it looks and smells like. It's where your memories are.

Where I was raised, in India, home during the retirement years was defined differently. Home is the place you will live until you take your last breath. Home is where you are 100 percent confident that you will be able to spend your last days without any worry or concern that you have to move.

This is how I define "home" for my *LifePlanning* clients. I call it the Forever Home.

What does this look like for Americans?

Your Forever Home is where the care is. If your health fails and you need care, your Forever Home is the place where you will be able to receive that care, without having to move. At the same time, you know where the money will come from to pay for that care. Your kids will not be your unpaid caregivers, but they will be close enough to you to keep an eye on the caregivers to make sure that these people show up when they're supposed to, don't take advantage of you, and don't leave you neglected.

Your Forever Home can be your current home, another private residence, an in-law suite in your child's home, or a retirement community.

You just need the assurance that wherever that home is, it's a place you won't have to leave when your health fails.

One of the most common questions I get when I talk about the Forever Home at workshops and seminars involves timing. When should you transition to your Forever Home?

If you're in good health, moving to your forever home isn't something you have to do the day you retire. You have some time. Generally speaking, make the move when you estimate that you will have about eight to ten years of good health ahead of you. None of us have a crystal ball, and there's no way to know for sure how long our health will hold up. For most of us, however, we should be in our Forever Home by about age 75. Most of us can expect to remain healthy to our mid-80s, though it's not a given.

If you're healthy enough at that age to play a round of golf or walk four to five miles, then you're probably going to be healthy for the next eight to ten years. If you're still climbing Mount Rainier—and yes, I have those clients—you might be able to push it out to 80. Conversely, if you start developing health issues at an earlier age, you may need to be in your Forever Home by the time you are 70.

Housing Options Overview

Now that you know what a Forever Home is, how does that translate into living options? Despite all the hype, you basically have two choices for housing as you age: a retirement community or not a retirement community.

When I say, "not a retirement community," I'm talking about a private residence of some kind. If that's what you choose to be your Forever Home, you have four basic options:

1. Remain in your current home
2. Move to a new age-friendly home
3. Move in with loved ones
4. Move to a lifestyle community.

Anything other than a private residence will most likely be some form of retirement community. Retirement communities fall into two broad categories:

1. Life Plan Communities, also known as Continuing Care Retirement Communities (CCRC)
2. Everything Else. This includes Independent Living, Assisted Living, Memory Care, Residential Care Homes (Adult Family Homes), and Skilled Nursing Facilities (Nursing Homes).

I will discuss each of these options in detail later in this chapter.

What Do You Want More?

When it comes to choosing a private residence or a retirement community as your Forever Home, it's important to remember that your choice will have a significant impact on you, your finances, and your family as you age. Your choice will determine to what extent you may burn through your retirement nest egg and to what extent you may burden your family. Traditional retirement planning doesn't take these factors into account, but the *LifePlanning* process does.

It all comes down to what's most important to you. Your housing decision involves tradeoffs.

Here's what's at stake:

Housing Option	Burden on Family	Financial Burn Rate	Social Contact
Private Residence	Higher	Lower	Lower
Retirement Community	Lower	Higher	Higher

If your goal is to leave a large inheritance to your family, choosing a private residence as your Forever Home makes that somewhat easier to accomplish. Choosing a private residence will also make you more reliant on family support as your health declines, so you won't be able to say that you don't want to become a burden. When you live in a private residence, you can minimize the burdens on your family, but not eliminate them.

If you want to avoid burdening your children with your needs as you age, a retirement community will help you accomplish that goal. You won't be burdening your children, but you will be busy spending their inheritance.

What do you want more? Is it more important not to be a burden? Or is it more important for you to leave as much of your estate as possible to your children? Your answers to those questions should guide your decision.

Aging in a Private Residence

Now that you have an overview of your housing options in retirement and the pros and cons of each, let's zoom in on the private residence option and what it takes to live there successfully for the entire length of your retirement—without going broke or placing excessive burdens on your family.

Remember, a private residence can be any one of the following four settings:

1. Your current home. This needs little explanation. This is the home you know and love, the place you are right now, modified as needed to make it age-friendly.

2. A new age-friendly home. This is a new (or a new-to-you) home purpose-built for the safety and convenience of older adults.

3. With loved ones. This might mean living in the same house with relatives or other loved ones, or living in an accessory dwelling like a granny pod or an in-law suite. Many Americans don't consider this a viable option, but it gives you a way to remain in a private residence.

4. A lifestyle community. These are usually 55-plus neighborhoods where you live in an age-friendly private residence and take advantage of amenities that make it easy to maintain social lives and healthy lifestyles. Frankly, this is my least favorite option. It can be great for a person in early retirement, but when you fall ill, you will probably have to move again.

Remember, the moment you decide you want to live your life in a private residence and access care at home instead of moving to a retirement community, you must concede that you will become a burden to your family to some degree. You must be able to live with the consequences.

You can minimize the burdens by making sure your loved ones don't have to become your unpaid caregivers. However, they will have an important role to play. If you've done the right planning, your family will be overseeing the people delivering your care, not providing that care themselves. They will make sure that the people you have hired show up to work, don't take advantage of you, and don't leave you neglected.

Requirements for Aging in a Private Residence

No matter which private residence option you choose, if you want to stay there as you age, your home must meet the following requirements:

1. It must be an age-friendly home, both in structure *and* location.

2. You must have family or social support to assist you when the time comes.

3. You must have financial resources to provide care to you at home if or when you need it.

Let's take a closer look at each requirement.

Age-Friendly Home: Structure and Location

I learned about the concept of the age-friendly home from a friend who was the general manager at a home health agency. Through him, I discovered their secret weapon: the occupational therapists they deployed to perform home assessments, recommend modifications, and help older adults prevent falls. These professionals wrote the play-book for the age-friendly home, which is what a private residence has to be if you want to grow old there.

An age-friendly home is a house that incorporates Universal Design principles.[97] These include:

- No-step entries
- Single-floor living, which eliminates the need to navigate stairs
- Switches and outlets reachable at any height
- Extra-wide hallways and doors to accommodate wheelchairs
- Lever-style door and faucet handles
- Walk-in (no threshold or low threshold) and sit-in showers

These features ensure that it is safe to remain in your home while you age. Unfortunately, it is estimated that less than four percent of homes in America have these six basic features that make a home age-friend-ly.[98] Less than one percent of rental units include all six features.[99]

How do you determine whether your home is age-friendly? An occu-pational therapist can assess your home and give you recommenda-tions.[100] Find an occupational therapist in your area at HealthGrades.com/occupational-therapy-directory.

If your home isn't age-friendly, what can you do? Remodeling is an option. It's a relatively easy matter to find a contractor who specializes in building or renovating homes according to the principles of Univer-sal Design.

The next thing to consider is whether your home is in an age-friendly neighborhood. Specifically, do you feel safe walking around? Are medical facilities nearby? Are emergency responders readily available? Are grocery stores and drugstores conveniently located? Try to imagine these considerations in a future where you may be slowing down, unable to drive, or more vulnerable than you are today. If your private residence is in an isolated area, it may not be suitable as your Forever Home as your health declines. You may end up being forced to move to be closer to services and support.

Family Support

If there is a lesson to be learned from the Ronald Reagan story, it is that without the unwavering support of a family member or a close friend, it will likely not be possible to age in place.

Without someone looking out for your well-being, you could be both vulnerable to being taken advantage of and of being neglected. Older people in their communities are often targets of scammers.[101] Scammers are not always outsiders; they may be family members, friends, neighbors, or care providers. If you're serious about aging in place, it is vitally important to live close to your support systems (children, siblings, or other relatives or friends you name as agents in your Power of Attorney). This also assumes that you will be willing to be open about your affairs with the people you plan to rely on for assistance, and that there is total transparency regarding your affairs among family members and agents.

One of the most important aspects of family support involves proximity. Many people fail to consider this aspect. A dream home in Hawaii doesn't do you much good when your children who are supposed to be your agents live in Germany. If you want to age in a private residence, it is ideal to live within two to five miles of the people who will be supporting you and checking on you every day if you're receiving care in the home. This greatly minimizes the burdens on your agents and increases the probability that you will be able to avoid institutional care. You will also want to consider forms of compensation for loved ones who provide care on a regular, prolonged basis. I'll talk more about that later.

I often suggest to clients that if they are going to live close to a family member, it might be just as easy to live on the same property. In most of the second and third world, and even in a few first-world nations such as Japan and Italy, joint family living tends to be the norm. Multiple generations come together under the same roof, creating an environment where, with rare exceptions, caring for an incapacitated loved one does not necessarily fall on the shoulders of a single person. In some cultures, including in India where I grew up, it is a commonly accepted social custom to have the oldest child (in some cases the oldest male child) care for aging parents, and by custom, the child who provides care for aging parents inherits the family home.

There is an interesting recent study with regard to multigenerational living. In America, one would assume that it is the children who are not open to having a parent live with them. However, the Gallup survey commissioned by Pfizer reported that while more than half (51 percent) of those 18 to 65 would accept having a parent live with them, only 25 percent of individuals over 65 would want to live with a younger relative if unable to care for themselves.[102]

Joint living is not for everyone. If a parent cannot stop parenting a child, then joint living is likely to fail from the word go. The same would be true for children who want to take over their parent's life. Successful families in joint living arrangements are the ones who know how to keep out of the business of other family members and will be there to support the decisions, no matter how much they cut against the lifestyle of the other.

To make joint living easier, it is not necessary to move into the existing home of a child or parent. It might be more beneficial to look for a new and larger home. It might be one property with two dwellings, or the possibility of adding a second building on one property. If this is the case, then one should look for housing units that may have or can be remodeled to have two totally separate living quarters, allowing both adult households to maintain their privacy, but at the same time allowing the child to provide aid to the parent. The joint living arrangement makes it possible for a client to be able to transfer a home to a child without having to worry about the Medicaid five-year look-back (if you are going to count on Medicaid as a way to have some or all of your long-term care costs covered). The hoped-for benefit will be that you will have a greater assurance of being able to stay at home because a loved one is there, and be able to otherwise have a happier life being close to your child(ren).

Financial Resources

It takes money to pay the people who will be bringing the care to you. As I have discussed in previous chapters, long-term care costs are the single biggest financial threat facing a retiree in America. Estimating the resources required isn't easy. No one can predict how much care you will need, for how long, and to what level. The best thing you can do to address these unknowns is to create a Financial Dashboard. I explain how to do this in Chapter 11. For now, let's focus on how costs that are not covered by the system can be addressed.

You don't need a huge nest egg to be able to age at home. If you have the right plan, you can pull it off for a lot less money than you might think. You can age at home with limited assets, but you'll need to understand how your various private assets and public benefits might work together to fund your care.

If you have more than $2 million in assets, you should be able to afford care at home for most normal situations. However, if you have less than $1.5 million in assets, or less than $300,000 in cash assets, there is a chance that you may not have enough resources to be able to cover the care costs you might face. You should be looking at either buying a long-term care insurance policy or planning on accessing either VA benefits, Medicaid benefits, or both. And if most of the equity in your estate is locked up in equity in your home, you should be considering establishing a line of credit against your home, preferably using a reverse mortgage. As I've mentioned before, no matter how you choose to cover possible long-term care costs, you must plan many years before you need the benefits, especially if you are single or you do not have children.

Aging in a Retirement Community

If you want to completely avoid burdening loved ones, your best bet is retirement community living. In addition to eliminating burdens on children and loved ones when you're incapacitated, retirement community living gives you a ready-made social life. If you are married, upon your incapacity or death, your spouse won't have to face isolation or worry about finding a new circle of friends. Many retirement communities also provide easier and less expensive access to the services you will need as you grow older. However, as I mentioned earlier, these benefits come at a price: you will be busy spending your children's inheritance.

There's another catch: not every retirement community is the same. If you choose the wrong one, you could still end up being forced to move when your health fails, losing money to unplanned care costs, and becoming a burden on your family. My goal is to help you understand your options so you can make an educated decision that gives you the best chance of avoiding these nightmares.

I mentioned earlier that there are two basic types of retirement communities:

1. Life Plan Communities, also known as Continuing Care Retirement Communities (CCRC)

2. Everything Else. This includes Independent Living, Assisted Living, Memory Care, Residential Care Homes (Adult Family Homes), and Skilled Nursing Facilities (Nursing Homes).

Choosing a retirement community can mean evaluating dozens of different factors, but it is my opinion that one factor is more important than any other. If you are serious about making a retirement community your Forever Home, the facility must give you contractual assurance (in writing) that upon moving into the community, you will never be asked to move out, either due to depleted funds or increased care needs due to deteriorating health.

Verbal assurances are not enough. We all know talk is cheap. You need these assurances in writing. My advice is designed to help you not only pick a retirement community that is right for your needs, but one that offers an ironclad guarantee that you won't have to move again.

While communities in both categories seek to serve the aging population, only CCRCs can offer the written assurance that once you move into that community, you will never have to move again, no matter your financial or health situation. If your estate is worth less than $1.5 million, retirement communities that do not accept Medicaid (or a similar program of their own creation, such as a benevolent fund designed to benefit residents) as a source of payment should be crossed off your list because they won't be able or willing to accommodate your needs as circumstances change.

Let's take a closer look at each type of retirement community.

Continuing Care Retirement Communities

Continuing Care Retirement Communities (CCRCs), also known as Life Plan Communities, offer older adults an attractive option for their future long-term care needs by allowing them to convert their home equity or other assets into housing and services, including health care. With features such as dining, health and wellness programs, social and recreational activities, transportation, and more within a secure environment and at a wide range of costs through a continuum of care needs, CCRCs generally enable residents to remain in the community and usually on a single campus regardless of their changing health care needs.

Unlike other senior housing options, CCRCs provide a method to keep costs stable, protect against the loss of accommodations and services if the resident exhausts his or her funds, and provide for a possible income tax deduction for certain fees paid to the CCRC for medical expenses.

Though there may not be a nationally recognized format for CCRCs, three fundamental components exist:

1. Access to a continuum of care (independent through skilled nursing)

2. Services and amenities to promote wellness and healthy living on and off campus

3. Maintenance for life (although this varies widely with what type of contract a resident chooses)

CCRCs generally require large entrance fees to get in, plus monthly fees.

The majority of CCRCs require an entrance fee, which averages about $320,000, up 3% from 2016, according to the National Investment Center for Seniors Housing & Care, an industry research group. The fee—based on the location, size of the residence, and whether it is single or double occupancy—can range from less than $100,000 to more than $1 million. CCRCs also assess monthly fees, which averaged

$3,266 nationwide in 2018. These, too, vary widely, from about $2,000 to more than $7,000 at some high-end CCRCs.[103]

A CCRC pools the fees to run the community and provide its residents with long-term care. Depending on the type of agreement, a portion of the entrance fee could be paid back to the estate after your death. CCRCs differ enormously in amenities, locations, and contract types, and these variations are reflected in their pricing models. About 80 percent of CCRCs are nonprofit. For many, providing support for a resident after the resident has run out of funds is seen as the fulfillment of the promise of buying into a CCRC.

CCRCs offer a variety of contracts. Here are the most common types:

Type A – Extensive or Lifecare Contract: This contract requires a substantial entry fee but sets a fairly stable monthly fee that will not change if you need to move to higher levels of care. This contract also likely has you paying more per month than the other contracts, but if you require long-term advanced health care, this contract will offer you financial stability. Under this contract, should your money run out and you are unable to pay, the CCRC will use the entrance fee you paid as collateral to cover the costs of living in the community. Finally, upon the death of the contract holder, part of the entry fee will be refunded to the heirs. NOTE: the final details of that refund differ between communities.

Type B – Modified Contract: This contract also requires an entry fee and produces a stable monthly cost (usually the same or lower than communities offering type A contracts). The difference is that you are only allowed a specified number of days at each level of care at the contracted rate before the rates are raised to market levels. This is good for most retirees since they usually face incapacity for a relatively short period of time and will not exceed the specified number of days.

However, should your advanced long-term care regularly exceed the specified days, you may find yourself paying more than if you were to go with a type A contract.

Type C – Fee for Service Contract: Like the other contracts, type C contracts require entry and monthly fees, but typically at a noticeably lower price than the previous two contract types. The caveat here is that you pay for additional services on an as-needed basis. Although you pay market price for these services, you benefit from often receiving priority or guaranteed admission for services.

Type D – Rental Agreement Contract: Instead of an entry fee, this contract allows you to rent your independent apartment in the community for a monthly fee. Like type C contracts, you also pay for additional services as needed at market price.

Type E – Equity Agreement Contract: Finally, this contract is much like the rental option, but you actually purchase your independent apartment in the community just like you would a house or condo. Like some of the other contracts, you still pay a monthly fee or home association fee for community amenities, and you would pay for additional services as needed at the market price.

Relocating to a CCRC is not a move to be made after experiencing a health setback. In fact, most CCRCs won't take you if you're sick because they are designed to accept new residents who are capable of living independently when they move in. Facilities minimize their risks of admitting high numbers of residents who will need care by requiring prospective residents to submit health information before being allowed to move in. Because many CCRCs also offer lifetime care, prospective tenants are also required to submit financial information and may be denied residency based on insufficient assets and income given a tenant's life expectancy.

Once you have decided to move into a CCRC, you have essentially chosen to live there for life. This is a big decision, so visit several CCRCs to narrow down your choices, and then spend a weekend at each of the top contenders. CCRCs are a very expensive investment, and the decision should be weighed carefully with the assistance of your attorney and a financial planner. With the cost of health care continuing to explode and the resulting changes in federal and state health care policies as an unknown, CCRCs can provide peace of mind.

My favorite Forever Home option is the CCRC because they offer a written guarantee that you won't have to move, and they offer a wide spectrum of care that ensures your needs are met no matter what. CCRCs also offer assurance that you won't end up isolated for health reasons or because of the passing of a spouse. The CCRC is, in effect, a form of long-term care insurance policy that pays with lifetime benefits. In fact, I think it's the cheapest long-term care insurance policy you can buy. A CCRC is a uniquely American retirement planning option for people who are serious about their desire not to be a burden to loved ones. You can say to your children, "I will never be a burden to you, and I will never have to worry about leaving my home if I fall ill because the care will come to me," and actually have a way to back up that promise.

There are a few drawbacks to CCRCs, though, including the fact that you're essentially renting with a large financial investment, meaning that you'll be likely to spend more money in this setting than in a house. If not being a burden is your top priority, the investment will be worth it.

And as you are considering CCRC options, also know that they are run as non-profit ventures (often by a religious denomination) or as for-profit businesses. Research tends to favor CCRC options run by non-profit organizations. These seem to have higher satisfaction rates, fewer rent increases, and fewer financial failures. These are all issues you should look into carefully before you choose your CCRC.

Everything Else

You've just heard me talk in glowing terms about CCRCs. While I think this option is the best one available today, it's not feasible for everyone. If you're not able to live independently, a CCRC won't work for you. If you've already been diagnosed with a chronic illness, a CCRC won't be an option for you. If the closest CCRC is in a place you don't want to live, a CCRC won't work for you. The entrance fees pose a particularly steep barrier to entry if you don't have the financial means.

That's where the rest of the retirement community options come into play.

In the introduction to this chapter, I grouped all the non-CCRC retirement community options into a single category. Below is a brief description of each option:

Independent Living Communities: For older adults who can function independently and don't require any assistance for day-to-day activities and needs. They often consist of smaller homes with easy access that eliminate the need to do yard work or maintenance.

Lifestyle Communities: Independent living communities enhanced with amenities like community centers, swimming pools, sporting activities, and other events, but none of the services you would find in assisted living facilities.

Assisted Living Communities: For those who are in need of some assistance during their day-to-day activities, but do not require 24/7 care or assistance.

Memory Care Facilities: For people facing cognitive decline who need 24/7 care and assistance for their own safety.

Residential Care Homes/Adult Family Homes: Licensed to provide services and care to a small number of older adults, usually between six and eight. These settings are typically in a relatively large house, with individuals residing in the bedrooms. Services include personal care, special care, and room and board, though specific services and care options vary with each location.

Skilled Nursing Facilities: Also known as nursing homes, convalescent homes, or long-term care facilities. These are facilities for people who do not need to be hospitalized but cannot be cared for at home. Most nursing homes have 24/7 caregivers and skilled nurses available to care for those with chronic illness, disabilities, or cognitive conditions. They basically provide assistance with activities of daily living and some health monitoring on a day-to-day basis. These facilities may also house rehabilitation beds and apartments.

How to Choose the Retirement Community That's Right for You

Whether you choose a CCRC or another type of retirement community, you will want to make sure that the place you choose is right for you. How do you assess whether a community is a good fit?

Fortunately, there are professionals who do this for a living. Just as you work with a real estate agent to find a house, you can work with a placement agency to find the right retirement community. Though some of these professionals earn a commission if they place you, it's possible to pay them privately to get more objective advice.

There's a caveat. One of the issues you will encounter when you work with placement professionals is that you will usually only see housing options that will pay them a commission. That's why it's important to offer to pay privately to see all the options.

Call a placement agent in your area and say this:

"I want to look at retirement community options where I can live until the end. My goal is to not have to move again, even if my health fails, and even if I run out of money. Please show me retirement communities that will help me reach this goal. I will pay you privately for the time you spend assisting me."

Your placement professional will generate a list of retirement communities that meet your criteria, then help you select a handful to visit.

When you start visiting, you will be glad you have a placement professional by your side. The salesperson who conducts your tour will show you the best parts of that community. They will have you talk to handpicked residents who may have a very biased view. This visit may not give you everything you need to know about this community. Your placement professional will take you on a walk around the rest of the campus so you can talk to residents not handpicked by the salesperson. That's the best way to get a more objective view of how residents feel about this community.

It's not enough just to have a sense of what the community feels like. It is also important that you have firsthand experience, even if you don't plan to move for a few more years. Once you find a community you like, but before you sign on the dotted line, spend a week living there. You wake up there, you eat the food, you sit with people, and you figure out what this community is all about.

Also, before you buy into a retirement community, make sure you ask about foreclosures and dues defaults, especially in cases where you are paying an entrance fee. Depending upon the type of community you choose, it may be incumbent upon you to hire either a financial advisor or an elder law attorney before making a final selection. Retirement communities come in all shapes and sizes. Making a budget for your anticipated expenses can help you narrow down your choices. If you had someone come in to do an assessment of your home or you've talked to a geriatric care manager, you can hone your choices even more.

When Money Is an Issue

I've talked a lot about private residence and retirement community housing options, but I would like to take a moment to address a topic that isn't often talked about during the retirement planning process.

What if you don't have a large lump sum to plunk down on a CCRC?

I have clients in this situation. They have modest estates in the $200,000 to $300,000 range, don't want to live in their own home, and don't want to be a burden on their kids.

What do you do if you're in that situation?

Fortunately, you are not without resources.

Assuming you're reasonably healthy, my advice is to start out in an independent living community with the expectation that you would have to move when your health fails. You would want to have a geriatric care manager standing by to help manage any housing transitions you might need as your ability to live independently changes. If you end up having to move to a more restrictive care setting, an adult family home might be an option. There are also subsidized housing options, including these programs in the U.S.:

Housing Choice Voucher Program: This program helps low-income families, seniors, and people with disabilities afford housing in the private market.[104]

Supportive Housing for the Elderly Program: This program subsidizes independent living-type apartments for seniors, and offers services like cleaning, cooking, and transportation.[105] Use the HUD Resource Locator at https://resources.hud.gov/ and choose "Find Affordable Elderly and Special Needs Housing."

Eldercare Locator: This site offers information and resources on housing options for older adults. Go to https://eldercare.acl.gov/Public/Index.aspx.

I'm also aware of many nonprofits whose mission is to create affordable housing for older adults. For example, a Washington State nonprofit called Sustainable Housing for Ageless Generation (SHAG) provides affordable rental apartment communities for low- and moderate-income seniors in the Puget Sound region. Learn more at https://www.housing4seniors.com/.

Another example is National Church Residences, the nation's largest nonprofit provider of senior housing, with 340 senior housing communities in 25 states. Learn more at https://www.nationalchurchresidences.org/about-us/.

The good news is that you don't have to be rich to find housing. You may have to adjust your expectations a bit, but if you integrate your plan for housing with your plans for health, finances, legal, and family issues, you will greatly lower the chance of being forced to move to a nursing home, going broke, or burdening your family.

The Ultimate Test: Coming Home After a Health Crisis

No matter which housing option you choose for your Forever Home, a health crisis is where the rubber meets the road. This is when the strength (or shortcomings) of your housing decisions will be revealed.

Simply telling your agents that you want to come back home after a health crisis without giving them the tools and resources to bring you home is not a plan. It's not realistic. That's why so many people end up in institutional care.

How do you prepare your family to bring you home after a health crisis?

Earlier in this book, I mentioned hospice as an example of an industry that's already set up to bring care to people living at home. We can apply this same approach to your care as you age by making arrangements in advance for a geriatric care manager to work with your family members to identify what you need and then make it happen. Identify the geriatric care manager in advance and let your agents know they are to contact this person. Do this *before* you fall and break your hip, not the day it happens.

Once you have identified your geriatric care manager resource, add this detail to your Power of Attorney so there is documentation of your wishes that is easy to find and easy to follow. I talk more about improving Powers of Attorney in Chapter 12, but I want to discuss a few more specifics related to an agent's role in housing.

Your Power of Attorney must give your agent clear direction about what you want them to do to help you achieve your goal of not being forced into institutional care. That guidance might look like the following language in your Power of Attorney:

> *When you make decisions for me using this Power of Attorney, it is tacit admission on my part that I am no longer able to manage my own affairs. At that time, I want to minimize the burdens you will need to shoulder on my behalf, and I want you to follow the directions which are designed to help me access whatever care I may need at home rather than in an institutional care setting. So, when I fall ill, you are 'required' by the terms of this Power of Attorney to use my assets to hire*

the services of a geriatric care manager. You will ask the geri-atric care manager, (hopefully one identified by you) to work with the social worker or discharge planner at the hospital to develop a plan to use the financial resources in my estate (or public benefits, if needed) to secure the care and services that will allow me to come back home without requiring you and other family members to be my unpaid caregivers. If it is not possible for me to return home, the geriatric care manager will help you determine which care setting I should move to, so I don't have to endure repeated moves to different care settings. Your role as my agent will be limited to making sure that the people who are hired to look after me fulfill their responsibili-ties, don't take advantage of me, or leave me neglected.

Next, you will need a solid commitment on the part of your loved ones and agents to bring you home after a health crisis. They need to understand and support your desire to come home. This won't happen unless you talk to them about your wishes and preferences. This is best accomplished at a Family Meeting, and I explain how to conduct one in Chapter 13.

You will also need to make sure your family and agents know exactly what to do when it's time for them to advocate for you. Your agents must know what to expect. They must know how to push back against the pressure they will inevitably face from well-meaning health care providers to move you to an institutional care setting. They must know how to respond to the social worker who asks, "Which rehab center?" Your agents must know to say that they are well within their rights to arrange your move back home. Instead of trying to figure out the logis-tics on their own, your agents will be contacting the geriatric care man-ager you have identified in advance. Your agents must know that they will be relying on the geriatric care manager to work with the hospital to manage the discharge.

You will be able to come back home because your agents are aware of your wishes, know what resources to use at the time, understand how to pay for those services, and are supportive of your goals.

Now, imagine that a health issue landed you in the hospital. At the moment of discharge, the social worker asks, "Which rehab center?"

Your agent responds that the goal is to meet your rehab needs at home and that the hospital will work with a geriatric care manager you have selected in advance to make this happen. The geriatric care manager comes to the hospital, reviews your chart, and tells the doctor that you want to rehabilitate in your home. Your geriatric care manager explains how they will arrange for the equipment, home improvements, and care providers to make your home safe and acceptable.

The hospital staff is more likely to agree to this arrangement, and you're back in your home.

A Closing Thought

Whether you are single or married, with or without children, our analysis has to be the same. You can live your life in your own home or a different home you purchase. Home doesn't mean the place you are living right now. You could move. You could live with a child, maybe not in the same house, but perhaps in a structure on the same property. Or, you can go to a retirement community, a place where they guarantee in writing that you won't have to move.

By now, you should be able to see very clearly why it's so important to have a plan for housing during your retirement years if you want to avoid institutional care. You've learned what you should be thinking about as you create that plan. You've seen how your plan for housing is connected with every other part of your retirement plan. Your housing plan has a legal component (writing your Power of Attorney), a financial component (planning to fund care), and a family component (communication, commitment, and support). You've seen how important it is to start planning eight to ten years before you fall ill, not when you're in the hospital.

It doesn't take magic. It takes planning.

CHAPTER 11

A BETTER WAY TO PLAN YOUR FINANCES

Foundational Insight

Traditional retirement planning is having a plan for accumulating money and buying products, such as long-term care insurance, annuities, etc.

LifePlanning is having a plan for the money you accumulate.

Introduction

In Part 1, you learned how the current focus of finances in the retirement planning process involves accumulating money and buying products. You saw how those actions alone can't help you achieve your goals of avoiding being forced into institutional care, not going broke, and not becoming a burden on your family.

I approach financial planning differently. I'm interested in bridging the gap between the goals that financial planners say they can help you achieve, and the goals I know you want to achieve. To me, financial planning is about more than just investment strategies, wealth accumulation, or product acquisition. Financial planning should help you achieve three fundamental goals:

Financial Planning Goal #1: Your fiduciaries have clarity on how they will use your assets, whatever the amount, to give you a life that is in keeping with your expectations and not those of a hospital discharge nurse or social worker who thinks that institutional care is automatically the best option.

Financial Planning Goal #2: You have a plan to use your assets to minimize the burdens that will be placed on your loved ones when your health fails and your agents are called upon to discharge their obligations under the various legal documents.

Financial Planning Goal #3: You have organized your finances in a way that means you won't outlive your money, regardless of how long you live, and even if your health fails.

The examples of Casey Kasem, Tim Conway, and others discussed in Part 1 of this book may seem extreme, but they make clear that planning around these three goals matters. Unless you let your agents know your goals and give them a clear path to follow to achieve them, you will end up with consequences you didn't intend.

The most important financial planning issue involves figuring out how large your financial nest egg (liquid cash, stocks, mutual funds, house, car, etc.) should be to preserve your lifestyle in retirement, and then coming up with a road map with your fiduciary, your family, and your friends to protect those assets so that they will be used in a manner that aligns with your expectations as your life comes to a close.

I'm not going to give you investment advice. That's outside my wheelhouse. My purpose here is to highlight the financial hurdles you're likely to face as you age and give you solutions for how to deal with them without being forced into institutional care, going broke, or becoming a burden on your family. In the process, you will learn what to ask your financial planner to do differently.

The Financial Dashboard

I was sitting at my desk one afternoon when my operations manager, friend, and co-worker of many years walked in. Saket and I had been advising our clients to ask their financial planners to help them think through retirement-related financial issues. I wanted these financial advisors to help my clients answer what I thought were simple questions that would help increase their confidence about their ability to achieve their goals of avoiding institutional care, not running out of money, and not being a burden. I wanted the financial planners to run some financial models for my clients, and the financial planners weren't interested in doing this. I wanted to know why.

"The problem is the industry," Saket, a financial planner himself, told me. "They don't get paid to run financial models to help people make decisions. Their business model isn't set up to collect revenue from that kind of work. They just want to invest and sell products because that's how they get paid."

Though the financial planners I encountered through my clients didn't seem interested in doing any projections, many claimed that their approach helped people live a good quality of life in retirement. Yet, when I looked to see if meaningful financial modeling had been done by these financial planners, it was usually missing. When the models had been done, they were more about providing assurance that one could live to a certain age, usually 90 or 95, without running out of money. There was no analysis of how the money would be used to keep the person out of institutional care or from becoming a burden on their family.

Their omission turned out to be a gift. Saket and I decided to lay the groundwork for what I now call the Financial Dashboard. We wanted this dashboard to answer questions like when to retire, whether to buy a long-term care policy, how much of your nest egg to withdraw each year, and more.

Saket and I worked on our Financial Dashboard for about six months, using a whiteboard to list all the issues we thought people should be looking at when they turn 50. We looked at the issues unique to people who hadn't yet retired, and to those who already had. We considered the issues of retirees who are financially secure, and those who retired without saving enough. In every case, I wanted my clients to know if their resources would last even if they lived to be over 100, and I wanted them to be able to use this dashboard to determine whether they had the financial resources to avoid institutional care, avoid losing money to unplanned long-term care costs, and avoid burdening their family. I wanted this dashboard to be better than a crystal ball.

Our next challenge was bringing the dashboard to life. We searched for a financial modeling program that would help us answer the questions we were asking, but no single financial modeling tool addressed everything. One program, ES Planner, came the closest, so we hired Julie Price, a local financial planner, to use ES Planner to create retirement dashboards the way Saket and I wanted them built.

Our Financial Dashboard did everything we hoped it would. Remember the problem of people leaving large amounts of money to their children or to beneficiaries that I talked about in the previous chapter? The Financial Dashboard showed us why. It included analysis of how much money they would need to be able to live out their life comfortably on a very conservative basis without running out. My clients knew without a doubt how much money they could withdraw from savings every year and use that money to take care of their kids and grandkids, give to charities, take exotic vacations, or whatever. If my clients wanted to leave money to children, why not give it to them while they're living? The Financial Dashboard showed them how. More importantly, it allowed people to see their intended beneficiaries, family members, and charities benefit from their money while they were still living, not after their death. In some cases, families found reasons to stop being overly generous.

Over time, the Financial Dashboard evolved into a set of questions that my clients could take to their financial planners. Today, my clients don't have any problem getting their financial planners to run these models.

How to Create a Financial Dashboard

If you want your financial plan for retirement to look great on paper, there's one simple trick: die young. A better plan is to expect longevity. The Financial Dashboard helps you do that. In fact, I consider it one of the most powerful tools in the *LifePlanning* arsenal. Below are the basic steps to follow to create a Financial Dashboard for your retirement.

Know What to Ask

Before you go to your financial planner, you need to know what questions you want the Financial Dashboard to answer. Those questions will vary based on your situation.

Some examples:

- If I am still working, when is the ideal time to retire?
- When should I start drawing Social Security benefits?
- How can I best maximize Social Security benefits?
- How much money would I need to live comfortably to age 105 without running out of money?
- How will I pay for long-term care if I need it?
- Should I invest in a long-term care insurance policy or not? If so, should it be a traditional policy or an asset-based policy?

How much can I afford in the way of premiums, both now and after I'm on a fixed income?

- If Medicaid or VA benefits will be a payment source for long-term care, what actions do I need to take (and when) to prepare?

- Should I convert my traditional IRA accounts to Roth IRAs? If yes, how can I convert them in a way that minimizes costs?

- How much of my nest egg can I gift/donate to see my intended heirs benefit now rather than later?

- Am I making a mistake in giving money to my children?

- Are my assets invested properly?

- What are the costs associated with my investments? Is there a way to lower those costs?

- And many more questions, based on your unique situation.

Establish Your Retirement Income Needs

The first step is gaining a clear understanding of how much it costs to maintain your current quality of life or to fund the quality of life you expect to have during your retirement years. I see this as a five-step process.

1. Start with your current net income (present-day dollars), which for most people, is enough to fund your current lifestyle. This number will need to be adjusted to account for inflation.

2. Next, catalog your expenses over the past several months and average them by month and by year.

3. Third, note any expenses that will end after a certain number of years, such as a loan payment or your children's educational expenses you may be covering.

4. Don't forget to include anticipated expenses. Each of these details will be helpful for a financial planner as they are projecting your spending into the future.

5. Finally, what is the minimum amount of inheritance, if any, you would like to leave for your loved ones or to charity?

This should let you get to a number, adjusted for inflation, that you can expect to need to be able to maintain your quality of life. I recommend printing this out in the form of a chart that you can see and relate to.

Understand Your Income Sources

Next, once you know your income needs, list your income sources. Most retirees will have Social Security, pensions, or other investments as primary sources of income.

Income from Social Security and pensions is easy to determine because they are fixed amounts each month. Both are also easy to obtain. If you have concerns about where Social Security is headed, create your income projections using 75 percent of the projected Social Security amount as the income you will be able to count on. If the Social Security Trust Fund goes bankrupt, you will still be able to get about 75 percent of your projected income from the contributions of current workers. You will also want to talk to your financial planner about creating a strategy for when you should start drawing Social Security.

Once you determine your fixed income—that is, income from Social Security and pensions—you will have a clear understanding of how much you need from your investments to maintain your quality of life. Not all of your income from investments will come from your gains. Some may be from the principal. Just keep in mind that the more you draw from your nest egg, the less space there is for return.

Identify a Safe Withdrawal Amount (SWA)

What is the right amount to withdraw from invested assets to fund your quality of life in retirement without running out of money, even if you live to be 105 years old? That's the question I want your financial planner to answer.

As I mentioned earlier, most financial planners are helping their clients plan in a way that will make their money last to age 85, 90, or 95. We know that we are unlikely to see our 105th birthday, but think of this. If you're one of the few freaks who makes it to age 105, what would happen if you planned for your money to last until age 90? However, if you plan to live to 105 and you end up dying at 90, your heirs get more. How bad could that be?

Your financial planner will help you find the sweet spot. The amount you can withdraw safely will then become your guide on how much to take on by way of expenditures without fearing spending money or overdoing it. You will need to repeat this exercise every two or three years with your financial planner.

Identify a Safe Gifting Amount

The Financial Dashboard exercise also includes having your financial planner map out a gifting strategy, focused heavily on the amount you can gift annually without running out of money. This will make it possible for the people you choose to benefit from your wealth while you're alive—but without jeopardizing your own security. If I am going to have a charity put up a plaque on its wall to recognize my generosity, would I not like to see it while I am living? Would I not like to see my children pay off debts or improve their lives while I am alive?

Create Scenarios

This step is all about the what-ifs. The most important what-if scenario involves long-term care expenses for you and your spouse, if you are married. What you want your financial planner to do is to help you understand how much disposable income you will have in retirement to cover long-term care insurance premiums. If developing the Financial Dashboard shows that you will run out of money before you die because the policy premiums will require an unduly large withdrawal amount, you are not the right candidate for a long-term care insurance policy. But, if you see that you can afford the premiums without running out of money, you will want to know what the dollar amount is—in other words, what is the most you can withdraw and dedicate to a long-term care insurance policy, without running out of money? You will then take this number to your insurance agent and ask them to give you options for that amount of money and not a penny more. I'll talk more about the types of long-term care insurance premiums later in the chapter.

Don't Put It Off

Whether you are closing in on retirement or you're already retired, you need to have a Financial Dashboard. It is more important than an investment plan. Even if you're 80 years old and think you don't have that much time left, a Financial Dashboard will give you the information you need to live out the rest of your life without worrying about going broke or being a financial burden on others. You'll know how much you can spend on fun, how much you can give to your family, and how much you can donate to charity—all without putting your future in jeopardy.

Choosing a Financial Planner

If you have a financial planner you trust, ask that planner to develop your Financial Dashboard for you.

If you don't have a financial planner, now is the time to find one. The best choice is a professional who meets the following criteria:

1. The professional holds the Certified Financial Planner (CFP) designation, the gold standard for financial planners.

2. You connect well with the financial planner on a personal level.

3. The financial planner is free from conflicts of interest. This will be the case if the planner will work with you on either a flat fee or an hourly basis instead of a percentage of "assets under management."

Let's take a moment to examine the two compensation models for financial planning.

Fee-only planners are generally free from commissions and, in my opinion, are better positioned to give you more objective advice. Fee-only planners charge either a flat fee or an hourly fee. They do not get paid by the financial firms they represent—they are paid by you. There aren't that many fee-only financial planners, but you can find them if you look. Some will offer fee-only financial planning as part of a larger service offering that also includes assets under management. Don't be afraid to work with a financial planner who offers both, as long as you have the option to pay for objective advice. Ask around to find a fee-only financial planner.

Fee-based planners most commonly receive a percentage of the total assets they manage in your account. Their compensation is much like a commission, but they may charge other fees in addition to the percentage as well. Generally, fee-based planners can only offer you financial products from the companies they represent, or products that their company has in its portfolio. This can cause a conflict of interest when the planner is aware of options outside of their company that would be more beneficial to you but cannot offer those options to you.

My advice: choose a fee-only planner, if you can find one.

Paying for Long-Term Care

As I've mentioned several times in this book, the single biggest financial threat that the average retiree will face in America is uncovered long-term care costs. The threat is particularly urgent for married people with estates valued at less than $1.5 million and around $1 million for single people, or if your estate has less than $300,000 in cash assets.

Long-term care costs can range from a few thousand dollars per month to upwards of $16,000 per month, depending on the level of care. These expenses have risen nearly three times the rate of inflation.

So, where will the money come from? Here's the typical triage:

1. First, look to your long-term care insurance policy if you have one.

2. If you don't have a long-term care insurance policy, the next option is to pay for care with private resources … a nice way of referring to your own pocket. If you have equity in your home and you want to live out your life in the home you know and love, a reverse mortgage is a great option.

3. If you are not willing to invest in a long-term care insurance policy or establish a line of credit using a reverse mortgage, learn how to hire caregivers directly, without going through a care agency.

4. If you don't have a long-term care insurance policy and a reverse mortgage isn't right for you, the next option is to look at VA and Medicaid benefits.

From a financial perspective, there are more options available to the average person than meets the eye. This section will introduce you to all of them.

Long-Term Care Insurance

Long-term care insurance helps pay for the costs associated with long-term care. Generally speaking, this type of insurance pays for care not covered by health insurance, Medicare, or public benefit programs like Medicaid and VA benefits. If you have a long-term care insurance policy and you find yourself in need of care, your insurance policy will be the first funding source you investigate.

Most people buy long-term care insurance to avoid having to spend their own money on long-term care expenses. For some people, even if they have the money to pay for long-term care, they often hesitate to spend their own funds because they're concerned about spending too much too soon and running out of money. If you know that you will be your own obstacle in spending money on long-term care costs when the time comes, you will be well served by purchasing a long-term care insurance policy.

There are two types of long-term care policies: traditional and asset-based.

Traditional Long-Term Care Insurance

The goal of traditional long-term care insurance is to provide the policyholder access to care services, then reimburse them the cost of those services. Traditional long-term care insurance policies only pay a benefit when you are no longer able to manage your own activities of daily living, also known as ADLs.

These ADLs include six major tasks or functions: eating, bathing hygiene, toilet incontinence, mobility transferring, dressing, and grooming. If it is determined that you are unable to do at least two of these, then the policy will start paying benefits.

I recommend starting your search for a traditional long-term care insurance policy around age 50. Premiums for a long-term care insurance policy vary based on age. It's important to understand both the terms of the policy and what will happen with the policy's premiums.

If you do consider buying a traditional long-term care policy, the question to ask is not whether you can afford the policy today, but whether you will be able to afford it ten, fifteen, or twenty years in the future when you are retired and on a fixed income. By that time, the premiums may have doubled or even tripled due to health care cost inflation. Your Financial Dashboard should factor in these rising premiums, and the results of your analysis will dictate whether this type of policy is right for you.

Rising premiums aren't the only consideration. Traditional long-term care insurance is a "use it or lose it" type of policy. If you are lucky enough to go to sleep one day and not wake up, the premiums you shelled out for this type of policy will be lost, and no benefits will be paid.

Asset-Based Hybrid Long-Term Care Insurance

If the "use it or lose it" nature of traditional long-term care insurance doesn't sound like an acceptable risk to you, consider an asset-based hybrid long-term care policy. These start as either annuities or life insurance policies, both of which have death benefits that address the "use it or lose it" concerns common with traditional policies. If you die without needing long-term care, your heirs receive a predetermined death benefit. The premiums you pay don't get squandered. You determine the amount of money you would like to have available to cover future long-term care costs, and the insurance company will present either an annuity or life insurance policy based on the sum.

Here's how it works. You give the insurance company a certain amount of money—let's say $200,000. The insurance company takes that money and puts it into a life insurance policy or an annuity. If you are lucky enough to go to sleep one day and not wake up, the insurance company will give this money to your heirs. If you end up needing long-term care, riders added to the policy allow you to use the benefits as long-term care insurance. The insurance company will give you a multiple of your original investment as a long-term care benefit. If you put $200,000 into the policy, then they may give you up to $600,000 in a long-term care benefit. The multiple will be determined based on your age and your health.

Asset-based hybrid long-term care policies tend to be very flexible, allowing various payment plans. You can pay monthly or annually, make a single payment, or make a set number of payments.

Also, because the policies are fixed in their benefits, there's no worry about future premium increases. Asset-based policies are a good option if you are still working and have the disposable income to pay off the policy before retirement or have the funds to pay it off with a single premium.

As I've mentioned before, I don't recommend going to a long-term care insurance agent to find out what type of long-term care insurance policy is for you and how much you can afford. With few exceptions, most insurance agents are interested in one thing only: selling you a policy, any policy, today. I know—I sold insurance earlier in my career. Your insurance agent is unlikely to assess the appropriateness and affordability issues that are more important than getting started with a policy today.

Go to your financial planner first and request a Financial Dashboard so you can answer questions like these:

- Should I invest in a long-term care policy?

- If so, what is the maximum amount of money I should be able to dedicate to this policy today, knowing that it's only going to be used sometime in the future?

- If I buy the traditional long-term care policy, can I afford increasing premiums in retirement on a fixed income?

- For a hybrid or an asset-based long-term care policy, can I afford to give the insurance company a large lump sum (e.g., $200,000 or more) upfront? What is the most I could afford to pay upfront, given that any funds I allocate to a lump sum won't be available to fund my other retirement needs? If I pay this lump sum, will I still be able to get enough return from the balance of my investment portfolio to meet my other needs?

A Financial Dashboard created by your financial planner can answer all these questions. This is the only way I know to get a truly objective look at the big picture.

Private Resources/Your Own Money

If you need to pay for long-term care, using private resources is another option. Most of us save money to fund medical expenses later in life. Savings, IRAs, 401(k)s, 403(b)s, brokerage, and other accounts can and should be used to help pay for long-term care when the need arises. While using your own funds to pay for care may work for some, for most Americans, there are a few concerns. First is the fact that long-term care is very expensive. A year or two in a nursing home can use up savings that took a lifetime to accumulate. Another major concern is for married couples. One spouse's illness can wipe out the couple's retirement savings, leaving little or nothing for the surviving spouse. When the surviving spouse becomes ill, now with a reduced nest egg, the result can be devastating.

Many couples are acutely aware of this possibility. The fear of running out of money is one of the most common reasons why people resist the idea of using their own funds to pay for care. However, it can be wise to minimize the risks of this spending by tapping into other ways to access private funds to pay for long-term care costs.

Private Resources/Reverse Mortgage

Reverse mortgages allow you to trade equity in your home for cash. You are not required to pay back the cash as long as you stay in the house.

This often-misunderstood financial tool has received bad press over the years. The good news is that the problems associated with reverse mortgages a generation ago have all been resolved. Gone are the sketchy operators and excessive fees. That's a good thing. If you are determined to age in place and you own your home but have limited cash assets to be able to cover these costs, a reverse mortgage is one way to access funds to pay for care. If used correctly and for the right reasons, a reverse mortgage can help you avoid institutional care.

Why consider a reverse mortgage over a traditional mortgage or a line of credit? A traditional mortgage always calls for a monthly payment. A reverse mortgage postpones that payment and makes the amount available to be used to pay for care costs, allowing you to age in your own home. A traditional mortgage is fixed in amount when you take one out; a reverse mortgage automatically increases in value over the years without the need to reapply or requalify. A traditional mortgage can be terminated by the bank or financial institution, but a reverse mortgage cannot be terminated so long as you are living in the house. A traditional mortgage will need to be paid back upon your death, as will a reverse mortgage, but with a reverse mortgage, the family members are allowed to buy the house for 5 percent less than the market value, giving your family a better chance of being able to keep the home if that is what they desire.

Who is the ideal candidate for a reverse mortgage? You must be living in an age-friendly home, close to your named agents, and you must have established a dependable plan where you can be sure that when the time comes, you will be able to access care at home, without turning your family members into your unpaid caregivers or running out of money before you run out of life. So, the decision to obtain a reverse mortgage should be made only after the housing issues have been sorted out.

If you are absolutely sure that aging in your current home is the right choice for you and that it is perfectly viable, then a reverse mortgage is the right tool for you to consider. At that point, you should ask your financial planner to include various scenarios of a reverse mortgage in your Financial Dashboard to see if they improve your outcome. Your financial planner may need to consult with a reverse mortgage specialist to ensure the details are input accurately.

With a reverse mortgage, your goal is to access the equity to pay caregivers, allowing you to age in place. When you establish the reverse mortgage, you will be given different options as to how you wish to access the equity: in a lump sum, in monthly payments, or by way of a line of credit that you can tap into later. If your financial planning around long-term care issues will include utilizing VA or Medicaid benefits, then I recommend establishing a line of credit using a reverse mortgage at your earliest opportunity. The line of credit will not interfere with your ability to access VA or Medicaid benefits; however, taking a lump sum or opting to receive monthly payments will have an adverse impact on your eligibility. Furthermore, by establishing a line of credit and not taking the funds in a lump sum or monthly payment, no interest or costs are being incurred other than the cost to establish the line of credit because you are not taking out a loan.

If you decide that a reverse mortgage is a suitable option for you, I encourage you to speak with your family and anyone designated as your caretaker about your decision.

Private Resources/Hiring Caregivers

If you need long-term care, you want the care to come to you, and you don't want your children to become your unpaid caregivers, you will need to hire professionals. This is an expense that needs to be factored into your financial plan.

At the time of this writing (2022), care agencies in the Seattle area charge between $35 and $60 per hour. At these prices, the bill for full-time care can exceed $40,000 a month. Though the hourly rate may be higher or lower in your area, the expense will add up fast no matter where you live.

How can you hire professional caregivers without breaking the bank? Fortunately, working through an agency isn't your only option. Hiring caregivers directly can greatly reduce the cost.

Where do you go to find direct-hire caregivers? The website Care.com is one option. Most cities also have employment agencies that help families find caregivers for direct hire. In 2022, these caregivers cost under $20 per hour.

If you want your health care agent to go the direct hire route, the geriatric care manager you have chosen will play a pivotal role in the caregiver recruitment and selection process. Your geriatric care manager can recruit and interview candidates, choose the best ones, give your health care agent a list of candidates to interview personally, and then help make the final selection.

When you go the direct hire route, you can often get round-the-clock in-home care for far less than the cost of care in a nursing home. However, there are downsides. If you hire a caregiver directly, you become the employer, which comes with obligations that you may (or may not) be willing to assume. When you hire caregivers directly, you become responsible for recruiting, interviewing, screening, hiring, training, payroll taxes, workers' compensation, and liability insurance. When the caregiver calls in sick, resigns, or just doesn't work out, it's up to you to find a replacement. When you work through an agency, all of these tasks are done for you—but that service comes at a price.

I have worked with many families that went the direct caregiver route with good results. Two sons I know who were in the market for caregivers for their elderly father relied on their dad's geriatric care manager to recruit and screen candidates, and then make a recommendation about whom to interview. After interviewing candidates in person, the sons ended up choosing a couple who came Monday through Friday. They also hired two older ladies who alternated weekend shifts on Saturday and Sunday. Between these two couples, they paid no more than $9,000 in any given month, far less than what a nursing home would have cost. Their father was able to continue to live at home, just as he wanted. In fact, his health improved during the first few years of this arrangement because, instead of living alone, he had people living with him, creating social connections that helped him thrive.

When you're deciding whether to hire caregivers through an agency or hire them directly, make sure to look at the advantages and disadvantages of each option.

Weighing the Options: A Brief Summary

Hiring a Caregiver on Your Own	
Pros	Cons
Less expensive	Difficulty finding candidates
Do your own screening	Need a backup plan if the caregiver isn't available
Choose whomever you want	
No middleman	You handle supervision and performance issues
	You are responsible for taxes, workers' comp, etc.

Hiring a Caregiver through an Agency	
Pros	Cons
More caregivers to choose from	More expensive
Most agencies offer backup caregiver	May not get the same caregiver every day
Handles screening and performance management	Less input on the selection process

Public Benefits

If long-term care insurance benefits, private funds, or a reverse mortgage aren't available or they aren't right for you, the final option involves turning to our nation's safety net. The two public benefit programs I discuss in this section are where older adults and their families land when they have no other options. These programs are Medicaid and Veteran's Affairs (VA) benefits. The discussion that follows is a general overview of these complicated public benefit programs. It's always a good idea to consult with an elder law attorney to discuss your unique situation.

Medicaid

Medicaid is a joint federal and state program that provides long-term care costs for those who meet its financial and medical criteria. The Medicaid program requires you to spend your money down to almost nothing before it will cover your costs.

Medicaid pays for medical and long-term care costs for those who meet three requirements:

1. Functional Eligibility: The applicant must functionally or physically need medical or long-term care assistance.

2. Income Eligibility: The applicant's income must be insufficient to cover the costs. Depending on your state, your income must be below a certain amount set by your state's Medicaid program. The income threshold varies from state to state.

3. Resource Eligibility: The applicant must have spent down their own assets to the allowable limit, which is very low.

Let's look at each of those requirements individually.

Functional Eligibility: The first requirement is that you need the assistance of a caregiver, such as in a nursing home, your own home, or another setting. You are automatically assumed to have met this requirement if you apply while living in a nursing home because your needs are obviously serious enough to require accommodation in that setting. For those not living in a nursing home, the state will conduct its own assessment to determine whether you meet your state's financial eligibility rule. Washington State, for example, will send a state-employed social worker who uses a rigid framework to evaluate whether you meet the requirements. If you do, the social worker will set the number of hours of care that the state will cover. It's always best to speak to an elder law attorney knowledgeable in Medicaid requirements because qualifications vary from state to state.

Income Eligibility: This is the second requirement for Medicaid, and the definition is strict. It is referred to as MAGI, or Modified Adjusted Gross Income. MAGI is calculated by adding your household's adjusted gross income and tax-exempt interest income together. You should be able to qualify for long-term care under Medicaid as long as your income is below the MAGI threshold, or slightly above to compensate for other medical expenses. It is also possible to qualify for benefits if your income exceeds the MAGI threshold under what's called the medically needy program, or by using certain types of Trusts. Different states have different rules on how one can work around the income eligibility issues, so it is important for you to speak to an elder law attorney in your state.

Resource Eligibility: The final requirement for Medicaid eligibility involves your assets and varies based on whether you are married or single.

If you are married and you are the ill spouse who is applying for Medicaid, you must have no more than between $1,500 and $2,000 in assets to your name to meet Medicaid's asset limit. (This limit varies by state.) However, if you are married, your spouse can have an unlimited amount of income, a home of any value, an automobile of any value, and other financial assets with specific limitations.

It's a bit different if you're not married. Single people are still only allowed between $1,500 and $2,000 in assets (this limit also varies by state), though the rules will allow you to have some other assets, such as a home with limited equity, personal property, etc. Since there is no spouse to transfer assets to, the five-year look-back rule applies. If you gift assets within this period, you may end up making yourself ineligible for Medicaid for a period of time, depending on the value of the assets transferred. Once you qualify for Medicaid, your assets could be subject to a state Medicaid lien to recoup some of the costs they are paying toward your care.

Most people aware of the asset limit might think that they can simply transfer the assets to their loved ones and then apply for the benefits. Anticipating that people will take these steps, both the VA and Medicaid programs have taken action to prevent this. To qualify for benefits you cannot have transferred assets of any value to anyone within three years for VA and five years for Medicaid.

It's important to note that there are no limits to the value of assets that the ill spouse can transfer to the healthy spouse. Also, Medicaid's five-year look-back period for gifting assets doesn't apply to married couples. With the right planning, most middle-class Americans should be able to qualify for Medicaid benefits without impoverishing their spouse.

Qualifying for Medicaid isn't a do-it-yourself project. You will be much better off if you work with an elder law attorney licensed to practice in your state.

VA Benefits

If you are a veteran of the U.S. military or are (or were) married to a veteran, you probably already know about the U.S. Department of Veterans Affairs—the VA—and the services it provides to veterans. What you might not know is that the VA offers several benefit programs that can provide monthly income during retirement to veterans and surviving spouses who qualify. When you're creating your financial plan for retirement and considering how you might pay for uncovered long-term care expenses, it's important to understand which VA programs might be available to you and your spouse.

In this section, I offer a brief tutorial on each type of VA benefit that might play a role in a veteran's financial plan for retirement. Keep in mind that this information is current at the time of writing, but may have changed by the time you read these words. VA rules and application requirements are complicated, to say the least. For that reason, it's a good idea to consult an elder law attorney or the VA website for the latest information. I always recommend working with a qualified elder law attorney to determine the best way to access the benefits that apply to you.

Let's start with a few definitions that will help you better understand what's available.

The VA recognizes two types of disability:

1. Service-connected: the veteran is disabled due to injury or illness that was incurred in or aggravated by military service.

2. Non-service-connected: the veteran is disabled due to injury or illness not related to military service.

A disability's link to a veteran's service is a key factor when it comes to determining which benefits might apply.

The VA offers two types of benefits to veterans: Compensation and Pension.

Compensation is paid to a veteran with service-connected disabilities. Pension is paid to a wartime veteran who is permanently and totally disabled from non-service-connected disabilities, and who has a very low income.

VA Disability Compensation

VA Disability Compensation offers a monthly tax-free payment to veterans who got sick or injured while serving in the military and to veterans whose service made an existing condition worse. Since it is an entitlement program as opposed to a means-tested program, the VA compensation program may entitle the veteran to a disability payment that is not dependent on that veteran's income or assets. Veterans who have become incapacitated to the point that they need assistance from others, either in their home or an institutional care setting, may be eligible for additional benefits. The reason behind the need for care must be directly tied to a service-related injury. The VA's website offers a complete description of the program, eligibility requirements, and the application process at https://www.va.gov/disability/.

Dependency and Indemnity Compensation (DIC)

The same is true with Dependency and Indemnity Compensation (DIC), a tax-free monthly benefit paid to eligible survivors of military service members who died in the line of duty, or to eligible survivors of veterans whose death resulted from a service-related injury or disease. This provides the widower or widow of the veteran with a continued disability benefit should the veteran die as a direct or indirect result of service-related injuries.

To be eligible for this benefit, you must be the surviving spouse or dependent child of a military service member or veteran who meets one of the following:

- Died while serving on active duty, or during active or inactive duty training.
- Died as a result of a service-connected injury or disease.
- Died as a result of a non-service-connected injury or disease, and who was totally disabled from his/her service-connected disabilities for any of the following:
  - At least 10 years immediately preceding death.
  - Since the veteran's release from active duty and for at least five years immediately preceding death.
  - At least one year immediately preceding death if the veteran was a former prisoner of war.

This is just a brief overview of eligibility requirements. The DIC Fact Sheet at https://benefits.va.gov/BENEFITS/factsheets/survivors/dic.pdf offers a good overview of eligibility criteria, benefit amounts, and how to apply. You can also learn more at https://www.va.gov/disability/dependency-indemnity-compensation/ and https://www.benefits.gov/benefit/290.

VA Aid and Attendance

VA Aid and Attendance is another disability program that can help cover long-term care costs for veterans who served during a declared war period and their surviving spouses.

The program provides monthly payments added to the amount of a monthly VA pension for qualified veterans and survivors. This tax-free benefit is designed to provide financial assistance to help cover the cost of long-term care in the home, in an assisted living facility, or in a nursing home. VA Aid and Attendance is for those who require the regular attendance of another person or caregiver in at least two of the activities of daily living such as bathing, dressing, eating, toileting, and transferring.

Unlike the VA compensation programs discussed earlier in this section, VA Aid and Attendance does not require the veteran to have suffered a wartime injury. Instead, the program qualifies veterans based on their financial situation—their "means."

The payouts can be substantial. Here's an overview of the benefit levels in 2022.

Status	Monthly Benefit	Annual Benefit
Surviving Spouse	$1,318	$15,816
Single Veteran	$2,050	$24,610
Married Veteran	$2,431	$29,175
Two Veterans, Married	$3,261	$39,036

Remember, these benefits are tax-free. You don't need a calculator to see the potential boost to your finances this could provide over the years.

In order to qualify for VA Aid and Attendance, the veteran must clear a number of hurdles:

- Served at least 90 days of active duty with at least one day during a declared wartime period[106]
- Left service with anything other than a Dishonorable discharge
- Be 65 years or older or totally disabled
- Require the assistance of another person to perform some of the activities of daily living
- Meet income and countable asset criteria established by the VA, which is very similar to that of the Medicaid program
- A surviving spouse must have been married to the veteran at the time of his passing, and not remarried unless to a wartime veteran

The program also assesses household income relative to medical costs. The applicant must show that their medical costs require them to pay so much out of their household income that what remains is below the threshold that the VA has established. The family is permitted to deduct any unreimbursed medical expenses such as insurance payments, co-payments for medical care, home care expenses, and amounts paid to adult family homes, assisted living facilities, boarding homes, nursing homes, etc.

The VA then looks at the remaining assets to determine the net income. If the income is below the allowable threshold, then the VA will add enough money to bring the income up to the allowable limits.

Let me give an example.

Let us assume that we are looking to apply for benefits for a married veteran whose household income is $2,500. Meanwhile, the family is incurring $3,000 per month to cover assisted living facility charges. Under this scenario, the VA will assume the family's household income is zero and add $2,431 per month to the household income for a married veteran.

The benefits are only available to those who have no more than $138,489 in resources. This amount changes annually and is the same amount used by the Medicaid system to establish the maximum spousal resource amount (CSRA). This amount does not consider one home situated on less than two acres of land, and automobiles. Veterans Affairs, like Medicaid, imposes a penalty if any assets have been transferred within three years preceding the application date, and the penalty cannot last for more than five years.

If you are a veteran or if you are married to one, VA Aid and Attendance benefits should be carefully considered as part of your strategy to pay for uncovered long-term care costs. There are many times when, even though you might qualify for VA benefits, it may be better to go for the Medicaid benefits and leave the VA benefits alone. This requires a case-by-case analysis that is best completed by a qualified elder law attorney in your home state.

Transferring Assets to Qualify for Public Benefits: Tax Implications for Retirement Accounts

If you intend to pay for long-term care with Medicaid and/or VA benefits, it is vital to plan around tax issues related to retirement accounts like a 401(k) and IRA. If you fall ill and need to move your assets to your spouse to qualify for public benefits, one of the most expensive assets to transfer is your traditional IRA.

Let's say that you're a veteran who needs long-term care and you want to access VA Aid and Attendance benefits. Let's say that your assets exceed the VA's resource limit by $200,000, the amount of an IRA you own. If you move that money out of your IRA and give it to your children so you can meet the VA's resource limit, you will be subject to a three-year look-back period, which will delay when you can start receiving the monthly VA Aid and Attendance benefit.

That's not the worst of it. You will have a tax problem. When you withdraw pre-tax funds from an IRA, you have to report the income to the IRS. You know what that means. You'll end up paying income tax on the withdrawal amount. Transferring this account can cost up to the highest marginal tax rate, currently 37 percent plus a 3.8 percent Medicaid surcharge.

As I like to say, when you poke the balloon, the air has to come out somewhere.

However, there is something you can do to mitigate this cost. Let's talk about the conversion of traditional retirement accounts to Roth accounts. Because of the tax costs on transfers of a traditional account, Roth accounts would be highly beneficial to you if you ever need to apply for Medicaid or VA programs.

If you have a traditional retirement account, you can convert part or all of it to a Roth account at any time. There are no amount or age limits to this conversion. There's just one catch: the amount you convert is taxed as income in the year you make the conversion.

Why would you pay taxes now to avoid paying the same taxes later? The key reason is tax brackets. The higher your income, the higher the percentage of taxes you must pay.

The advantage of converting to a Roth account is that you can decide how much to convert. You can convert a portion of the account each year. That way, you pay less in total taxes over a longer period of time.

Most financial advisors consider only the marginal tax savings of a Roth conversion strategy, and therefore may not recommend it. But with this additional information, you can insist on adding flexibility to your financial plan by converting your traditional retirement accounts to Roth IRAs over time.

Addressing Financial Burdens

You've already seen how counting on your family members and agents to manage your financial affairs when you're incapacitated is a recipe for creating heavy burdens. The fiduciary is essentially expected to act on your behalf without much direction, making even the simplest tasks a challenge and a hardship.

If you're serious about not being a burden on those you love, you have to take deliberate action in advance to make things easy for them.

How do you do this? You will want to meet and consult with your fiduciaries to make your wishes very clear and specific. You will also want to come up with a very detailed and specific outline for your fiduciaries. Your goal is to make sure they have sufficient guidance and resources to act on your behalf when you cannot.

Financial tasks that are expected of your fiduciaries fall under three broad categories:

1. Managing your financial holdings such as investments or properties
2. Paying bills
3. Filing taxes

Beyond your finances, your agent will be responsible for:

- Arranging a go-to health care professional who can coordinate your care the way you want
- Coordinating your health care professional's access to your personal information

These weighty burdens can be lightened by creating a team of professionals and additional resources to assist your designated agents.

Assemble Your Resource Team

Let's identify ways to ease the burden for your agents and fiduciaries (often members of your family) by creating a team of professionals and providing resources to guide them through the tasks of managing your affairs.

Here's exactly what to do:

Select a Geriatric Care Manager

Naming a geriatric care manager in your Power of Attorney documents is crucial. Here's why: if you fall and end up in the hospital, and the nurse asks your agent which rehab center to send you to, what do you want them to say? Hopefully by now you realize that it is possible to give your family the tools to bring you home if at all possible. The nurse won't be able to authorize you to be discharged to your home on the word of your agent alone, and that's where the geriatric care manager comes in. A geriatric care manager will establish and obtain the equipment and support you need for care in your home. By pre-interviewing and selecting a geriatric care manager, and then writing them into your legal documents, your agent is empowered to call them at this critical moment. The geriatric care manager can come in, talk to the nurse and doctors, outline an agreeable plan of care, and you wake up in your own home, just as you planned.

Acquire a Financial Planner

If you become incapacitated, you will most likely be relying on your agents to manage your financial assets. Arranging to have a financial planner not only protects you and your assets, but it also gives your fiduciaries a reliable source of knowledge and advice to lean on for help. Make sure that the financial planner you choose to oversee your documents and assist your fiduciaries is someone you trust and have worked with in the past. Make sure the financial planner you include in your resource list has a succession plan that you are comfortable with in case they retire or go out of business. You will want to name this person as the professional you want your fiduciaries to work with.

Arrange for a Property Manager or a Handyman

Consider hiring a property manager or a handyman if you have rental properties. Not everyone is comfortable with managing properties, and your fiduciary may not be interested in managing a property they have no connection to. Having a manager deal with your properties can alleviate a major burden to your loved ones. Consider delegating tasks to potential property managers to build a relationship and determine whether they are right for the job. Once you identify someone, be sure to name them in your Power of Attorney documents.

Even if you don't own rental properties, your agent will need to handle maintenance issues with your home. Suppose the plumbing starts leaking, the refrigerator goes out, or the roof is damaged by hail. When that happens, your agent will need to attend to these issues. Having a handyman's name or a property manager's number to call will make the task easier for your agent to handle.

Set Up Bill Pay

When you're no longer able to manage your affairs, one of the first tasks your fiduciary will have to tackle is paying your bills. Without guidance, figuring out what bills need to be paid, to whom, when, and how much, is one of the biggest challenges your fiduciary will face. There are several ways to reduce this burden. One is to use software your fiduciary can access to track and pay your bills. Banks offer this service, but if you or your fiduciary choose to change banks, you will lose your electronic history. Another option is to use a program not attached to any single institution, such as QuickBooks®, Quicken®, and Mvelopes®, among others. These programs give you a way to track income, expenses, deductions, and other financial data. If you choose to use a program to track your bills, make sure that your fiduciary becomes familiar with the program while you're healthy.

If you want to completely eliminate the bill-paying burdens, consider arranging for an accountant or bookkeeper to take over the role, assisting your fiduciary when the time comes. Ask your current accountant if they can help your fiduciary in this role. If they can't, consider finding an accountant who is willing. When you have found an accountant with whom you are comfortable, you will want to name that accountant in your Power of Attorney documents, so your fiduciary knows whom to contact.

Hire an Accountant for Taxes

Filing your taxes is another financial issue that your fiduciary may struggle with. Filing taxes is difficult even in the best of times; having to file someone else's taxes without any guidance or knowledge of their finances is an extreme burden. Consider hiring a local accountant to manage your taxes rather than turning to a national tax preparation chain. Working with a local provider means building a professional relationship and establishing trust. When you choose a local provider that you know and trust, you will be more confident that your fiduciaries will receive competent and reliable service from your tax preparer. Again, make sure to request a succession plan from your firm. It's important that your accountant have competent and trustworthy people who can step in if your accountant retires or leaves the business.

If you are dead set against hiring an accounting professional to prepare your taxes when you can't do it yourself, I suggest that you sit down with your fiduciaries and prepare your taxes with them for a few years in a row so that they are familiar with your financial situation and your process.

Don't Forget Password and Log-in ID Management

Just about everything these days requires you to log in to something, yet password management is one of the most often overlooked parts of the planning process. If you don't give your agents a list of login credentials, passwords, and the account information they will need to manage your online accounts, you will make their life a living hell. You can avoid all that by creating a spreadsheet with all your password information, and then giving it to your agent.

I dealt with this kind of issue after my mom died. I ended up with her cell phone and I tried to open it. I knew what her password was, but somewhere along the line, someone tried to log in unsuccessfully one too many times, and her phone ended up locked. I spent a lot of time troubleshooting this.

Now that I've told you to give your agents all your passwords, I need to share this caveat: For most sites, it is illegal to impersonate a real user—meaning that others should not log into the system using your ID and conduct business as if they were you. Though there are a few ways for your agents to be able to quickly and easily manage your affairs without your credentials, it is extremely difficult to give them the same authority over your accounts that you have. Proceed with this recommendation with caution, and make sure that your agents know that they cannot access your accounts and impersonate you. A better option might be for you to have your Power of Attorney provide your agent the power to be able to deal with your online accounts.

Prepay Final Expenses

Consider prepaying final expenses and being clear about what kind of funeral you want. By making those choices in advance and then prepaying those expenses, you not only save money, but you also save your loved ones the burden of having to make those decisions during a time of mourning, and then having to foot the bill themselves.

You should also decide how you want your remains handled and then communicate your wishes to your family. For instance, if you decide you want to be cremated, what do you want your loved ones to do with your ashes? Should they be interred in a columbarium, scattered in the ocean, used to nourish plants and trees, made into jewelry, shot into space, or something else?

By making these decisions well before your death and then talking openly about your decisions with your loved ones, you are sparing them from painful burdens at an emotional and difficult time of their lives.

Prepaying final expenses doesn't just relieve burdens for your loved ones; it can help if you need to qualify for public benefits. Under current Medicaid rules, prepaid funeral and burial costs are not counted as part of your estate, which makes prepaying these expenses an important part of the Medicaid planning process. Veterans can also receive aid under the VA burial benefits. The VA does not cover costs related to handling remains, so consider prepaying these expenses.

Prepaying final expenses and deciding in advance how you want your remains to be handled is a subject that has financial implications. But that's not all. There are also legal, psychological, and family implications. I will talk more about those in the next few chapters.

Conclusion

Remember, you don't need to have a lot of money in your estate to enjoy a good quality of life all the way to the end. What's more important is your plan to use that money to help you reach your goals: avoid the nursing home, avoid going broke, and avoid being a burden.

CHAPTER 12

A BETTER WAY TO CREATE
A LEGAL PLAN

Foundational Insight

L egal documents in traditional retirement planning are focused more on issues related to death rather than those related to living, and that includes Powers of Attorney.

Legal documents in *LifePlanning* are about laying down a path for your named fiduciaries (trustees, agents, Powers of Attorney, etc.) to follow so they know what goals they are striving to achieve on your behalf, what resources they have available to them, and what other rules they are to follow. This will give you the ability to live your best life until the end—without being forced into institutional care, going broke, or creating burdens for others.

Introduction

In Part 1, you learned that when you go to a lawyer, you are working with a professional who is trained to help you with three things:

1. Who gets what when you die? (Will or Trust)
2. How do you want to die? (Living Will or Advance Directive)
3. In the case that you cannot manage your own affairs, who will manage your affairs until you die? (Powers of Attorney)

Attorneys are trained to create Die-Die-Die estate plans. Law schools teach the law, but they don't teach how to create legal documents that will help you avoid the nursing home, avoid losing money to unplanned long-term care costs, and avoid burdening your family.

As you read earlier, your estate plan needs to include end-of-life-focused legal documents, but it shouldn't stop there. You need more than just a Die-Die-Die estate plan if you want to achieve your goals.

What you need is an elder law attorney familiar with *LifePlanning* concepts, not just legal concepts. *LifePlanning* coordinates your legal planning with your planning for health, housing, and finances.

The legal planning you do as part of a *LifePlan* helps you achieve two primary goals:

1. Protect assets from long-term care expenses, estate taxes, bad actors, and other threats using a Safe Harbor Trust
2. Minimize the burdens your illness and/or death will create for the family members who will be involved in implementing your plan

What follows are the lessons I learned from the experiences of Bill and Vivian Wallace, as well as those of the thousands of clients I have had the opportunity to assist during my more than twenty years of practicing law.

The Solution Comes into Focus

In law school, I learned about the ways you can legally qualify a person for Medicaid benefits without having to spend down his or her asset base to $2,000 (the maximum amount allowed for a single person in Washington State). If a client had too much money in his or her name, the excess assets could be transferred or gifted to family members or placed in a Special Needs Trust.

Not long after graduating from law school, I worked with two sons who wanted help qualifying their mother for Medicaid benefits to pay for nursing home care. This is the story of Eileen that I shared in Chapter 4. To recap, Eileen was single and had an estate worth about $130,000. I helped her protect $80,000. When I visited her in the nursing home a year later, I discovered that the money I had helped her protect wasn't being used to enhance her quality of life in any way.

As you may recall, Eileen's situation troubled me greatly. It wasn't that her sons were at fault. They weren't. They cared deeply about her well-being. They wanted her to have the best life possible, but, like so many other family caregivers in similar situations, they didn't think there was much else they could do. Eileen was in a facility where she was safe, well fed, and looked after. They visited her. They loved on her. They did their best to manage her affairs. What more could they do?

Eileen's sons didn't realize at the time that there were three questions they should have been asking me, and I didn't realize at the time that providing the answers to these questions was within the scope of my role as their elder law attorney.

The Three Questions

1. What can we do to help our loved one live as good a quality of life as possible in his or her current setting?

2. What can we do to get our loved one the care they need without running out of money?

3. How can we get our loved one the care they need (and manage their affairs) without being crushed by burdens or losing our sanity in the process?

These are questions that almost no family members think to ask when they're sitting in the elder law attorney's office dealing with the aftermath of a loved one's health crisis.

Eileen's sons didn't know to ask me these questions. And I, their elder law attorney at the time, wouldn't have had a way to answer them.

My experience with Eileen and her sons started me thinking about how we protect assets from long-term care costs. Eileen's situation showed me the limitations of Trusts with the primary goal of protecting assets so they can sit in a bank account, accrue interest, and enrich the heirs after the older adult's death. I wanted to design Trusts that would require the trustees to use the protected assets to make life better for the older adult—while also making life easier for the family.

This situation underscores one of the major gaps between Die-Die-Die legal planning and *LifePlanning*. If you want to avoid the nursing home, avoid going broke, and avoid being a burden on your family, you will create a legal plan for retirement that answers the three questions you read earlier in this section, and you will do it long before your health fails.

How do you design a legal plan that achieves these goals? You start by writing Trusts differently.

The Safe Harbor Trust

For me, elder law was never *just* about protecting money. It was about helping my clients age with as much dignity and independence as possible, regardless of their financial status. It wasn't until I started using the Safe Harbor Trust that I really felt like I was making a difference.

I could write a separate book about Safe Harbor Trusts and how they work, but I will spare you the technical details. Instead, I will focus this discussion on what a Safe Harbor Trust is, what it can help you accomplish, and the scenarios where it will be useful when you are creating your plan for retirement.

A Safe Harbor Trust is an extremely versatile legal tool that achieves three goals that are vitally important if you want to avoid the nursing home, avoid going broke, and avoid becoming a burden.

Safe Harbor Trust Goal #1: Asset Protection
The Safe Harbor Trust can protect assets from a variety of threats. As you have already seen, small- to mid-sized estates face the threat of uncovered medical and long-term care costs; large estates face the threat of estate taxes; and all estates face the threat of bad actors. A Safe Harbor Trust can protect assets from all these threats—and more.

Safe Harbor Trust Goal #2: Quality of Life
The Safe Harbor Trust is designed with the express goal of using the protected assets to make life better for the beneficiary.

Safe Harbor Trust Goal #3: Family Guidance
A Safe Harbor Trust creates a predetermined path for your family to follow in the aftermath of your health crisis to ensure your quality of life and to achieve your goals of not ending up in institutional care, not going broke, and not being a burden.

Now that you've seen the three major goals for a Safe Harbor Trust, let's look at how it meets each one.

Safe Harbor Trust Asset Protection Scenarios

Let's take a closer look at four scenarios where a Safe Harbor Trust can protect assets:

- Uncovered medical and long-term care costs
- Estate taxes
- Subsequent relationships and bad actors
- Inheritances

Uncovered Medical and Long-Term Care Costs

The majority of Americans are middle-class people without access to large fortunes. For the average middle-class American, the single biggest financial threat to their financial security in retirement is having to deal with uncovered medical and long-term care costs because of how Medicare works. As I see it, for estates exceeding $2 million (at least in Washington State), the focus will be more on protecting estates from estate tax. For estates under $1.5 million, the focus should be on protecting the estate from uncovered medical and long-term care costs. Regardless of estate size, everyone should be worried about bad actors.

Assets placed in a Safe Harbor Trust as a result of the death of the owner or transfer by the owner results in the assets being exempt from the spend-down requirement for means-tested benefits like Medicaid. For smaller estates, this means that the Safe Harbor Trust keeps those assets from being exhausted before a person can qualify for medical and long-term care benefits from VA or Medicaid. Since both programs require you to first use your own assets to cover care costs, which could leave the remaining spouse without a means to support themselves, a Safe Harbor Trust can make a big difference in quality of life.

When I look back at Bill Wallace's situation with the knowledge I have now, I can see how the right kind of planning, one involving a Safe Harbor Trust, would have made all the difference. Bill wouldn't have been forced into a nursing home, and Vivian wouldn't have had to face impoverishment to access Medicaid benefits to pay for Bill's care.

What Bill and Vivian needed was a plan involving two relatively simple steps. First, the plan would have required Vivian to work with a geriatric care manager who would have found a way for Bill to access care at home. Second, the plan would have required Vivian to work with an elder law attorney familiar with VA and Medicaid rules so those benefits could be used to cover some of Bill's care costs.

Estate Taxes

For the smaller subset of the total American population, the very wealthy, a Safe Harbor Trust can offer protection from estate taxes. Assets placed in a Safe Harbor Trust as a result of the death of the owner or transfer by the owner results in the assets being exempt from estate taxes.

At the federal level, the issue of estate taxes in the current climate only touches people with estates valued at more than $12.06 million for single people and $24.12 million for married couples. There's a caveat, however. These limits are only good through 2025, and then the limit drops back to *about* $5.4 million per person because the law that increases the federal estate tax exemption limits sunsets in 2025.

As of this writing, 17 states impose state estate taxes or state inheritance taxes.[107] The exemption limit ranges from between $1 million in some states to over $2 million in others. The state of Washington, for example, imposes a tax on any estate valued over $2.193 million.

Both the federal and state exemption limits are per individual, meaning that for a married couple, and with the proper planning, any estate can escape any incidence of state or federal estate tax up to twice the individual level. For example, with proper planning, in the state of Washington, one can avoid paying taxes for estates valued at up to $4.386 million, and up to $24.12 million at the federal level.

However, to have an estate escape the estate tax at the state or federal level, all assets in excess of an amount that will make the surviving spouse's share exceed the individual exemption limit will need to be kept out of the surviving spouse's estate. This is generally accomplished by incorporating the protections of a Safe Harbor Trust (aka Credit Shelter Trust, aka Exemption Tax Trust, and many other names) as part of your estate plan. The Safe Harbor Trust can include legal language that sets aside half of the estate when the first spouse dies and protects that half from estate taxes.

Subsequent Relationships & Bad Actors

Safe Harbor Trusts offer legal protections that guarantee your share of the community estate is only available for your spouse and your children after you die. This protects a widowed spouse from the predators and bad actors I described in Chapter 4.

Please allow me to use this fictional story from my wife, Jamie's, perspective to illustrate how a Safe Harbor Trust protects the vulnerable from bad actors.

The event that sets this story in motion is my untimely death.

Naturally, Jamie is consumed by grief. Once she returned from India after sending my ashes down the Ganges, Jamie rarely ventured out of the house. She forced herself to get up every morning and maintain some semblance of a routine.

One summer morning, almost a year to the day after my death, Jamie was at the Federal Way Farmers' Market in search of a watermelon to take to a cookout that our daughter, Abby, was planning. On her way out, Jamie bumped into a tall man she had never seen before. The watermelon bounced out of her arms and landed with a splat at her feet.

"I can't believe that just happened," said the man, looking around for something to clean up the mess. "I'm sorry. I'm such a klutz. I'll buy you a new one."

"You don't have to do that," Jamie said.

"Oh, but I do," he laughed. "And that's not all. Let me buy you a cup of coffee as a peace offering. By the way, my name is Ned."

It was the first time in many months that Jamie had interacted with a man other than a grocery clerk, delivery driver, or one of our sons. Ned was attractive, he seemed nice, and he also looked like he might have a South Asian grandmother. What was the harm in letting him buy her a cup of coffee?

After coffee and conversation, they exchanged phone numbers. Ned promised to call. Jamie drove home feeling better than she had in a long time.

The next day, Ned called. "Let's go see a movie," he said. "Will you be my date?"

A week later, he showed up at her house with a bottle of wine.

A month later, he whisked her off to Chicago for a weekend.

Three months later, he moved in. Jamie was walking on air. She noticed little things about Ned, such as his penchant for spending money on extravagances, but she didn't care. She felt alive again.

Six months later, they were married. Everyone was concerned, especially our children.

What Jamie didn't know is that Ned was a charlatan. Their meeting at the farmers' market was no accident. Ned was looking for a rich widow to marry and fleece. Jamie fit the bill perfectly because she had been married to a successful lawyer who had a radio show. In fact, Ned had been a regular listener. What Ned didn't count on was that this successful lawyer had planned for the day when someone like Ned might show up.

A few months later, Ned asked to see Jamie's estate plan. "I want to make sure that everything is current," he said. "Now that we're married, we should update all the documents."

Fortunately, the Safe Harbor Trust that I had drafted for Jamie and me would save the day.

The Safe Harbor Trust limited Ned's access to only Jamie's half of the estate. Because I allocated my half of the estate in a Safe Harbor Trust for Jamie, she now is guaranteed that this money can only be used for her and our three children. Ned can't get to that portion of the estate.

Remember, this story is fiction. I have no idea what Jamie would do if I passed away. She's a smart woman, and I would like to think that she would make good decisions. However, as I've seen in my law practice time and time again, grief and loneliness are powerful emotions that can make people vulnerable to the machinations of bad actors like Ned. No one likes to think that they would fall prey to such schemes, but people do every day.

When you're working on your estate plan and one of your goals is to protect assets from bad actors, tell your attorney about your desires and ask him or her to build those provisions into your Safe Harbor Trust.

Inheritances

An Inheritance Protection Trust, a type of Safe Harbor Trust, can be used to protect your children's inheritance from themselves and others. Some of my clients are concerned about their children's ability to handle money responsibly. Others may be dealing with children who have drug or gambling issues, while still others may be dealing with children who are on their tenth marriage, making the eleventh a near certainty. All these issues have my clients worrying about leaving money that they know could be lost, and they are looking for a way to protect the inheritance.

Each concern I mentioned above would require a different solution. For example, if you are concerned about your child's ability to responsibly manage their inheritance, and you are worried that they will lose the money faster than they can get their hands on it, then you can leave the money to a Trust where the beneficiary will be a co-trustee along with another person, and will not be able to access the assets for at least a period of time set by you (I suggest two years). This cooling-off period allows the beneficiary to get used to the idea of the money that's coming their way, and it keeps them from getting at the funds without some serious thinking. You might even require the beneficiary to work with a financial planner before the funds are released. The financial planner would help the beneficiary come up with a plan to make the funds last the beneficiary's lifetime. You could also require the funds to be distributed to the beneficiary over time, so no single hasty decision sinks the entire inheritance.

If you have a child with a drug or gambling habit, you may want to leave the assets to a Trust and name a professional trustee to manage it. You might ask the trustee to distribute assets for specific expenses, such as rent, utilities, food, clothing, etc., and provide a small stipend to cover basic needs.

If your concern is that the beneficiary might get divorced, you can protect the asset from being lost to the divorcing spouse by leaving the money in a Trust naming the beneficiary and a co-trustee to agree on any distribution that needs to be made. Then, if a court orders a judgment against the beneficiary, the beneficiary can sign the check as directed by the court, but with knowledge that the check will not clear without the second signature of the co-trustee over whom the court has no jurisdiction.

These are just a few examples of the many ways that a Safe Harbor Trust can protect your hard-earned assets.

As you can see, the Safe Harbor Trust is an extremely flexible tool, much more so than single-use Trusts such as a Special Needs Trust.

If you end up instituting a Safe Harbor Trust for the purpose of an inheritance, it will be in the form of a testamentary Safe Harbor Trust. This means that the Trust exists as a clause inside another Trust or Will and becomes a full-fledged Trust with all of its protections when the person passes away.

There may be other uses, depending on your specific need. A Safe Harbor Trust, therefore, is a global term. Just because it's called a Safe Harbor Trust doesn't mean that it can't function as a Tax Trust, a Special Needs Trust, or an Asset Protection Trust.

When you sit down with the attorney who is preparing your estate plan, explain all your concerns. A competent lawyer will be able to include all the protections needed to reach your goals and allay your fears. I offer guidance on how to do this in Chapter 12, but your best bet is to work with an attorney familiar with the *LifePlanning* process.

Safe Harbor Trust Quality of Life & Family Guidance Scenarios

I address Quality of Life and Family Guidance together because they are inextricably intertwined. Quality of Life is what the Safe Harbor Trust helps you to achieve, and the Family Guidance provisions within the Safe Harbor Trust lay out a path for your family to achieve it.

The asset protection mechanism in the Safe Harbor Trust creates a pool of funds that does more than just sit in a bank account and accrue interest. This money is put to work. Regardless of the size of the estate of the client I am helping, the Safe Harbor Trust requires the trustee to use Trust assets to improve your quality of life. This is especially important if you are living in a care facility of some sort instead of in a private residence. You can be very specific about what the trustee must do to better your quality of life.

The language in a Safe Harbor Trust lays out a specific sequence of events that will happen when an older adult's health fails (we will assume the older adult is you), starting with an assessment by a geriatric care manager, whose findings are incorporated by reference into the Trust language. The plan of action recommended by the geriatric care manager will help your family (the trustee) allow you, the beneficiary, to access care without moving, if at all possible, and to identify the most appropriate way to give you the best quality of life possible under the conditions. This plan of action makes it easier for your family to manage your situation because the Safe Harbor Trust, your Power of Attorney, and other elements of your *LifePlan* already outline where you want to access care, what resources will be available to pay for that care, and how you will get the care you need without recruiting family members into service as your unpaid caregivers.

The Safe Harbor Trust considers your needs and preferences—for living arrangements, for care, and for the demands placed on family members. The Safe Harbor Trust then lays out a pathway for the trustee to follow so as to give you predictability that your intended outcomes will come true, without the task becoming a burden on the trustee.

This turns the Safe Harbor Trust into a document that actually "documents" your hopes and wishes, and the pathway upon which the trustee is guided to make your hopes come true.

A Safe Harbor Trust could have made a big difference in Eileen's life. If the $80,000 I was able to protect for her had been placed in a Safe Harbor Trust, here's what might have happened:

The trustee of Eileen's Safe Harbor Trust, most likely one or both of her sons, would have been directed to contact a geriatric care manager to conduct an assessment to see how Eileen's quality of life in the facility might be improved. Funds from the Trust would be used to pay for this assessment.

One of the geriatric care manager's first recommendations might be to get Eileen a private room. Funds from the Trust could be used to pay for this upgrade.

Another recommendation might be to bring in private caregivers to give Eileen a shower once a day, instead of once each week as is the norm in her facility. Her sons could have taken Eileen out to a restaurant for a meal or two each week. They could have brought in services that Eileen couldn't access at the facility, such as a hairdresser to set Eileen's hair each week, and a nail technician to give Eileen the manicures she enjoyed so much. All of these expenses could be funded with protected assets in the Safe Harbor Trust.

Eileen isn't the only one who would benefit from the Safe Harbor Trust. Because this Trust is coordinated with Eileen's other legal documents, including her Power of Attorney, her sons would have access to detailed instructions about how to handle every task they would be called to perform, including paying her bills, filing her taxes, managing her financial portfolio, attending to the maintenance of her home and her car, and many other tasks. These detailed instructions would greatly minimize the burden of managing her affairs.

How to Create a Safe Harbor Trust

How do you create a Safe Harbor Trust? First off, this is definitely not a do-it-yourself project or something you can do with documents downloaded from the internet. Work with an elder law attorney, preferably someone who is familiar with Safe Harbor Trusts. As I have shared earlier, don't assume that all attorneys, even all elder law or estate planning attorneys, will be familiar with the Safe Harbor Trust. That is why I want you to be able to go to your chosen elder law attorney prepared. You need to show up armed with basic knowledge of how a Safe Harbor Trust works, and you should be able to tell your attorney exactly what you hope to achieve. This will make you a more empowered consumer.

Let's look at how to create a Safe Harbor Trust that protects assets from uncovered medical and long-term care expenses. We will look at married couples first.

When you're married, life in retirement can go in one of several ways:

- One of you is healthy and the other falls ill, or
- One of you is healthy and the other dies

In both instances, a Safe Harbor Trust can protect assets from uncovered medical and long-term care costs.

How does it work? Let's look at our first scenario—one spouse healthy, one spouse ill, using my own life as an example.

Imagine that my wife, Jamie, and I are both retired and enjoying our lives.

Out of the blue, I have a stroke. I need long-term care at home and Jamie needs to access Medicaid to help pay for it.

Before I continue, I want to mention an important technical detail about the Safe Harbor Trust that I haven't mentioned yet. A Safe Harbor Trust is a legal entity that does not exist while you're alive. It comes into being after your death.

When I share this point with live audiences, a few hands in the audience inevitably go up.

"What's the purpose of a Trust that doesn't exist when you're alive?" someone always asks.

It's a good question. We don't need the Safe Harbor Trust if Jamie is living, and here's why.

As an ill spouse who needs to qualify for Medicaid, I can have no more than $2,000 in assets. The healthy spouse, Jamie, can have one house, one car, between *around* $60,000 to $130,000 in other assets, along with other miscellaneous assets such as a prepaid funeral plan and an unlimited amount of income.[108] To get me on Medicaid, Jamie will work with an elder law attorney to transfer assets in my name to her until I meet the $2,000 asset limit. The rest of the assets will end up in Jamie's hands. If she has more than the allowed amount of assets (about $60,000 to $130,000), then she will convert the excess assets into income coming to her name, because her income has no bearing on my qualifications. She will have all the assets protected that will allow her to carry on life without the worry of losing all our assets to my care costs, and I will be able to access Medicaid benefits without waiting for her to spend down the money to $2,000.

So, if I can qualify for Medicaid without needing the Trust, why the Trust? Here is why: This solution works perfectly to qualify me for Medicaid; that is, unless Jamie falls ill and dies before me. You read about how this scenario creates problems in Chapter 5.

There's no way Jamie can guarantee that she won't fall ill and die before me. If she didn't have a Safe Harbor Trust before she died, and if I was still living and receiving Medicaid benefits, who would she leave her assets to when she died? She would leave them to me.

Remember, I'm on Medicaid and am limited to no more than $2,000 in assets.

Without a Safe Harbor Trust, if Jamie dies before me, what happens to all the assets I transferred to her so I could meet the Medicaid asset limit? The house, the cars, the retirement accounts, the cash—it all transfers back to me. What happens then? I no longer qualify for Medicaid because I have more than $2,000 in assets.

If I want Medicaid to keep paying for my long-term care, the only option I have is to transfer these assets to my children. You have already seen that transferring assets to anyone other than your spouse triggers Medicaid's five-year look-back period and an often-lengthy penalty period where you must pay for long-term care with your own funds. Jamie's death has the unpleasant side effect of kicking me off Medicaid and imposing a penalty period before I can get back on.

With a properly written Safe Harbor Trust, you can avoid this whole sorry scenario.

Here's how. If Jamie happens to die before me with a Safe Harbor Trust as part of her planning, her assets don't transfer to me after her death; they transfer instead to the Safe Harbor Trust, with our children as trustees of the Trust. My children will then use the Trust assets to hire people to do the things for me that Jamie was doing for me. I'm still able to get the care I need while still living at home. I'm able to access Medicaid benefits to help offset the costs, and I'm not requiring my children to become my unpaid caregivers because there is money in the Safe Harbor Trust to pay for the care I need.

Now, let's look at the second scenario where a Safe Harbor Trust can help a married couple protect assets from long-term care costs: one spouse is healthy and the other spouse dies, leaving the widow a single person. Again, let's use my life as an example.

Who's to say that I will end up with a long-term illness that renders me incapacitated for years? I may be one of the lucky ones who dies in my sleep. I could die sitting up at the kitchen table while eating breakfast and reading the paper. I could also fall ill and die after a day or two.

If any of these events come to pass, my wife, Jamie, will find herself single. This creates problems if she needs to access Medicaid benefits to help pay for long-term care in the future.

Without a Safe Harbor Trust, Jamie inherits my 50 percent of the estate after my death. When she needs long-term care, she will have to spend down the assets and/or gift them to our children to reach the $2,000 asset limit. Medicaid's five-year look-back period will kick in and she will have to wait out the penalty period before she can access Medicaid.

Why would I do that when a Safe Harbor Trust can make things so much easier? During the estate planning process, I create a Safe Harbor Trust that says when I die, my share of the estate is transferred not to Jamie, but to a Safe Harbor Trust for the benefit of Jamie if she needs long-term care in the future. In the meantime, Jamie still retains control over her half of the estate, which means she will still have money of her own. She won't have to ask the kids for money to buy a hamburger. If someone decides to take advantage of Jamie, they can run off with her 50 percent. My half is in the Safe Harbor Trust, giving Jamie an ironclad guarantee that she will never die broke because someone took advantage of her, she will never be a financial burden on our children, and the kids will always have resources available to augment what Medicaid covers. This is a necessity because Medicaid will never provide 24-hour care in a person's home. In Washington State, we are lucky to get Medicaid to pay for five or six hours of care. With money in the Safe Harbor Trust, our kids can hire caregivers to cover what Medicaid won't. Jamie can continue to stay at home without recruiting the kids to be her unpaid caregivers.

Lest you assume that the Safe Harbor Trust is only a viable option for married people, let me clarify that the Safe Harbor Trust can be just as effective for single people. The way the Trust would work would be different, but the protections would be just as potent. For a single person, the Medicaid requirement that the applicant has no more than $2,000 is key. On the day you need to apply for Medicaid, you must not have more than $2,000 in assets to your name, and you must not have given away any assets of value in the five years preceding the date of the application.

If you are a single person, what does that mean for you? It means that you should consider gifting assets out of your name while you are still healthy. The goal is to avoid being penalized by the five-year look-back period. The gift can be made directly to a family member, to a trusted individual, or to a Safe Harbor Trust. On the day the gift is made, the five-year look-back clock starts ticking.

Whether you are single or married, with or without children, there's a form of a Safe Harbor Trust that can help you achieve your goal of not being forced into a nursing home, not losing assets to long-term care costs, and not becoming a burden on your family.

Safe Harbor Trusts and Probate

As you are considering your planning options, it's important to know how a Safe Harbor Trust impacts Probate. A Safe Harbor Trust is designed to help protect money from Medicaid, and if you have a Safe Harbor Trust, your estate will need to go through Probate to activate that protection. This is true in most states, but it is state-specific. Depending on where you live, you may be able to avoid Probate in your specific state, while also having a Safe Harbor Trust.

If you are wondering why Probate is an issue, there is a good reason. The federal statute that enables protection from uncovered medical and care costs requires the Trust to be created inside of a Will, and a Will is only recognized after it goes through a Probate process. If you make provisions outside of a Probate process to enable the protection, you will likely be taking a chance on whether the Trust will be honored or not—unless you live in one of the few states where the laws do not require the Trust to be created inside a Will, such as California.

Subjecting your estate to the Probate process shouldn't bother you. Here is why: Probate is a one-time cost of a few thousand dollars at most (in the majority of situations), which is a drop in the bucket compared to the $5,000, $10,000, $15,000 or more you would pay each month to access care services at home or in a care facility. Ultimately, if your estate is valued at less than $1.5 million, it's worth your time to set up a Safe Harbor Trust for the Medicaid-related asset protection it offers.

If you decide to incorporate the protections of a Safe Harbor Trust, be sure to change your beneficiary designations on life insurance policies, bank accounts, annuities, financial holdings, and the like to align with your planning around the Safe Harbor Trust in your Will or Trust. This is because the designations in your other financial documents generally outweigh your Will or Trust, meaning that if you do not change your beneficiary designations in your other documents, your wishes may not be realized.

Finally, at the death of beneficiaries (the surviving spouse in the theoretical example involving me and my wife, Jamie), assets in the Safe Harbor Trust would avoid Probate.

A WORD OF CAUTION: Although your hope may be that assets you gift to others are placed in a separate Safe Harbor Trust for your benefit, there is absolutely no guarantee or duty of the person receiving the gift to make them available to you in the future, and you can have no expectation that the person establishes such a Trust for your benefit. However, if the assets are placed in a Safe Harbor Trust for your benefit, they would be available first to supplement your long-term care needs, and the remainder would be passed on to your heirs as you would have otherwise directed in a Will.

Safe Harbor Trusts involve nuanced concepts beyond the pale of most estate planning attorneys. My suggestion is that if the notion of a Safe Harbor Trust appeals to you for all the benefits I have described in this section, you should learn everything you can about this type of Trust, get clear about what you want to accomplish, and then find a good elder law attorney in your state and seek out input before implementing the Safe Harbor Trust.

The Living Will

As you saw in Chapter 4, a Living Will gives guidance to your agents about your preferences to be kept alive by external means. There are many variables that go into these decisions along with how and when these Living Wills come into effect. The most important things to keep in mind when you create your Living Will are who your agent is, and what laws govern life support in your state.

When you have a good understanding of your state laws and an agent who you can trust, one who is very clear about your wishes, it is possible to create a Living Will that doesn't cause more problems than it solves.

Here's an example of how a Living Will can work when there's dissension in the family.

Nathan, age 78, was in the hospital, brain dead after a massive cerebral hemorrhage. His Living Will was clear about artificial means of life support. He didn't want it. Yet, there he was, lying there in a hospital bed being kept alive by machines.

His wife, Jean, and their three adult children gathered around his bed.

The doctor walked in. "It's not looking good for Nathan," he said carefully. "He's unlikely to regain consciousness. It's time to decide whether you want to continue life support."

Jean looked at the kids. Their eyes were filled with tears. The moment they had all been dreading was finally here.

"I'll leave you to talk," the doctor said, closing the door behind him.

"Your dad was adamant about not being kept alive by artificial means," Jean said. "I think we should try to honor that."

"I know that Dad wouldn't want to live this way," said Melissa, her oldest. "I don't want to see him go, but I agree that we should do what he asked."

Jeff, one of the two brothers, was seated in the corner, his head in his hands. After a long pause, he spoke. "Yes, I agree. Let's just pull the plug and get it over with."

Carl, the youngest son, looked stricken. "I can't believe we're having this conversation," he shouted. "Who are you people? I can't believe you would give up hope that fast. Dad just got here. It has only been 24 hours. I don't want Dad to die if there's even the smallest chance he might get better."

Jean was Nathan's health care agent. She was the one the doctors were looking to for a decision. Jean needed to make a decision, yet not everyone agreed that ending life support was the best option. What should she do?

Fortunately, Nathan and Jean had done their legal planning with me as part of their *LifePlan*, and his Living Will document had the answers. Living Wills, the way I write them, go beyond the boilerplate language that says little more than pull the plug if there's no hope. The Living Wills I write have instructions for just this kind of moment, providing a road map for decision-making, one that ensures that every family member is at peace with the decision, whatever it might be.

If there is any dissension among family members, you follow the process in the Living Will to resolve it.

Fortunately, Nathan and Jean had talked about this. She knew that the Living Will explained the steps she should take, so she pulled it up on her phone.

"Here's what it says," Jean read. "With respect to any life-sustaining treatment, I do not want my life to be prolonged and I do not want life-sustaining treatment if:

1. I'm diagnosed to be either in a terminal condition, or

2. In a Permanent Unconscious Condition, and

3. My agent, working in concert with all family members, who are given the opportunity to voice their opinion within a reasonable amount of time, agrees with the diagnosis that continuation of artificial means of life support is futile, then:

    a. I do not want cardiopulmonary resuscitation.

    b. I do not want to have artificially provided hydration.

    c. I do not want to have artificially provided nutrition.

    d. I do not want to receive antibiotic therapy.

    e. I do not want heroic measures.

    f. I do want to be kept comfortable and pain-free to the maximum extent possible.

4. If there is any dissension among my family members, then I direct the agent to seek another opinion about the diagnosis before agreeing to the termination of life support measures. And to the extent practical and possible, I suggest that the physician providing a new opinion not be working in the same medical system as the physician or physicians making the original diagnosis. I wish to allow all family members reasonable opportunity to be at peace with the final decision, but I'm also clear that in the end, it is the acting agent

who shall make the final decision. That agent's decision shall not be challenged by others.

5. The agent should work with the geriatric care manager set out in the Health Care Power of Attorney for help locating a physician for such a second opinion."

"There's also the Terri Schiavo Provision," Jean said, continuing to read. "With respect to any life-sustaining treatment, I also do not want my life to be prolonged and I do not want life-sustaining treatment in situations where I may have a medical diagnosis of being terminally ill or I may be in a permanent vegetative state."

Jean put her phone down. "Well, it looks like the first thing we should do is get everyone's input, which we've just done. The next step is that I need to seek a second opinion about Dad's diagnosis because not all family members agree that it is time to pull the plug. And, thankfully, it looks like I should be able to call Dad's geriatric care manager to have her coordinate a second opinion from another doctor who doesn't work in this hospital system."

The kids agreed to suspend the removal of life support until a second opinion was obtained. Asking for a second opinion put the brakes on the hospital's efforts to terminate life support and bought the family time to gather more information.

Jean called the geriatric care manager, who arranged for a second opinion. A few days later, the family met with the geriatric care manager and Nathan's attending physician to review the findings from the doctor who had provided the second opinion.

"The second opinion is in 100 percent agreement with your doctor's recommendation," said the geriatric care manager. "She concurs that there is little likelihood that Nathan will ever regain consciousness, let alone recover."

As Nathan's health care agent, Jean knew that the decision was hers to make, but she wanted to check in with her children to see if their feelings had changed. She wanted them to be at peace with the decision, whatever it might be.

She turned to them. "What do you think?" she asked. "There's no chance that Dad will recover. Two doctors agree. Should we end his life support?"

Melissa and Jeff nodded. Jean looked at Carl. His eyes were filled with tears. "Yes," he said finally. "Yes."

Not too many lawyers write Living Wills with detailed instructions beyond a list of heroic measures the person does or doesn't want. I think that's a mistake. What I want you to know is that it's possible for your Living Will to provide this kind of guidance. You just have to know to ask for it.

As you can probably see from the family story I just told, the Terri Schiavo case taught me a lot about how Living Wills should be written. My Living Wills incorporate language that requires the agent to look not only at the medical status of the person (e.g., in a persistent vegetative state or terminally ill) but also at the quality-of-life indicators when rendering a decision about allowing the removal of artificial means of life support.

To be sure that you understand how a Living Will works, I want to give you this explanation. First of all, the only situations where a Living Will can be used to withhold life-sustaining treatment is when you have a medical diagnosis of either being: (1) in a persistent vegetative state or (2) terminally ill and in a condition where you cannot communicate your own wishes.

A persistent vegetative state is a diagnosis which requires the medical community to do everything reasonably in their power to cure. Generally, this would be an effort that will take anywhere from a few weeks to a few months, depending on the situation. If your loved ones are not sure that all reasonable efforts have been expended, then they can ask for a second and a third opinion and keep the efforts going. The same is also true with the terminal illness diagnosis. Just because one physician says that you are terminally ill does not mean that another physician would agree.

The point of a Living Will is to say to your family that, should you be in a situation where your body cannot maintain itself without outside interference AND there is no reasonable chance of getting you better, then you do not wish to stay alive. Alternatively, you can also say that you wish to be kept alive no matter what. Whatever your decision, your loved ones will know what you want. Even if you said that you do not wish to linger, it does not mean that your loved ones cannot challenge the diagnosis of a persistent vegetative state or terminal illness and buy time to satisfy themselves that all efforts have been expended.

If you can educate your chosen agents (which is one of the things we cover in the Family Meeting), signing a Living Will does not mean that you will be left to die without any efforts being expended to get you better.

POLST vs. Living Will

No discussion of legal planning for retirement would be complete without talking about the Physician Orders for Life-Sustaining Treatment, also known as the POLST form. Prepared by a physician, this document serves as a portable guideline regarding your wishes for emergency care providers to follow in the event of a medical emergency. The POLST form acts very much like a Living Will, which is why I want to talk about it. I want you to understand which document you should rely on—the POLST or the Living Will—as both can conceivably accomplish the same goal. To make your decision, here is what you should know.

If you have ever accessed care in a hospital or other institutional setting, the provider has probably asked you to fill out a POLST form. A POLST form is not the same as a Living Will. Both forms address the same issue—your wishes regarding being kept alive by artificial means—but they do it differently. A Living Will is a legal document; a POLST form is a doctor's order, which means that the instructions on the POLST form must be carried out by everyone in the health care community, even if the attending physician is unavailable for consultation. In my opinion, a POLST form should be used only in a setting where you have medical oversight or when you are frail and nearing the end of life. It should be used with great caution.

Consider this example.

Sally, age 86, had a lung disease that required periodic treatment in the hospital. During her most recent visit, she was asked to complete a POLST form, and she did. This was a doctor's order not to revive Sally in the event of a medical emergency. Sally signed the brightly colored (usually pink or green) POLST form, took it home, and stuck it to her refrigerator door with a magnet.

At home, a week later, Sally felt a strange tingling in her head. She fell to the floor and used her life alert to request an ambulance. Sally quickly lost consciousness. When the EMTs entered her home, they came in through a door that led to her kitchen where Sally lay unconscious. One of the EMTs spotted the telltale brightly colored POLST form stuck to the refrigerator. When they saw the doctor's order not to revive Sally, they complied. Sally died that day.

This is by no means an outlier. Emergency providers lack consensus on what action to take when they encounter (POLST) forms.[109]

In a survey of emergency physicians and pre-hospital providers, responders were given scenarios in which the patient had a POLST.

The providers were then asked to decide what to do. Unfortunately, providers often know that the form exists but fail to read it, making assumptions about what it says. For example, DNR orders are equated with "do not treat" orders.

My counsel to most of my clients is to rely on a Living Will and forego the use of a POLST for now. If you do sign a POLST in a hospital setting, revoke it (by tearing it up) as soon as you leave the hospital. If you don't, you could risk ending up like Sally.

For the most up-to-date information on laws around Living Wills and POLST forms, it's always a good idea to consult a knowledgeable elder law attorney licensed to practice in your state.

A Better Power of Attorney

Over the years, as I watched my clients dealing with the consequences of Power of Attorney documents that assigned authority and responsibility, but offered no guidance, I started wondering. Why not just write the Power of Attorney differently? Why not include those missing details? Why not have it read like a manual of instructions?

If I had my way, there would be no more leaving it up to agents to figure "it" out. My Power of Attorney would unpack the pronoun, removing all ambiguity from the nebulous "it." My Power of Attorney would define "it," list all the resources the agent could work with to accomplish "it," and state clearly what the desired outcome of "it" should be.

My Power of Attorney would help clients accomplish the most important "it" of all: avoiding institutional care, not going broke, and not being a burden.

Not only would my Power of Attorney identify who would be responsible for each task, but it would also say exactly what the agent would be doing, and it would explain in detail how to do it. I wanted my

Power of Attorney to do more than offer a false sense of security. I wanted it to provide absolute clarity to the people who would be using it—the agents.

I started asking my clients detailed questions about how they wanted their affairs managed. It didn't matter who they were—young, old, single, married—I asked them all.

"If your executor or personal representative has to deal with Probate, who do you want them to work with?" I asked one couple.

"Um … you?" said the husband, looking confused. He turned to his wife, who shrugged. They hadn't thought it through. "What if your executor is working with someone who has a totally different idea about what the Probate process needs to look like?" I asked an older man who was widowed and had five children. "How do you want the executor to handle that?"

He stared at me. "I guess they'll call you," he said.

One woman, let's call her Barbara, came to see me because she had heard me on the radio. She told me that she didn't want to be a burden on her son, whom she had named as her agent.

"Who will he be working with to manage your affairs when you're incapacitated?" I asked.

Barbara gave me the name of her financial planner.

"No, I don't think you understand," I said. "What do you expect your son to do for you if you are incapacitated?"

She thought for a moment. "Well, he will have to pay my bills and file my taxes."

"What if the plumbing in your house breaks?" I asked. "Will you expect him to fix that?"

"I would expect him to call the plumber," Barbara said.

"Do you have pets?"

She nodded.

"What happens when the dog starts barfing on the carpet?" I asked. "What do you want your son to do? Do you expect your son to clean up the mess and take the dog to the vet?"

"Yes," she said.

"And you don't want to be a what? A burden?"

Barbara looked uncomfortable, but I could see the light coming on. She hadn't considered that managing a person's affairs included more than just handling the money.

"If you don't want to be a burden, you can't expect your son to manage every part of your life on his own. He will need to pay your bills, file your taxes, manage your investments, maintain your home, look after your pets, take care of your cars, and do whatever else needs to be done. Who have you lined up to help him do that?"

"No one," she admitted. "I just never thought about it."

"This is the kind of thing you need to be thinking about if you are serious about not being a burden," I told her. "If you don't plan in advance for these things, you will most certainly be a burden."

Barbara wasn't the only one who hadn't thought things through. It was like this with every client I saw. I knew I was onto something, so I kept asking questions designed to help them drill down to the details about what their agents would have to do for them, and then identifying the professionals who would carry out those tasks. Most of my clients did not rely on professionals to complete these tasks because they were used to doing it themselves. In these cases, I would challenge them to at least identify professionals who their children would be able to work with, and then establish some type of a working relationship with those professionals in advance. If my client didn't want to involve professionals, I advised them to identify the child who would take on the task, but pair the responsibility with compensation, so that the child wouldn't feel taken advantage of in the process.

The list of names and contact information was just the beginning, though. An agent could have that list and still end up being burdened by the tasks of managing an elderly loved one's affairs.

Stan, a divorced man in his late 60s, is a good example of how this plays out. He had attended one of my seminars, listened to me on the radio, and then scheduled an appointment to talk about creating a *LifePlan*. At the end of our first meeting, he handed me a sheet of notebook paper with a list of professionals and their contact information.

"I've heard you talk about this, so I figured I would work ahead and get this part done," said Stan as he handed me the sheet. He looked proud, like a student eager for extra credit for a special project. "My daughter will be serving as my agent, and this will make things easy for her."

"That's great," I said, surveying the list. "Do you think this list will be everything your daughter will need?"

Stan nodded. "Everything is there, including phone numbers and email addresses," he said. "She should be all set."

We were on the verge of a teaching moment. The list gave Stan's daughter a list of people to call, but it offered no guidance about what he wanted his daughter to tell these professionals to do. Stan was only a fraction as prepared as he thought he was. I had to break it to him gently, as I do to all my clients.

I decided to make this point by doing a drill-down into the tasks related to the management of his financial portfolio. Just about everyone can relate to this.

"When you're incapacitated, do you want your daughter to manage your investments?" I asked.

Stan nodded.

"Does your daughter know how to access your account information?"

He thought for a moment. "No," he admitted. "I haven't given her any of my passwords."

"Does your daughter know about your preferences for how your money is managed?" I continued. "Does she know how you want it done? Does she know your risk tolerance? She's younger than you, which means she may have very different ideas about how things should be done."

Stan shifted in his seat. "We've never really talked about it."

I held up the list and pointed to the financial contact. "Who is this?" I asked.

"It's her financial planner," he replied. "There's a guy I work with, but I figured it would be easiest if she worked with someone she knew."

"It's great that you're looking out for her, but if you have a specific way you want her to manage your finances, in addition to discussing your preferences with her, you might want to consider having her work with the financial planner you already have a relationship with," I explained. "As I see it, your daughter has two jobs when it comes to managing your investments. The first job is to make sure the financial planner isn't taking advantage of you. The second job is to manage your money according to your preferences. You've built a nice portfolio over the years. You don't want her to disrupt that, do you?"

"No, I don't," he said. "It's obvious that I have more to do."

I ask the same sort of detailed questions about every aspect of my clients' lives. These discussions are often uncomfortable, and my questions related to health are often the toughest ones to answer, even for people who believe they have been proactive about their planning.

We're taught to talk about money and legal documents, not the fact that we will get sick. No one likes to plan for the day their health fails, but if you don't, the chances are much greater that you'll end up living in an institution, losing your money to long-term care costs, and burdening your family.

I confronted this reluctance in my clients every day.

One interaction in particular drove this point home.

I was meeting with Julie, a woman in her 50s who came to me to create a *LifePlan*. When I asked what she expected her agents (in this case, her children) to do for her when she got sick, her response was like that of so many others I see.

"It depends on what happens to me," Julie said. "They'll have to figure it out at the time."

She seemed uncomfortable. It was clear that she didn't want to talk about this.

Julie is not the only one. It is deeply ingrained in our culture not to talk about the reality of physical decline, let alone the aftermath. Almost no one knows how to explain what they want to happen after an incapacitating illness. No one understands what is possible. Our country's "system" for elder care has everyone convinced that it's impossible to plan, and that institutional care is the only option.

If you want to keep retirement from turning into a nightmare, you must plan.

"Why did you make this appointment today?" I asked.

"I don't want to end up in a nursing home," Julie replied. "I don't want to die broke, and I don't want to be a burden."

"If you want to accomplish those goals, your family is going to need instructions from you about how to get it done," I said. "Expecting them to just figure it out at the time, is about the best way I know to end up living in some sort of institution."

I could tell by the look on Julie's face that she hadn't considered this before.

"It doesn't matter how or why you fall ill," I explained. "You write instructions into your Power of Attorney documents that give your agents step-by-step instructions about what to do. Your agents will know that you don't want to go to a rehab center if it can be avoided. They will know that when it's time for you to be discharged from the hospital, the health care staff will pressure them to move you to a rehab center. They won't be surprised when this happens because you will have prepared them for it. They will know that you want to come home, and they will know how to make that happen."

"That's exactly what I want," she said. "I didn't know it was possible."

"Almost no one realizes this can be done, but it can," I said. "Your Power of Attorney will have instructions so that your agents will know what to do. They will know to call a geriatric care manager *you* have selected (which means you have more work to do before the Power of Attorney can be effectively written), because you will add their name and contact information to your Power of Attorney. Your agent will know what to ask the geriatric care manager to do so you can come back home. If coming home isn't an option, then your agent will know to rely on the geriatric care manager to help them find a place where you can live so you won't have to move again, even if your health gets worse and your care needs to increase."

"What about my kids?" Julie asked. "I don't want to burden them."

"You won't," I reassured her. "It will be written right into your Power of Attorney that you don't want to be a burden, nor do you want family members to be your unpaid caregivers. If they provide care, they will know that you want them to be compensated for their services in the same way that you would be willing to pay a professional. They will know that you don't want to be their charity."

Julie shook her head in disbelief. "I had no idea you could do this."

Almost no one realizes that if you are clear about what you want your agent to strive for and give them resources that they can use to seek out the outcomes you desire, you can avoid the retirement nightmare trifecta: broke, a burden, and stuck in a nursing home.

"You have to think through what you want in advance," I said. "You can't prepare a good Power of Attorney unless you know what you want your future to look like when you are no longer the captain of your own ship. You should have a clear sense of what your housing goals are, and what role you want each child to play. You cannot simply make these decisions on your own; you have to run them by your kids so they know what you expect them to do. They can then voice their support or their objections to the proposition."

Just as I was about to move to the next set of questions, Julie spoke. "This all sounds great, but it seems like a lot of work."

"It is," I admitted. "But if you don't do this work, do you think it disappears? Do you think it goes away? It doesn't. You pass it on to your agents, creating the burdens you said you didn't want."

Instead of writing Power of Attorney documents that almost no one reads, you're partnering with your attorney to create a document that reads like a manual of instructions for your family, and then giving them the financial and professional resources needed to help you reach your goals. The result? You live out your years in the place you choose—without running out of money and without becoming a burden on your family.

Choosing Fiduciaries

Most of the legal documents for estate planning require you to name someone who will act on your behalf. Any of these roles, whether it's a trustee of a Trust or an agent named in your Power of Attorney, is generally referred to as a fiduciary. Legally speaking, a fiduciary is a person who holds a legal or ethical relationship of trust with one or more other parties. Typically, a fiduciary prudently takes care of money or other assets for another person, which makes choosing your fiduciaries one of the most important and delicate aspects of planning.

Your fiduciaries will be legally empowered to act on your behalf when you are no longer able to do so yourself, both in life and death. Because of this, it is important that you choose fiduciaries that you trust completely, and that you communicate your wishes with them clearly.

Consider Family First

Whom should you choose? My recommendation to my clients is that they consider a member of the family. Why? Aging is a family affair.

Children are often the first choice, but some people bypass their children and choose another family member instead, maybe a brother, sister, or cousin. This usually happens when the children aren't interested in taking on the responsibility. When considering family members as your fiduciaries, keep in mind that we all age. For that reason, those who are of similar age will also age along with you and may not be much more capable than you when the time comes to step in and act.

Why would someone not want to choose a family member? The biggest concern involves the possibility of disputes. The *LifePlanning* process has a way to minimize those concerns: the Family Meeting. That's where you make your plans and preferences clear to everyone, it's where you explain who is responsible for what, and it's where you explain why you chose whom for each role. The Family Meeting is also the place where you will make everyone aware that you expect total transparency from your agent. This does not guarantee that there will not be trouble, but it will minimize the chances.

I always tell my clients to look at the legal planning process as less a mechanical process and more as a spiritual journey. Dealing with the death or illness of a loved one is generally a rite of passage, especially for a child dealing with the needs of a parent. When you create a *Life-Plan* for retirement and choose family members as fiduciaries, you are teaching them powerful lessons about how to plan for life in old age, lessons that they will most likely apply in their own lives.

If you are thinking that your children are not prepared to deal with the responsibilities of managing your affairs, or you are concerned that they won't manage those issues effectively, remember that the role you want your children to play is not that of a financial planner, accountant, doctor, plumber, property manager, or the provider of the services you need. The role they will be filling is that of the agent, the project manager who oversees the professionals you want them to work with and to make sure that these professionals are not taking advantage of you or leaving you neglected. That limited role is one that most children will be able to manage successfully. Most will grow from it.

Whenever my clients tell me they want to name someone other than their children to be their fiduciary, I always encourage them to think carefully about this decision. Unless you have compelling reasons not to, I recommend naming your children, holding a Family Meeting, and seeking their input about your decision. If your child says no to the responsibility, you can name someone else at that time. Ultimately, you need to listen to your sixth sense about this issue and make the decision that feels right for you.

Co-Fiduciaries

Some of my clients ask to name one or more people as co-fiduciaries. It usually happens when parents are worried that the children not selected for a fiduciary role will feel slighted.

Sometimes naming co-fiduciaries works; sometimes it doesn't. Situations related to illness and death are especially problematic. Emotions run high, old rivalries may surface, and the resulting disagreements could be disastrous for everyone. When family members let their emotions cloud their judgment, it can lead to family rifts that never heal. You don't want that. I think it's better to have one cook in the kitchen. At least the food will be cooked. It might be too salty for the taste of someone, but the food will be cooked. The Family Meeting is the place to address these concerns. If, after the meeting, a family member expresses concern about being left out or not being treated equally, you can always revisit the issue and make the changes.

Professional Fiduciaries

Whether you are a single person with no children or relatives, or part of a family where conflicts are common, you might be wondering who will serve as your fiduciary.

There is an entire industry dedicated to playing the role of fiduciary. Every guardianship court in America has a registry of professionals who can fulfill these roles. I call them "professional children," and they are easy to find.

A professional fiduciary will charge for their time. This can be a mutually beneficial arrangement, but it does cost more on average than a paid family member.

You can authorize a law firm or other professional to elect a professional fiduciary for you. Most are familiar with what is required for agents under Powers of Attorney, and some offer fiduciary services themselves. However, you should know that going this route may cause a conflict of interest with whomever you hire to serve as your agent.

When you're in the market for a professional fiduciary, interview at least three companies/individuals who offer this service. Providers fall into two broad categories: individual providers and companies. Individual providers tend to be less expensive and often more caring, but their availability may be limited due to illness or personal circumstances. If you go with an individual, make sure that he or she has a backup plan. Companies tend to be more reliable, but their service can seem impersonal. Companies also tend to be more expensive than individuals.

If you decide to hire a professional fiduciary firm to serve as your agent, I have two words of caution.

First, do whatever you can to avoid having the court appoint the professional fiduciary firm. You want to make these arrangements long before you will need them.

Second, know that some professional fiduciary firms will try to force you to work with the professionals on their roster. Don't let that happen.

A man I know, a 75-year-old named Scott, dealt with this. He decided to hire a professional fiduciary to serve as his agent. He wanted the firm to oversee the activities of the professionals he had already selected to pay his bills, manage his investments, file his taxes, and so on.

Scott interviewed several firms. The one he liked most had its own Trust department. He read the fine print and saw that this firm required that they manage his assets, and that they charged 1.5 basis points to do that.

Scott had spent years building a portfolio with a financial planner. He was happy with the results and had no desire to switch. A closer look at the contract revealed more of the same. The firm required that Scott use their bill pay service, their tax preparation service, their property management services, and so on.

Scott doesn't have to agree to those terms, and neither do you. The firm you hire to serve as your agent should not be the firm that is also providing the professional services that the agent is supposed to oversee. Your agent is supposed to be the one who keeps the professional service providers from taking advantage of you, and that's harder to do when both are working for the same company.

My advice to Scott—and to you—is this: When you hire a professional fiduciary, tell them that the only role you want them to play is that of the agent who manages the group of professionals you have already selected to manage your affairs. If they won't do that, don't sign the contract. Find someone else.

This gives you the checks and balances you need to make sure you're not taken advantage of by the professionals who will be managing your affairs.

Mental Health Advance Directives

In Chapter 4, I discussed one of the problems in the retirement planning process that no one likes to talk about: the loss of mental capacity.

The stories I shared in that chapter illustrate how family members and fiduciaries often struggle with issues stemming from the older adult's behavior in that long and often hard-to-define gray area between mental capacity and incapacity.

Your family will probably be the first to notice changes in your behavior and judgment. The changes might give them cause for concern. It won't be easy for them to raise their concerns to you, but when they do, odds are good that you will deny the suggestion that anything is wrong. You might even be insulted by what you hear as an accusation.

If the people you trust—your family members and your fiduciaries—have concerns about your mental health, and you aren't cooperative, it will make it harder for them to advocate effectively for you. As you saw in Chapter 4, if you don't have a Mental Health Advance Directive, the guardianship process, a long, expensive, and conflict-generating ordeal, is your only option.

I've watched situations like this unfold time and again, always with great sadness. I vowed that I would find a way to help prevent this from happening to any more of my clients. The way I do that is with the Mental Health Advance Directive. Let's take a look at how it works.

Remember Roger from Chapter 4, who was communicating with his alleged cousin, the Nigerian prince? Remember how Roger's wife, Margaret, was told that guardianship proceedings were her only option?

Had Roger executed a Mental Health Advance Directive while he was mentally capable, it would have given Margaret a better way to deal with his declining mental state. First, I will explain what a Mental Health Advance Directive is and what it can do, and then I will explain how this document could have been used in Roger's situation.

A Mental Health Advance Directive is much like a Living Will for health care. A person with or without a mental illness can specify how treatment decisions should be made if he or she becomes unable to make sound choices due to their mental illness.

Many states, including Washington State, allow you to create a directive that gives someone else the legal authority to make decisions for you if you are unable to make sound decisions yourself. You can specify what type of decisions you want made for you, and even what those decisions should be.

The person you choose to make these decisions is called an agent. You can also write down instructions about the treatment you wish to receive. For instance, the directive can say what medication you do or do not want and why, or describe ways to calm you when you are upset. You can have a directive that only appoints an agent or one that only provides instructions about treatment, or a directive that does both.

Each state has its own laws related to Mental Health Advance Directives, so it's important to consult with an elder law attorney in your state if you choose to make this document part of your legal plan. In Washington State, a Mental Health Advance Directive goes into effect only if a person becomes incapacitated. If you live in Washington State and you have a Mental Health Advance Directive, you can choose in advance whether you can change or cancel the instructions in the directive if you become incapacitated. If you choose not to be able to change or cancel the directive, on becoming incapacitated, you may receive treatment based on the directive even if you say you do not want to be treated at the time.

I've used the term "incapacitated" several times in this section, so let me take a moment to define it. "Incapacitated," as a legal term, generally means that a person cannot make sound decisions about his or her care or treatment. Before a person can be declared incapacitated, certain health care providers or a court must examine the person and decide whether he or she understands information that is needed to make decisions regarding his or her health care. If the person is found to be incapacitated, then the Mental Health Advance Directive will apply.

If you are concerned about someone using your Mental Health Advance Directive against you, it's important to choose your agent carefully. The person you choose to make mental health decisions for you should be someone you trust. Unless the person is also your spouse, adult child, brother, or sister, you cannot pick the following people as your agent: your doctor, an employee of your doctor, or an administrator, owner, or employee of a health care facility in which you live or are a patient.

How does a Mental Health Advance Directive work with a Living Will or Durable Power of Attorney for Health Care? If you already have a Living Will and/or a Durable Power of Attorney for Health Care that applies to medical decisions, you should review what it says. The Living Will and Durable Power of Attorney for medical decisions will be in effect except where they conflict with what your Mental Health Advance Directive says. To avoid confusion, you may want to consider having only one person be your agent to make health care decisions for both mental health and medical decisions. You will want your elder law attorney to review how the documents fit together.

If you want to prepare a Mental Health Advance Directive, most states offer standard forms. Consult with an elder law attorney in your state for assistance in crafting your Mental Health Advance Directive.

Now, let's return to the story of Roger and Margaret from Chapter 4. Roger's Mental Health Advance Directive would give his agent (in this case, Margaret), the authority to request a psychiatric evaluation at the first sign of mental health problems. For Margaret, that moment would have undoubtedly been when Roger first mentioned sending money to the Nigerian prince. Though Roger would most likely oppose this psychiatric evaluation, the presence of the Mental Health Advance Directive gives Margaret the legal right to get this vital assessment completed. She would have been able to commit Roger to a mental health facility for a maximum of 14 days for an assessment. This admission would allow the doctors to assess Roger's situation and then suggest a course of action.

Lest Roger be concerned about giving up his rights permanently, the Mental Health Advance Directive would only empower Margaret to enforce Roger's prior directions for mental health treatment in spite of his later refusals while in a confused state. For treatment to continue beyond 14 days, the doctors or Margaret would have to seek guardianship or subject Roger to involuntary civil commitment proceedings, both of which impose an extremely high standard of proof. If either action is needed, it can be obtained much faster because the psychiatric evaluation is already complete.

A properly created Mental Health Advance Directive can have as many safeguards as the person executing the document desires. It can state, without limitation:

- Preferences and instructions for mental health treatment
- Consent to specific types of mental health treatment
- Refusal to consent to specific types of mental health treatment
- Consent to admission to and retention in a facility for mental health treatment for up to 14 days
- Descriptions of situations that may cause the principal to experience a mental health crisis
- Suggested alternative responses that may supplement or substitute direct mental health treatment, such as treatment approaches from other providers

- Appointment of an agent to make mental health treatment decisions on the principal's behalf, including authorizing the agent to provide consent on the principal's behalf to voluntary admission to inpatient mental health treatment

- The principal's nomination of a guardian or limited guardian for consideration by the court if guardianship proceedings are commenced

People do not go from sane to insane overnight. It happens over time. During the twilight period, where a person has sufficient mental capacity to fool the world, but not the family, much mayhem can take place. Without a Mental Health Advance Directive, the only option available to your family will likely be a guardianship, which will take months to complete and destroy family harmony, often permanently.

Powers of Attorney that Read Like Manuals of Instructions

Now that we've covered the documents you will encounter in your legal plan and how to think through whom to name as fiduciaries, let's connect these concepts at a level deeper than traditional planning.

If you're serious about minimizing the burden on your agents and fiduciaries, your best bet is to build that goal into your Power of Attorney. You do that by writing your Powers of Attorney so they read like a manual of instructions.

Let's take a look at some of the key areas to map out in your Power of Attorney.

Name Service Providers

One of the main failings of a traditional Power of Attorney document is that, while it is intended to ease the burden on your loved ones, in most cases it lacks the guidance to deliver on that benefit. You can and should include in your Power of Attorney detailed guidance as to whom your agents should work with when dealing with your affairs.

Your Powers of Attorney should list every professional your agents might need to work with, including a geriatric care manager, your financial planner, an accountant or bookkeeper to aid with taxes or bills, a property manager, a specific geriatrician or geriatric physician, the company involved in your final arrangements, and so on. This eliminates much of the legwork that your agents need to do to carry out your wishes and provide you with the care you both need and want.

Your list should also include backup professionals. Keep in mind that it may be many years before your agents need to use this list. What if one of the professionals on the list is retired or has gone out of business? It's a good idea to include one or two backups for each category.

Care **Management** Provisions

If you are serious about avoiding the nursing home, not going broke, and not being a burden, then your Power of Attorney must include guidance for your agent to work with a geriatric care manager. Let me explain why.

There may come a time when you are unable to care for your own needs. Your agent may need to step in and arrange for the necessary care. He or she may not have the training, skills, knowledge, or desire to evaluate your situation. He or she may not know how to get you the care you need in any setting other than a nursing home. Agents may also find themselves struggling to find the time and resources necessary to monitor the care you are receiving from others, or they may not have the skills to know if you are being over-medicated, ill-treated, and the like.

As you've already seen, if you assume that your agents will figure "it" out on their own without any instructions or guidance, you are already halfway to the nursing home. The "it," of course, is keeping you out of institutional care. It's your responsibility to help your agents figure out what to do with you so you don't end up in institutional care.

How do you do that?

You got your first peek at the answer to this question back in Chapter 3 when I talked about hospice, an approach to care that makes it possible for people with less than six months to live to take their last breath at home. In the hospice model, a team of care providers from different disciplines work under the guidance of a professional who coordinates their activities. Everything they do is designed to help the patient stay at home until the end.

The hospice model isn't just for people who have a terminal illness. It works just as well for people who need care for any reason—but would rather receive that care at home. There's just one catch: if you have more than six months to live, the services of a hospice-style team providing care at home won't be covered by insurance. However, it will be highly effective in helping you avoid being forced into a care facility when you would rather stay at home.

So, how do you create a hospice-style team to help you receive care at home after a health crisis? You do it by adding care management provisions to your Power of Attorney and Safe Harbor Trust. The guidance in this section of your Power of Attorney directs your agents to enlist the help of a geriatric care manager, using the assets in your estate to pay for these services. You can direct your agents to call a specific geriatric care manager if you fall ill and name that geriatric care manager right in your legal documents.

At the very least, a geriatric care manager will be able to complete an initial assessment and develop a care plan. This will give your agents direction about what needs to be done to help you achieve your goals of staying out of the nursing home, not going broke, and not becoming a burden.

Geriatric care managers know what services are available in your area. They know which providers are top-notch, and which ones should be avoided. They can provide essential insight into how best to provide for your needs in the least restrictive setting without resorting to drastic measures such as nursing home placement.

Because the geriatric care manager is compensated with assets protected by the Safe Harbor Trust, there is no financial burden to your family members. An additional benefit is that they do not have to spend the extraordinary amount of time and effort required to understand your care needs and figure out how to meet them.

Care management provisions in your Power of Attorney might include language like this:

> *The first time that I fall ill, and you, my agent, have to advocate for me, you are required by the terms of this document to call a geriatric care manager, a person familiar with end-of-life issues and familiar with how to bring me back home even when I do not have a hospice diagnosis. You are required to ask the geriatric care manager what it will take for you to be able to help me access care at home.*

Duty to Work with Professionals

This language acknowledges that your care needs will place additional and unavoidable burdens on the agents you've named to manage your financial and personal affairs; therefore, it is your desire that your agent retain professionals to help manage your affairs. In this part of your Power of Attorney, you include a list of suggested professionals for your agent to work with and you attach that list as an exhibit to your Power of Attorney. This won't just be your financial planner. This list will include names and contact information for the people who will do everything that needs to be done to manage your life, not just manage your finances. You will list who you want to mow your lawn, maintain your car, fix things around the house, manage your properties, pay your bills, prepare your taxes, and everything else. If you are serious about not being a burden, you will take as much time as needed to gather this information well in advance of a health crisis.

Prohibition Against Arbitration Agreements

If you end up in a rehab center, nursing home, or other type of long-term care facility, you need to think about the agreements your agent will be asked to sign on your behalf. These facilities work with a lot of lawyers. One of the ways the lawyers try to minimize risk is by forcing residents into arbitration to resolve disputes. Every long-term care facility does this, including assisted living facilities, adult family homes, nursing homes, group homes, and larger communities. They will all try to get your agents to sign an agreement that says, if we have a fight, you are not going to sue. You will go into arbitration. These agreements are generally placed in front of family members during times of high stress, like moving to an assisted living facility or a nursing home.

The facilities' lawyers are prepared, so you should be, too. Your Power of Attorney can include provisions that prohibit your agents from signing voluntary arbitration agreements, arbitration agreements, or documents that forfeit your right to sue a housing facility in situations of negligence or inaction that led to your injury. You can include specific instructions for this situation. Any arbitration agreement your agents may sign to get you accepted into a facility becomes invalid. Your agent can still sign the insurance application like normal.

But if a situation later arose that necessitated litigation, this provision would allow you and your agent more options to fight for your rights. Even though one of the main reasons to draft your Power of Attorney is to have a say in who provides your care, sadly, it may not always be the case. In guardianship proceedings where the court becomes involved, who handles your affairs may be forced on your agents by disgruntled relatives or professional service providers who claim to be working in your best interests but are, in reality, looking out for themselves.

Bar Against Guardianships

Finally, the point of a Power of Attorney is to avoid possible future guardianship proceedings. Sadly, that goal is not always achieved. There are many individuals who have signed a Power of Attorney and are still subjected to a guardianship proceeding because a relative felt that the agent was not acting in the older adult's best interest. Once a court gets involved in your life, it will judge the family issue using a standard that they may not want it judged against. Even if you are made subject to the guardianship proceeding, it's important that your faith in children, family members, or others named as agents be made clear. If a guardian is to be appointed, final decisions about health and finances need to be in the hands of chosen fiduciaries, family members, or others and not outsiders who will want to dictate their own ethos and morality on your life.

Admission into a Long-Term Care Facility

Your Power of Attorney might include detailed instructions related to your preference to avoid being placed in a long-term care facility. I have a few clients who were concerned that their agents would be too quick to follow the guidance of health care workers who are biased in favor of institutional care for older adults. These clients did not want to end up in long-term care facilities after a health crisis. Their Powers of Attorney included language that explained the process their agents should follow in the aftermath of a health crisis, including enlisting the services of a geriatric care manager to complete an assessment of what it would take to avoid institutional care.

These are just a few of the many topics that your enhanced Power of Attorney can cover. Your goal is simple. Your Powers of Attorney should read like manuals of instruction. That's how you avoid institutional care, going broke, and being a burden.

Compensation

Don't take your agents and loved ones for granted. Ensure that they are fairly compensated for the time and effort it takes to make sure you are well cared for. It can be disastrous to assume that they don't expect any compensation because of your relationship. While this may be true at first, by not compensating them, you will more than likely burden them financially, socially, and mentally. Few people want to be someone else's charity—even family.

How do you determine what to pay? A good starting point is to understand what a professional fiduciary would cost. You don't need to provide the same level of compensation, particularly since a loved one is probably not a professional in this area. Knowing the going rate for professional fiduciaries gives you a starting point for what the right compensation might be. Alternatively, in some families, there is a home that might make sense to gift to the family member who is serving as fiduciary while the rest of the heirs split everything else. There are several ways to handle compensation, so work through your unique circumstances with an estate or elder law attorney.

Lighten the Load for Financial Fiduciaries

If you're serious about not being a burden, one of the best things you can do is to have a Family Meeting and talk to the people you have named as your agents and fiduciaries. Ask them whether they're comfortable taking this chore on. If they aren't, find someone else.

When you've settled on an agent, you will want to meet with him or her to make your wishes clear. You will also want to come up with a detailed and specific outline for your fiduciary, ensuring that they have sufficient guidance and resources to act on your behalf when you cannot.

Financial tasks that are expected of your fiduciary fall into three broad categories: managing your financial holdings (such as investments or properties), paying bills, and filing taxes. You will also want to connect your fiduciaries with a geriatric care manager who can coordinate your care if you fall ill.

There's a lot to do, so let's discuss ways to lighten the load for your fiduciaries.

Fiduciary Tasks: Paying Your Bills

Perhaps the most pressing task your fiduciary will perform is to manage your bills and pay them on time. The toughest challenge your fiduciary will face will be figuring out whom to pay, how much to pay, and when to pay.

You may think this is a no-brainer, and maybe it is for you. You know all the bills. They're all on autopay, except for those two or three bills that come in from time to time that you know about, but no one else does.

If something happens to you and you haven't prepared your fiduciary in advance, payments may be missed, and services may get cut off during the time when your fiduciary is turning their life (and your files) upside down to figure everything out. Why not spare them the chaos? Why not just go ahead and talk to your fiduciary today about what they need to do? Have them work with you as you pay bills when you're still healthy, so they know where everything is. Or, come up with a system that they understand that makes it easy for them to step into the fiduciary role if you are incapacitated.

It will make your fiduciary's life a whole lot easier if you have a bill paying system set up that tracks your payments and perhaps even pays your bills automatically. One option to reduce this burden is to use software your fiduciary can access to track and pay your bills. Banks offer this service, but if you or your fiduciary chooses to change banks, you will lose your electronic history. Alternatively, you can use a program not attached to any single institution. Quick-Books, Quicken, and Mvelopes are a few examples. These programs give you a way to track income, expenses, deductions, and other financial histories.

You could even lift your fiduciary's burden altogether and hire an accountant to become your bill manager. Ask your current accountant if they can help your fiduciary in this role. If they can't, consider finding an accountant who can. When you have found an accountant you are comfortable with, name that accountant in your Power of Attorney documents so your fiduciary knows whom to contact.

Fiduciary Tasks: Filing Your Taxes

This is another task that could be tricky for your fiduciary to navigate if you don't sit down with him or her in advance. Filing taxes is hard in the best of times. Having to file someone else's taxes without any guidance or knowledge of their finances is an extreme burden. It might seem easy for you—you're retired, and your income streams seem fairly straightforward, but for someone just becoming familiar with your financial affairs, the task can be daunting.

Or maybe you decide you don't want your children to have to file your taxes. You would much rather pay an accountant $500 a year to do it for you, which is hardly an expensive proposition these days.

You write that direction into your Power of Attorney. Say, "When I fall ill, you (agent) will go to this accountant, and they'll prepare the taxes."

If your agents say they can do it, then include that in your Power of Attorney and build in provisions to pay your agent for that service, the same way you would pay any professional.

Consider hiring a local accountant to manage your taxes. I recommend someone with whom you can establish a professional relationship, trust, and have history with as opposed to a tax preparation factory. By having a history and trust with this accountant, you can be confident that your fiduciaries will receive good services when it comes to preparing your taxes. You should also make sure that your accountant has competent and trustworthy people who can take over your account if your accountant should retire or leave the business.

If you are currently working with an accountant that helps you file your taxes, inquire whether that accountant can also manage your bills. Be sure to introduce your accountant to your fiduciary so that they can coordinate the management of your bills.

If you do not wish to hire an accountant to prepare your taxes in the event that you can no longer handle your affairs, we suggest that you sit down with your fiduciaries and do your taxes together a few years in a row so that they're familiar with your process and your financial situation.

Fiduciary Tasks: Managing Your Holdings

If you're managing money yourself, great. But when your children have to step up to the plate, will they know what to do? Will they change things? Will they do things the way you want them done? Now is the time to plan.

You are likely leaving financial assets in the hands of your fiduciary. Arranging to have a financial planner manage your holdings not only protects you and your assets, but it also gives your fiduciary a reliable source of knowledge and advice to lean on for help. Make sure that the financial planner you choose to oversee your documents and assist your fiduciary is someone you have worked with in the past. You will want to name this person as the professional you want your fiduciary to work with. Make sure your financial planner has a succession plan that you are comfortable with in case they retire or go out of business.

If you own and rent out property, I suggest that you hire a property manager to oversee your rentals. Though it might seem like an extravagance, you'll be making the burden that much lighter for your fiduciary. If you feel more comfortable managing your properties today, at least consider finding a property manager for the future so that should a handoff be necessary, it will be as seamless as possible. Also, don't forget to name your property manager in your Power of Attorney.

As for your other investments, make sure that your fiduciary is aware of them and, most importantly, can access them easily. Since many of these investments will probably require online access, it is important that you create a system for granting online access that is both secure and easy for your fiduciary to follow.

I suggest that you gather your login IDs and passwords and move them to an online password management system. There are a number of password software programs including LastPass, 1Password, and KeePass. They all offer slightly different benefits. Some charge fees and some are free. You could also choose to write your access keys down on paper.

However you choose to aggregate your access data, remember to review with your fiduciary how to access it. Don't forget to add their responsibilities toward your holdings in your Power of Attorney document.

Fiduciary Tasks: Paying Final Expenses

In the last chapter, I introduced the concept of prepaying final expenses and identifying in advance how you want your remains to be handled. In this chapter, I will explain more about how to do this—and why it's so important.

As you have already seen, prepaying your final expenses does more than just save money; it makes it possible for your loved ones to avoid the burden of having to both make the arrangements and foot the bill during their time of grief. When you do these things in advance, you are giving a lovely gift to your family.

Now, let's talk about your remains. It's a sensitive subject, one that almost no one enjoys discussing. Have you decided how yours will be handled? The estate planning document that you will use to record your answer to this question is called the Directive of Disposition of Remains or Disposition Authorization. This document is used to outline your preferences—whether you want a burial, cremation, or something else.

In American culture, we treat the handling of remains rather callously. Ask any random person what they want to be done with their remains, and you're likely to hear a flippant response. "I don't care, flush me down the toilet," is not an uncommon response.

Since the dawn of humanity, every society has had rituals about what they do with the remains of a person who dies. These rituals are important. It's not just about disposing of your body. It's about creating closure for the people you are leaving behind—the people who live. Closure happens when you're done dealing with the last physical manifestation of a person's being. I see it as a spiritual issue.

Each culture has its own traditions, and I respect them all.

Whatever your decision, it's important to document it in detail so your family knows what you want.

If you want to be buried, share your plans, including the arrangements you have made for the funeral home, memorial service, burial location, and other details, along with any information about pre-paid funerals.

If you decide to donate your remains to a university or medical school, please tell your family about your desire, and make sure they know what will happen to your remains afterward. Many institutions cremate the remains and return them to the family.

Whether you opt for cremation immediately after your death or you are cremated after you've donated your remains to an organization, it is critically important to decide exactly what you want your loved ones to do with the ashes, and then include those directions in your documentation.

For instance, if you want your family to scatter your ashes in the western basin of Lake Erie, write something like this: "Within 90 days of my passing, you will take my ashes to Port Clinton, Ohio, where the Portage River empties into Lake Erie, and you will let me go." If you aren't specific about what you want to be done with your remains, you're likely to end up sitting in someone's garage atop some spare tires, on a mantel next to a commemorative gnome, or in some closet under last year's overcoats.

This is as much a psychological issue as it is a mechanical issue of handling remains. Not telling your family what you want to be done with your ashes—or making a request that's difficult to fulfill—will create unexpected burdens.

Not long ago, I talked to a man who told me a story that drives this point home. Charles was visiting his family in South Florida. During a walk on the beach one morning with his brother, Joe, Charles noticed something bobbing in the surf, and he waded out to retrieve a small ziplock baggie containing a beautiful, intricately patterned container about the size of a whiskey shot glass.

"What do you think it is?" Joe asked while holding it up in the light to inspect it.

"It looks to me like someone's drug stash," replied Charles. "Might as well throw it back in."

Just then, Charles noticed a man with a surfboard running up the shore toward him.

"Is this yours?" Joe asked, holding up the baggie.

"Yes," said the man, out of breath from the run. "It's my dad."

It took a moment for Charles and Joe to process what he was saying. "Oh," Joe said. "It's your dad's ashes."

The man nodded. "Dad was a surfer and he wanted to be buried on the fourth reef, but I dropped him almost as soon as I got on the board," he said. "This is only the second time in my life that I've ever been on a surfboard. Not really my thing."

The man took the baggie and tucked it into a pocket in his wetsuit. "I'm so glad you found him. Thank you." Then he paddled out into the surf.

This encounter illustrates why it's so important to think about what your request might mean for your family. What actions might be required? Will those actions be easy to complete, or will they create challenges like the ones faced by the man Charles and Joe met on the beach?

By making these decisions well beforehand and offering your fiduciaries and loved ones a clear guide, you are saving them time and money. You are also freeing them from the burden of having to make these decisions for you during a very emotional and difficult time of their lives.

Conclusion

Die-Die-Die estate planning isn't bad, it's just shortsighted. With a few tweaks, your legal plan for retirement can plan for the challenges of life as you age *and* for the day when you die. Legal documents created within the context of a *LifePlan* will protect your wishes, ensure that your decisions are legally protected, and legally empower your fiduciaries to carry out your wishes.

We certainly don't intend for you to draft these documents yourself. You will benefit from working with competent legal counsel who can advise you and help create these documents for you.

CHAPTER 13

A BETTER WAY TO INVOLVE YOUR FAMILY

Foundational Insight

Traditional retirement planning assumes that your family will always be there for you.

LifePlanning is about laying down a path for your loved ones to follow in order to create predictability of outcome while minimizing burdens to family members.

Introduction

As you have already seen, your family will play an integral role in every part of your retirement plan. In many ways, your loved ones become the stars of the show, especially when your health fails.

Every aspect of your planning—health, housing, finances, and legal—will involve your family in some way when you cannot manage your own affairs due to illness or death. It's not a matter of whether you are going to get old; the issue is, when you do get old and need the involvement of others in your life, how will your family respond?

They can step into the situation unprepared, without a clear understanding of your wishes, left at the mercy of the opinions of medical professionals who likely will be more focused on their needs and less on yours, or they can step into a situation where they not only know how you wish to live the rest of your life, but they also know the exact steps to take in order to give you the best chance to live that life.

The more your loved ones know about how you want things handled when you become incapacitated and the more you organize the information they will need when it is their time to act, the less burdensome this period of interdependence will be.

One of the criticisms I often hear about *LifePlanning* is that it involves a lot of work. My critics are right. There is no escaping the fact that *Life-Planning* involves more work than most of us are used to. Most of us go to a lawyer and talk for a while, and then come back after a few weeks to be handed a binder full of documents. These documents give our agents the responsibility to manage our lives and the authority to take whatever actions are needed, but they don't give our agents a shred of direction about what to do. That's why so many older Americans become a burden on their families, and it's a big reason why so many have nagging fears about what will happen as they age. But, as you are now seeing, with a bit of work, this problem can be easily remedied. It is possible to provide explicit direction to your family about what you want them to do in order to help you achieve your goals of not ending up in institutional care, not going broke, and not being a burden on your family. Sadly, in the traditional retirement planning process, this work is almost never done.

You have to do the work. As I mentioned in the previous chapter, if you don't do this work, who do you think will do it? It gets pushed downstream to your family—to your agents. Your unwillingness to do the work in advance is what creates the burden. You have to come to grips with the fact that cheap work delivers cheap results. If you don't want to put in the effort, then somebody else will have to.

Once you have gone through the process of planning how to handle aging from health, housing, financial, and legal perspectives, it is time to bring your family in and get them involved by holding a Family Meeting.

The Family Meeting

In the *LifePlanning* process, the Family Meeting paves the way for the people you have chosen for roles in your plan to act in a way that is in keeping with your desire to avoid institutional care, avoid losing assets to uncovered long-term care costs, and avoid burdening family members.

The Family Meeting accomplishes four things:

1. **Mutual Understanding:** The Family Meeting gives your family a chance to hear you talk about what you want each of them to do (and how) when it's time for them to step in.

2. **Role Acceptance:** The Family Meeting creates a forum where the people you choose accept their responsibilities and duties with the rest of the family as witnesses.

3. **Transparency:** The Family Meeting makes clear your desire for transparency, along with the actions you expect the agent to take to achieve that outcome.

4. **Conflict Avoidance:** Addressing the previous three items minimizes the chance of family feuds over your decisions.

I didn't invent the concept of the Family Meeting. It has been around for millennia. Since the beginning of time, family groups have been meeting to have conversations about all sorts of topics. It's only here in America, in the last century or two, that the concept of the "Family Meeting" (regarding the care of older relatives) has fallen out of fashion, or at least has become less effective.

Certainly, it is out of fashion with professionals who help consumers with retirement planning. The concept of a Family Meeting was not covered in law school at any level, nor have I taken any continuing education classes on this topic. To be sure, there is a smattering of discussion by a few individual practitioners, but there is no best practice on how a good Family Meeting can be held. Why is this? At the consumer level, the reason why, in my opinion, is that we have no idea how life will unfold when an elderly person falls ill. We know what we would like to happen (stay out of the nursing home), but we don't know how to effectively bring it up with loved ones. And we know, or should know, that loved ones assuring us that they will see to it that we don't end up in a nursing home is a well-meaning gesture, without much grounding of the realities that will need to be addressed when the time comes. We watch our friends end up in nursing homes, yet we have little knowledge of how to keep it from happening to us. And if *we* don't know, how can we tell our family what to do? And at the professional level, it appears that industries are busy churning out wisdom that furthers the financial interests of the industry and its constituents, leaving the rest to the consumer to figure out.

LifePlanning changes that reality and gives you a way to answer all of these questions, and the Family Meeting is the place where you share your answers with your family.

The Family Meeting is the time and place to share all the planning you've done for your retirement years, and, most importantly, to test the assumptions upon which those plans are based and then make any necessary adjustments.

Family Meetings are powerful, but they're not easy conversations to have. Think about the subject matter. We are talking frankly and openly about life coming to an end as we have known it thus far. I have facilitated thousands of Family Meetings for my clients over the years, and there have been many emotional—and some tearful—moments. Expect these moments and let the tears flow. You are giving your family a tremendous gift by doing this work. You are showing them how to take responsibility for your life by planning ahead for your own incapacity and death instead of refusing to face it like so many people do. In the process, you are showing your family what it means to live.

It is important to remember that, given the subject matter, there likely will not be a second chance to get the meeting right. So, it is important to be well prepared for the meeting. What follows is guidance based on my own experience in holding Family Meetings. There is no right or wrong way to conduct a Family Meeting, but there is a minimum amount of information that needs to be organized and conveyed, so preparation is key.

Family members will have roles in your life. Will they be willing to assume those roles? You want to make sure that you are conveying all the details of your plan clearly. You want everyone in that room to come away with a detailed blueprint of their role in your plan, as well as an idea of how to fulfill that role. The Family Meeting is the place to share your expectations and then hear what your loved ones are willing to do for you. The most important thing that happens in Family Meetings is that the children and named agents walk away with a very clear understanding of what their roles and responsibilities are going to be. They have a meaningful opportunity to push back or tell you to do it differently or tell you that they're not going to do it at all.

An effectively held Family Meeting will diffuse problems later. Here is an example of how that happens. One couple I worked with, let's call them Bill and Diana, assumed that their daughter, Kendall, would be their agent for all their Power of Attorney documents. Bill and Diana were in their mid-60s; Kendall was an artist in her mid-30s.

On the day of the Family Meeting, we all gathered in my office. Bill and Diana had been looking forward to this day for many months. They were confident that sharing their *LifePlan* with Kendall would be as much of a relief to her as creating the *LifePlan* had been for them.

When it was time to talk about the Power of Attorney and who would serve in the agent role, something happened that Bill and Diana didn't expect.

"Kendall, we want you to serve as our agent," Bill said. "We've thought through everything. We have a list of professionals for you to work with and we have documented all our preferences and instructions in our Power of Attorney. We want to make things as easy for you as possible."

As I always do in Family Meetings, I asked Kendall to read selected parts of the Power of Attorney document aloud.

Kendall read a few paragraphs and then she stopped. The expression on her face was a combination of terror and guilt.

"Kendall, what do you think of this?" I asked.

She sighed, then broke out into huge sobs, her head in her hands.

Bill and Diana looked shocked. I wasn't. I could tell from Kendall's reaction that she didn't want the responsibilities. Now she had to admit that to her parents.

I have to give Kendall credit. She didn't run out of the room like I've seen some people do. I reached over to my desk, grabbed a few tissues, and handed them to her. "What's on your mind, Kendall?" I asked softly.

"I can't do it," she whispered.

"Oh, Kendall, why?" asked Diana.

"I'm moving to Europe," she said. "I haven't had a chance to tell you yet. I have no idea where I'll be. I can't commit to this. Please don't hate me."

Though Bill and Diana were surprised by Kendall's refusal, they were grateful for the Family Meeting and its ability to surface this issue ahead of time.

"We just assumed that she would be happy to do it," Bill told me afterward. "The Family Meeting showed me that it's never safe to make assumptions about something this important."

The couple ended up hiring a professional fiduciary to serve as their agent.

The Family Meeting is one of the most powerful parts of the *LifePlanning* process. It's the place where everything comes together, where all those unspoken assumptions can finally be brought out into the open. It's where the plan becomes real.

I have facilitated hundreds of Family Meetings where the plans my clients had going in didn't align with what their children were willing to do. As a result, some of my clients ended up changing their housing decisions. I have seen situations where people who were determined to age in place make the move to a retirement community. I have seen people dead set against living with their kids agree to live in a wing of their child's home, or move closer to them, many times out of state. The Family Meeting has an amazing ability to raise these issues so they can be worked through in a constructive way.

Disputes can happen over the smallest things while you're still alive and after you're gone. Nearly all conflicts can be avoided when you bring transparency to the planning process. The Family Meeting is the place to explain whom you have chosen for decision-making responsibilities. Be as transparent in the meeting as you can be (though you do not have to share information about the assets in your estate, or whom you are going to leave what—that will happen at the right time), and make sure that everyone understands that when you're naming one child to be your agent, that child is going to be transparent in what they're doing with all other family members.

The Family Meeting is also the place to talk frankly about the reality that not everyone will agree with all decisions, but you want to prevent disputes from creating ill will. The Family Meeting sets the stage for compromise rather than confrontation.

Remember, although it is your plan for retirement, you will not be the one who implements it once your health fails. Your agents will. The Family Meeting ensures that everyone is on the same page when it comes to your needs and desires, that they know what help is available, and where to turn to when the time comes. You will talk about all the resources you have assembled for agents to use, make sure everyone knows what your ultimate goals are, and provide the best possible assurance that your wishes will be respected.

Where to Hold the Meeting

I recommend having the meeting in person if at all possible, although the meeting can be effective on Zoom or a similar online platform. You will collect valuable data about the feasibility of your plans. For instance, if a named agent is unable to make it to your Family Meeting with plenty of advance notice and when everything is running smoothly, will that person be the best choice to carry out your wishes in a crisis at the drop of a hat? Another reason to conduct the meeting in person is so that you can see how everyone reacts to your plan. Are they involved? Do they interrupt? Do they seem satisfied with your plan? You can learn a lot about what your family and loved ones think by watching how they react when you tell them your wishes.

Who Should Lead the Meeting

Though you can lead a Family Meeting yourself, most families have a more productive discussion when a neutral third party facilitates the meeting. In my experience, the chances are high that this meeting will be charged with emotion. Some people in your family might not want to hear some of the tougher details of your plan. They might become defensive. They might be offended that you might think them incapable of such an action. They might believe they have a better idea for how to take care of you than you do. They just might not listen to everything you have to say.

When a neutral third party mediates the meeting, the information tends to be internalized differently than from family members. They don't necessarily take it as personally as they would if it came directly from you. When they are led by an objective third party, Family Meetings clear the air, bring transparency, reduce the risk of family fights, and draw loved ones closer.

When to Conduct the Meeting

If you're tempted to rush into the Family Meeting, my advice is to wait until you are totally ready. Being ready for your Family Meeting means you have completed three things:

First: You have taken a good long look at the rest of your life, you understand the housing options available to you, and you have chosen the one that makes the most sense for you. As you learned in Chapter 10, you need to pick a path:

- Live life in your own home, which makes you more dependent on your children, if you have them, or

- Living in a retirement community so you won't be a burden, even though it means you will burn through your children's inheritance faster.

Second: You have thought through how your planning will impact your loved ones or named fiduciaries. You will want to discuss how you plan on financing uncovered long-term care costs. If you have included the protections of a Safe Harbor Trust, you will want to review the way the Trust works. If you have a long-term care insurance policy, you will want to share the details, and suggest to the agent to work with a geriatric care manager to trigger the policy benefits, which can be notoriously tricky to do. If you are going to count on paying privately, you will want to share that you would like the agent to work with a geriatric care manager to hire direct caregivers to keep the costs down. If you are going to choose to add a line of credit against the equity of your home, you will want to share that detail as well.

Third: You have determined how open you want to be about your plans with your named agents. As I mentioned earlier, you do not have to share knowledge of the magnitude of your estate or income, or who will get what when you die. That is not the purpose of this meeting. The purpose is for people to know what the role calls for, what your hopes are, and what resources you have made available to them for the agents and loved ones to fulfill their roles. You are looking for acceptance of the roles, and affirmation of your hopes that the family will not end up fighting when decisions are being made.

What to Bring

You should bring a detailed inventory of your decisions and designations in the areas of health, housing, finances, and legal. You should also bring all relevant legal documents to the meeting other than your Will or Trust. I recommend that you don't bring a Will or Trust because, at any time after the meeting, you might want to alter it. If you decide to change it and your children or loved ones saw the previous version, it could cause ill will, especially if the changes you make leave them with less than what was originally stated. Instead of bringing the

Will or Trust, make sure that you leave detailed instructions on how to obtain either document should the time arise.

Who Should Attend

I recommend inviting anyone named as fiduciary, agent, or beneficiary. If there are other family members who aren't named as a fiduciary, agent, or beneficiary but are close enough to you that they would feel left out if they weren't invited, ask them to attend as well.

I recommend that you also invite the spouses of your named agents, fiduciaries, and beneficiaries. They will most likely hear about your plans, and it's usually better for them to hear about those plans from the source. However, if you decide to not invite one spouse, for whatever reason, it is probably wise to not invite any spouses in order to avoid ill feelings.

Proposed Agenda

Though I don't believe there is an overarching rule that governs how you conduct your Family Meeting, there are a few key points that I believe you should hit.

Housing

The most important topic to broach is your plan for housing in the event you become incapacitated. You will want to tell your family that you either plan on aging in your home or moving to a retirement community. All other decisions, roles, and expenditures will flow from this decision. Discussing your housing decision first will allow you to gauge how supportive your family members and your named agents are of the plan you have created. Go through a hypothetical situation where you fall ill. Walk your children through the specific parts of the Health Care Power of Attorney that determine the action they are to take.

Let me give you an example of why this is the most important decision to begin with and how it can influence your decisions, or that of your agents. During one Family Meeting, my clients, a couple in their mid-70s (I'll call them Fell and Lisa), came with their children, twin daughters, Lisette and Mary, who were in their late 40s. Everyone had a copy of the Health Care Power of Attorney.

As I mentioned in the story of Bill, Diana, and Kendall in the previous section, I don't read the Health Care Power of Attorney to the family. I have the named agent (if it's someone other than the spouse) read the section about working with a geriatric care manager when the client falls ill.

Since Fell and Lisa were both the primary agent for each other, they had named Lisette the first successor agent. Mary was the second successor agent.

"Mary, will you read section 13, which talks about how your mom and dad want you to handle things if they are in the hospital?" I asked.

Mary started reading.

> "I recognize should I face incapacity or disability, my care needs related to my disability may place additional and unavoidable burdens on my agent. In order to minimize these burdens and allow my agent to have a life of her own, my agent shall be required to hire the services of a geriatric care manager (GCM) to obtain a first assessment, which shall outline my needs and determine the course of action and the support systems necessary to address my quality-of-life issues and long-term care. It is my intent that such assessment addresses my needs with the aim of educating my agent on what will be needed in order to allow me to continue to access care at home, including facilities and services that will be needed to enhance or maintain my

quality of life, and communicates those findings to my health care agent. My health care agent may, using her discretion, implement the suggestions.

"Once obtaining this first assessment, my health care agent shall no longer be obligated to hire a GCM. Should my agent feel that the GCM's recommendations are improper, nothing would prohibit my agent from obtaining a second opinion from another independent GCM. In the end, it is my agent who will have the authority to make the final decision, a decision which shall not be challenged by others.

"For the purposes of this Durable Power of Attorney for Health Care, the term 'geriatric care manager' is to be broadly construed and shall include a certified geriatric care manager, a social worker, a registered nurse, or any similarly situated professional qualified to assist a disabled person with care coordination issues. If my agent is not familiar with the industry and does not know whom to hire, I direct the agent to go to AgingLifeCare.org and select a care management company from the listed providers."

Mary took a deep breath. "That's a lot," she said.

"It is," I agreed, "but can you see how it's designed to reduce burdens on the agent?"

She nodded.

I looked at Lisette, who, as the first successor agent, would be the one to assume responsibility for the parent who needed care after the other died. "You heard what Mary just read," I said. "What does that mean to you?"

Lisette thought for a moment. "Well, the first thing that comes to mind is that Mom and Dad want to be able to come back home after an illness," she said. "They want me to call the geriatric care manager to figure out how to do that."

"Are you willing to do that?" I asked.

"Yes," Lisette said.

"There are two things I want to emphasize," I said. "You just shared one of them. This section of the document directs you to work with a geriatric care manager so your mom or dad can access care at home. But that's not all. This language also gives the agent the authority to make the final decision about what's to be done."

"I have a question," Lisette said. "If Mom or Dad is in the hospital, what will actually happen? How will I use this information? I'm not sure I understand exactly what I'm supposed to say."

I was happy she asked the question. I could see that Mary was wondering the same thing. Both daughters were on the edge of their seats. This was a good sign.

"Let me give you a hypothetical situation," I said. "Let's say your mom died a few years ago, and now your dad has a stroke. After a week or two in the hospital, the discharge nurse comes to you and tells you that he is ready to be discharged from the hospital to a rehab center. The nurse will say it like it's the next logical step in the process. It won't sound like you have a choice in the matter."

"But we do have a choice," Mary said.

"Yes, you do have a choice, and you exercise that choice by knowing the right thing to say to the nurse at this critical moment," I explained. "Mary, what do you think you might say to the nurse?"

Mary paused to think, glancing down at her Health Care Power of Attorney. "I would say that we want Dad to come home and that the nurse should call the geriatric care manager to talk about how to make that happen."

"That's good." I turned to Lisette. "Is there anything you would add to that?"

I could see things click in her head. "Yes," she said. "I would tell the nurse this: 'Dad told us his preferences awhile back. He doesn't want to go to a rehab center. He wants to go back home. The only problem is that I don't know how to do it. I'm going to give you the phone number of a geriatric care manager that my dad chose in advance. That's who your discharge department will work with to bring him home.'"

Lisette nailed it. During the Family Meeting, that's the answer you want to hear from your agent. That's the response that proves they understand your goals. "You've got it," I said. "And if it turns out that it's not advisable to bring your dad home, the geriatric care manager will know how to help you figure out the best place for him."

I turned to Fell and Lisa. "Even though this document tells your daughter to go to AgingLifeCare.org and pick a geriatric care manager, I want *you* to go to that website, interview a few geriatric care managers, choose the one you like in advance, and then include their name and contact information in the appendix to this Health Care Power of Attorney. That will make things as easy as possible for her."

This, I believe, is what it takes to empower your family to achieve your goal of avoiding institutional care.

Before we leave this topic, I want to acknowledge that returning to care at home after an illness may not always be the best move. There may be situations where care in a facility is the best option. When you require your agents to work with a geriatric care manager and then tell them exactly how to do that at your Family Meeting, you are giving your agents a precious gift. They don't have to make this difficult decision alone. They will be guided by a geriatric care manager who will help your agents find the right care option for you.

Agents and Roles

After you have outlined your housing decision, I recommend that you tell each of your named agents the role you would like them to play. You will want to give them all the information that is relevant to that role, including the contact information of your geriatric care manager, lawyers, and accountants. Supply all the relevant passwords to access any needed online resources. And you'll want to outline what steps they should take should you become incapacitated.

Mental Health Advance Directive

During the planning process, there is often a lingering question about what will happen if you disagree with the actions your agent wants to take, not because of opposition from an informed person, but because of your own declining mental health. Though few have heard of the legal solution that addresses this issue (the Mental Health Advance Directive), it is important to understand and include this solution as part of your planning, and then talk about it during the Family Meeting.

As you've already seen, and as the stories in Chapter 4 vividly illustrate, people don't go from sane to insane overnight. It's almost always a long and drawn-out process, and the person usually can't recognize that their cognitive abilities are fading.

During the Family Meeting, we talk openly about this denial—and the often-unspoken fears about being unfairly stripped of rights by unscrupulous family members—conversations that almost never happen otherwise.

Here is an example of a time when this delicate topic came up at a Family Meeting. One client, Matt, a married man in his 60s, had initially balked at creating a Mental Health Advance Directive when he and his wife, Jane, met with me to create a *LifePlan*. "What if my kid uses it against me?" he asked at the time we met to discuss that document.

His concerns were understandable. Peel away the reluctance and there's always a trust issue driven by fear. That was the central issue for Matt. Though he trusted his wife, Jane, to take the right action on his behalf, could he trust that, if Jane died first, their 50-year-old son, Mark, would do right by him when the time came?

When we arrived at this point on the Family Meeting agenda, I set the context. "I find that fiduciaries and families often struggle with issues stemming from a principal (in this case, Matt) being in a state that's between total capacity and incapacity. A Health Care Power of Attorney anticipates this gray area, but it doesn't give us a good way to address it. Matt, if you lose capacity due to dementia, Alzheimer's disease, or another illness, you may not recognize your loss of capacity, and you may not be cooperative when your family members try to take steps to make sure you are safe."

I turned to Mark. "Let's say your mom has already died. Your dad is in the early stages of dementia, but you don't know it yet. You know he's been forgetful lately, but you don't think much of it. Now, let's say you get a call from your dad's bank because they've seen some suspicious transactions go through. After doing a little digging, you get your dad to admit that he has been sending money to a person online, someone who claims to be heir to a large fortune. That person asks your dad to send $10,000 to cover legal fees to get the money released, and he falls for it. Then, your dad meets someone online who claims to be in love with him, but she needs $5,000 to book a ticket to come meet him in person. He falls for it."

"It's hard to imagine Dad not in his right mind, but I know that there are scammers out there who target older people," Mark said.

"Let's say that you confront your dad about this, and he gets defensive," I continued. "He tells you to mind your own business."

Everyone laughed. "Yeah, that's probably what would happen," Matt said.

I paused and let the moment of humor linger. I was about to venture into the most delicate subject of all: Matt's guns. An avid hunter, trap shooter, and Second Amendment advocate, Matt had been collecting firearms for years. He had hundreds of them locked away in gun safes in his home, and a few handguns hidden in drawers in case of emergency.

Mark, on the other hand, didn't share his father's passion for firearms. The two often argued about gun rights.

"Mark, let's say that you notice that your dad's mental decline includes paranoia, which can happen with dementia," I said. "Let's say that he mistakes the mailman for an intruder and threatens him with a gun."

"That's not out of the realm of possibility right now," Jane joked.

Matt didn't smile. "This Mental Health Advance Directive was the hardest part of this whole *LifePlanning* process for me," he said, looking at Jane. Then he turned to Mark. "If your mom goes first and I end up senile, I want to know that you're taking my guns for the right reasons."

Mark looked uncomfortable. "Dad, I love you," he said. "I know that you and I don't see eye-to-eye on this issue, but when you end up with dementia or Alzheimer's, my goal will be to keep you safe, not to prove a point. My goal will be to keep you from blowing someone's head off because you don't realize what you're doing."

Matt had shared his concern, and Mark had responded. I let that sit for a moment.

"Remember, the Mental Health Advance Directive simply gives Mark the authority to seek a psychiatric evaluation if he thinks there is a reason to do so," I told Matt. "There's a level of trust involved here, and I'm hearing that Mark cares about your well-being more than he does about your position on the gun debate. Mark, am I reading that right?"

Mark nodded.

"Ultimately, Matt, trusting Mark to be your agent if Jane passes first will help you meet one of the goals you said was most important to you, which is to not be a burden on Mark. The alternative is a guardianship process, which takes six to nine months and can cost thousands of dollars. The two of you will be at war, possibly forever. Trust me, that is a burden like no other. You don't want that."

Living Will

Where the topic of the Mental Health Advance Directive is likely to bring up issues regarding trust, the Living Will is usually where the emotions run the highest. Tears are common. I always have several boxes of tissue at the ready.

In Chapter 12, you saw how my approach to the Living Will does more than just state what kinds of treatment you do and don't want; it gives your family a process that they can use to reach a decision when the time comes.

The goal during this portion of the Family Meeting is to make sure that everyone understands what you want, what roles everyone will play, how the decision to remove life support will be made, and what to do if not everyone agrees. It's also a time for everyone to ask their questions about the process. Nearly everyone has them, and I find myself dispelling many misconceptions.

One Family Meeting stands out in my mind. Joanne and George, a couple in their early 70s, came to my office for a Family Meeting with their four children, Mike, Karen, Paul, and Kathy, all in their 40s.

When we came to the Living Will portion of the agenda, before Joanne and George even shared their document, Kathy, the oldest, started to cry. She was aware that she had been named a successor agent in her parents' Living Will.

"Kathy, what's on your mind?" I asked.

"I can't be the one to make the decision," she sobbed. "I just can't. It's too much pressure. I don't want the responsibility."

I paused. This kind of sentiment wasn't at all unusual. It wasn't the first time I had seen tears during this part of a Family Meeting, and it wouldn't be the last. "I understand," I said. "How about we go through the document to see what it says? Then we can talk about your concerns."

When it comes to Living Wills, misinformation is rampant. Living Wills aren't just about pulling the plug, as so many people think. The language in these documents requires the agent to look not only at the medical status of the person (e.g., in a persistent vegetative state or terminally ill) but also at quality-of-life indicators when rendering a decision about whether to remove artificial means of life support.

I asked George and Joanne to read the document aloud. When they finished, they looked at Kathy, who was still weeping quietly with her head in her hands, and then at me.

"Kathy," I said, "you've just heard a lot of legalese about what kind of treatment your mom and dad do and don't want. Let me explain how the Living Will works. First, the only time when a Living Will can be used to withhold life-sustaining treatment is when there is a medical diagnosis that says your mom or dad is (1) in a persistent vegetative state, or (2) terminally ill and in a condition where they can't communicate their wishes. Your mom or dad may never be in that situation, but if they are, you won't be alone in making that decision. It won't be your burden to bear by yourself."

Kathy looked up. "I thought that as the agent, I had to make the decision alone."

I shook my head. "No, you don't. Let me tell you how it works."

Kathy needed some context. Most people do. Almost everyone has heard the phrases "he's a vegetable" and "pull the plug," but almost no one really understands what those phrases mean.

I explained that a persistent vegetative state is a diagnosis. If a person receives that diagnosis, the medical community must do everything reasonably in its power to find a cure. This can take anywhere from a few weeks to a few months, depending on the situation.

"If you and your siblings aren't sure that all reasonable efforts have been expended, you can ask for a second or third opinion and keep the efforts going," I said. "It's the same with the diagnosis of a terminal illness. Just because one physician says that you are terminally ill does not mean that another physician would agree."

"I want to jump in here," said Joanne. "Kathy, this isn't just for you, it's for all of you. The point of this Living Will is to say to all of you kids that if either one of us is in a situation where our bodies can't stay alive without outside interference, and there is no reasonable chance of getting better, then we don't want to be kept alive."

"But there's a gray area," Karen said. "Who determines whether there's a reasonable chance you will get better?"

"There's a process for that," I said. "Let's say your mom is the one being kept alive by artificial means and the doctor says there's no hope and you need to decide whether to continue life support. The Living Will tells you that the next step is to contact the geriatric care manager your parents have identified, and have that person contact another doctor in a different hospital system to give a second opinion. You can request as many opinions as you want, and you can rely on the geriatric care manager to coordinate that for you."

"If I were in Kathy's shoes, I would be worried about what to do if we didn't agree on the same course of action," Paul added. "How do you resolve that?"

I offered a silent thank-you to Paul for airing the concern that I suspect was at the root of Kathy's concerns. "The Living Will gives you a way to do that. Kathy, your job is to make sure that everyone gives their input, and that the geriatric care manager continues to get the additional medical input you need," I said. "Every time there's new information, the geriatric care manager gets you together to discuss it. That's how you know you've done everything possible for them. That's how you reach consensus."

Handling of Remains

In Chapter 12, I talked about creating a plan for the handling of your remains and then documenting those preferences so your family can honor your wishes. The Family Meeting is where you will make your wishes known. This is another topic that can bring up uncomfortable emotions.

Whatever method you've chosen, the Family Meeting is where you share your plans with your family, and then ask for their questions, comments, and input. Don't forget that the whole point is for your loved ones to take part in the ceremony you have chosen—whatever that might be.

The act of releasing, whether it's the scattering of ashes or the sprinkling of dirt on a coffin, is about one chapter coming to an end so another can begin. By talking frankly and openly about the arrangements for your death at the Family Meeting, you will be showing your family how it's done. There is no more powerful legacy than that.

The Promises

When I'm conducting a Family Meeting, one of my objectives is to make sure that all parties are committed to their roles. This is something you will want to do in your Family Meeting.

I check this commitment by asking the parents to make promises to their child, children, or other named agents (I will refer to named agents as "children" from here on out for the sake of brevity). I also ask the children to make promises to their parents.

Below are the topics I always make sure to include. You may have other topics you want to cover.

I ask the parents to promise that when their children come to them with concerns, the parents will listen. They won't just blow off the children's concerns.

I ask the parents to promise that if something happens that concerns the children and they want to call in the geriatric care manager, the parent won't push back. The parent will allow the geriatric care manager to get involved.

When it comes to the children, one of the most important promises I ask them to make involves what action they will take after a parent's health crisis.

I ask the children to promise that when they are asked by a hospital social worker, nurse, discharge planner, or other health care professional which care facility they want the parent to be discharged to, that the children will push back on that request. The children promise to bring in the geriatric care manager to work with the hospital to arrange for care in the home, if at all possible.

I ask the children to promise that they will not stir up conflict with each other and that they will work together to help the parents achieve their goals of aging where they choose, without going broke, and without being a burden on the family.

If there are multiple children and the parents have chosen one of them to serve as their agent, I ask the children to promise that they will let the child chosen as the agent make the final decision and they will support the agent in that decision, no matter how much they disagree.

There is something powerful about voicing these promises aloud. That's why I always ask families to do this. It's often an emotional experience, and one that ultimately brings the family closer together. I encourage you to take this approach in your Family Meeting.

Open Discussion

After you have said your piece and outlined everything you wanted to discuss, open the floor to questions from your family and loved ones. You want to leave the meeting confident that your family understands your wishes and knows exactly how to carry them out. Take as much time as you need to answer their questions.

NOTE: After the initial Family Meeting, I recommend that you wait 90 days and reassess the situation with your family and loved ones.

What Not to Discuss

Finally, the one topic I recommend not discussing is your exact financial situation. Of course, this is an individual choice, but there is a reason I discourage such a conversation. If your heirs and beneficiaries know exactly what assets you are holding, they may come to expect an inheritance of some kind. This expectation could affect how they decide to fulfill their role in your plan.

Don't Blow It Off

Over the years, a small percentage of my *LifePlanning* clients told me that they did not want me to facilitate their Family Meetings. Some claimed that they were confident they could handle the discussions themselves. Others didn't intend to talk to their kids at all.

So, if you're reading this and you don't want to talk to your kids, I'm going to give it to you straight. If you want to avoid the nursing home, avoid going broke, and avoid being a burden, you must share your plans and preferences with the members of your family who will be looking after you when you can't look after yourself. No matter how proud you are, no matter how independent you are, no matter how tough you are, the day you fall ill is the day that you will be counting on your kids to figure everything out. Don't make it harder for them than it has to be. Have the Family Meeting!

Family Meeting Examples

In the previous sections, you have seen how I guide my clients and their family members through discussions related to specific documents we cover during a typical Family Meeting. Now, I would like to share the view from a broader perspective. I have worked with thousands of clients whose Family Meetings have resulted in dramatic revelations. The following examples demonstrate the power of these gatherings.

Fred and Janice

Fred and Janice came to work with me after attending one of my seminars in the Seattle area. They were interested in a *LifePlan*, so I took them through my process. They had two kids, a son, Jake, and a daughter, Elise. Elise had just been through a divorce.

After the planning was complete, we held the Family Meeting. After explaining Fred and Janice's plan, I went through the legal documents and laid out how Fred and Janice had divided the agent responsibilities between their children. Elise would be the agent for their Health Care Power of Attorney; Jake would be the agent for their Financial Power of Attorney. When I reviewed this division of labor, everyone agreed. I left that meeting feeling good about what we had accomplished.

The next morning, the phone rang. It was Fred. "Boy, that went over like a lead balloon with Jake," he said. I could hear the concern in his voice.

"I thought things went well," I said. "What was his beef?"

"Well, Jake is telling me that Elise is a drug addict and shouldn't be in charge of anything, let alone our health care decisions," Fred explained. "I've never seen Elise use drugs or be under the influence of anything, even alcohol, so I don't know what to make of it. That's all news to me."

The Family Meeting is designed to get things out in the open, things like assumptions about who will do what, preferences for how things should go, and the like. This was the first time I had seen a secret come to light. The Family Meeting was doing its job, just not in the way I originally intended.

"I've never seen a situation like this before," I admitted, "but if Elise really does have a drug problem, or any substance abuse issue for that matter, you are better off confronting the situation now. If you don't, if you just give her your Health Care Power of Attorney and then she's not able to perform as your health care agent, it will just create a problem, won't it?"

Fred took my advice and talked to Elise, who admitted that she had a problem. In fact, her drug use was the reason her marriage had failed. Elise was more than happy to let her brother handle the health care agent responsibilities, so we ended up changing the Health Care Power of Attorney.

If that Family Meeting hadn't happened, Fred and Janice would have had no idea that the person they had named as their health care agent was not up to the task. Fred and Janice probably wouldn't have shared their overall plan with both kids, and Jake wouldn't have had the opportunity to share his concerns. When the health care issues would arise, as they always do, Elise would be the one making decisions, with Jake fully aware of her impairments due to drug use. The end result could have been a disaster. Fred and Janice might not have achieved their goal of not living in institutional care, going broke, or being a burden. The conflict between Elise and Jake also brought with it a very real risk of estrangement.

About two years after Fred and Janice's Family Meeting, Elise died of a drug overdose, bringing a sad resolution to the case. When I heard the news, I thought back to that Family Meeting. When everyone sits down together in a facilitated environment, the truth can come out and the parents can deal with it in a way that helps to avoid problems later. But if there's never a sit-down with the whole family, the truth won't ever come out, which almost guarantees that there will be problems, conflicts, feuds, and resentments among the kids, while the parents end up forced into institutional care, going broke, and becoming a burden.

The Story of Shelley Frankel

Another Family Meeting victory involved one of my tax law professors from law school, Shelley Frankel. He was instrumental in my development as an attorney and was also a good friend.

One day when I was facilitating a Family Meeting for a client, Shelley attended with his wife, who was serving as an agent for her sister, my client. When he walked in, Shelley stood in the doorway, beaming like a proud dad.

After the Family Meeting was finished, Shelley walked over to me. "I always knew you were going to do something different and something big," he said. "This process was great to watch."

Less than a year later, I got a call from Shelley's brother-in-law, the client whose Family Meeting Shelley had witnessed. "Shelley has pancreatic cancer," he said. "You need to call him. It's not looking good."

When I called Shelley, he picked up immediately. "Rajiv, I need something to distract me," he said. "How about you and I publish something?"

"What do you want to write about?" I asked.

"Let's talk about tax issues and the work that you are doing," he said.

I emailed Shelley an outline and we started working on the project. We didn't finish. Shelley's condition worsened quickly, and a few months later, he died.

One Saturday morning not long after the funeral, Shelley's wife called my radio show. I spoke to her live on the air.

"Rajiv, I need to say thank you," she said, the grief still evident in her voice. "If it hadn't been for you and that Family Meeting we attended, Shelley would not have died at home. Had I not heard that it is possible for people to advocate for their loved ones to be at home, Shelley would have died in a hospice house. He didn't want that. He died at home because I put my foot down. I said he wouldn't be leaving this house. He died overlooking the bay, which is exactly where he wanted to be. It was because of you, Rajiv. You gave me the knowledge and the courage to be able to stand up and advocate for that."

The Family Meeting had been a powerful education to Shelley's wife, like it has been to thousands of others.

CHAPTER 14

INTEGRATION & ACTION

Foundational Insight

Traditional retirement planning says, "Trust the experts."

LifePlanning says, "Trust yourself and question the experts."

Introduction

Now that you've seen what your plans for health, housing, finances, legal issues, and family need to include, how do you pull it all together?

If you're getting nervous about what it might take, let me reassure you.

You can do this!

I want you to see that it's possible to focus on what *you* want to achieve, not what others think you should strive for. You don't need other people to create this focus.

The first thing you need to know is that you can't count on the traditional retirement planning process or the financial planners and lawyers who are part of it to answer your most important questions. Questions like these:

1. How can I avoid the nursing home?
2. How can I avoid dying broke?

3. How can I avoid being a burden on my loved ones?

If financial planners and lawyers had the answers, 70 percent of Americans would not end up taking their last breath in institutional care.

How do you trust yourself to create a retirement plan that will deliver the answers you want?

First: Educate yourself on how to identify the gaps and holes in your current retirement plan. It's up to YOU to understand what's missing, how to get it, and how to connect all the elements of your planning so you get the results you want.

- Health care = Prevention. You avoid (or postpone) getting sick.

- Housing = Predictability of outcome. You aren't forced to move after an illness.

- Finance = A plan for how to use your money, which is more important than how much you have.

- Legal = Not just documents, but manuals of instructions.

Either you go to a *LifePlanner* who can help you pull this all together (find one at https://agingoptions.com/), or you educate yourself by reading this book, buying a *LifePlanning* workbook, attending a *Life-Planning* workshop, or joining the *LifePlanning* Portal for access to AgingOptions Academy.

Second: Once you have identified the gaps and holes in your planning, the next step is to eliminate them by taking specific directions to professionals and saying, "*This* is what I want you to help me do to eliminate these gaps and holes."

Third: Once you have worked with professionals to eliminate those gaps and holes, you turn your planning into a family affair. Why?

You're not going to be the one reading the Will when you're dead. Your executor is.

You won't be the one reading the Power of Attorney when you're ill. Your agents are.

They need to understand your goals, how the documents you've given them help you achieve those goals, and what their role will be in the process.

I will show you how.

You Are the Architect First, then the General Contractor

As you have already seen, bumble bee planning, flitting from one professional to the next to create plans to protect your health, housing, financial, and legal well-being in retirement, is no guarantee that you will avoid institutional care, avoid going broke, or avoid becoming a burden on your family. This fragmented approach is one of the reasons for the dismal success rate of traditional retirement plans.

If you want your plan to succeed, YOU NEED TO HELP YOUR-SELF, and you do that first by accepting the facts about working with professionals that I laid out for you in Part 1. Here's a quick review:

Reality #1: Professionals will give you only the advice that makes them money.

Reality #2: There are conflicts of interest built into the system.

Reality #3: Each professional is focused on helping you meet goals as viewed through the lens of their profession. No professional is working to meet your goals of avoiding the nursing home, not going broke, and not being a burden.

- Lawyers give you Die-Die-Die planning.

- Financial planners tell you to buy products and invest your money.

- Doctors tell you to call when you're sick, and then give you a pill, therapy, or surgery.

Let me say it again: YOU MUST HELP YOURSELF. To do that, you need to know how.

Remember the construction analogy I used earlier in this book? If you want a coordinated retirement plan, someone needs to design the plan and then manage the overall project. Someone needs to serve as the architect, and then the general contractor who oversees the actions of specialized subcontractors building your plan—in your case, the financial planner, attorney, real estate agents, and health care professionals.

Who will supervise the efforts of each professional and bring about this coordination?

It has to be you. YOU must commit to being the project manager of your *LifePlan*.

One of the most common questions I get from people involves how to hold doctors accountable. Given our current health care system, it may seem like there's nothing you can do, but that's not the case. If you need a reminder, go back to Chapter 9 and read about my own experience with Longevity Health Clinic.

Know What to Request

You've just seen how to use the health care system to stay healthy. Knowing what to ask for is vital, but few of us know how to do this, or even realize we can. As consumers, we have been taught to blindly follow the advice of professionals who allegedly know more than we do about specialized subjects. We rely heavily on outside influences to tell us what we should be doing, but these outside influences can often lead us astray. No one has been teaching us what to ask for—what to demand—from the professionals we pay to advise us. Most of us have no idea what to demand.

While there's no substitute for education and experience in specialized fields, you owe it to yourself and your family to become an informed buyer of professional services. You don't have to be an expert in that field, you just need to know what to ask for.

Instead of walking into the office of your lawyer, financial planner, doctor, or real estate professional and asking them what they recommend, I want you to walk in and tell them what you want them to help you accomplish. Half the battle is knowing what to ask professionals to do for you. I want you to know how to hold your professional service providers accountable, and how to set parameters on what you should expect from them. I want you to get what you want, not what's in their best interest to give you.

Finally, don't be surprised if the professionals you rely on to create the various elements of your *LifePlan* push back when you tell them about your desire to hold them to a higher standard. Many of the industries most involved in retirement planning have been resistant to change, especially those whose professionals bill themselves as the "quarterback" of your planning team. That's one of the reasons why retirement plans have so many gaps. *LifePlanning* eliminates those gaps by empowering you with the knowledge and confidence you need to make sure the professionals work in your best interest.

The next section explains how to do this with the professionals you trust to develop your plans for legal, financial, housing, and health.

Integrate Your Legal Plan

In Chapter 4, I talked about the problems with traditional legal planning, and in Chapter 12, I outlined the solutions. In this section, I will explain how those solutions translate into action.

First, let's review the goals of legal planning in the *LifePlanning* process:

1. Instead of limiting your planning to protecting assets from Probate and estate taxes, your legal planning must also protect assets from uncovered long-term care costs and bad actors.

2. Instead of limiting your planning to documents that assign responsibility and grant authority, your legal documents should read like manuals of instructions.

3. Instead of viewing legal planning as a "once-and-done" task, you need to view it as a "living" plan that you update regularly.

When you're working with your attorney to draft legal documents for your *LifePlan*, keep in mind that you are creating detailed written instructions for your agents to follow if you become disabled or die. Your legal documents must address subjects that the typical estate planning or elder law attorney may find unfamiliar. While most lawyers are trained to help you protect your estate from estate taxes and to avoid Probate and its associated costs, few attorneys will offer to help you protect your estate from bad actors, and even fewer will offer to help you avoid uncovered long-term care costs.

You have to take matters into your own hands.

As you learned in Chapter 4, a bad actor is anyone who has the potential to get their hands on assets you have allocated to someone else. You will want your attorney to create an estate plan that makes certain your money transfers to the persons you choose after your death—and no one else.

Ask your attorney to include the following provisions in your Will or Trust:

1. Include language that specifies that the funds you leave to your spouse or partner are to be made available only to your spouse or partner so long as the spouse or partner is alive, and include provisions that make it nearly impossible for a bad actor to convince the spouse to take a wrong action.

2. When that person dies, your funds then go to the beneficiaries you choose. This is especially important if your spouse or partner ends up with someone else after you die.

3. You want protections built into your Will or Trust that state if your spouse or partner were to get into another relationship after your death, or they remarry, your share of the estate will not be vulnerable to being lost to the whims of the new partner or spouse.

Our nation's legal system depends on prenuptial and property status agreements for such protections. However, there is a stigma attached to this type of planning. It's much easier to build in protections from bad actors from the very beginning.

Uncovered Medical & Long-Term Care Costs

It is common for lawyers to protect assets from estate taxes and Probate, but not uncovered medical and long-term care costs. Yet, the single biggest financial threat that you will be facing is the possibility that Medicare will refuse to cover the cost of a medical illness. If Medicare won't pay, VA and/or Medicaid might, but only if you have very little in the way of assets. Your legal plan needs to include a way for you to preserve assets in the event a spend down is necessary to qualify for Medicaid.

Ask your attorney to work with you to create a plan to accomplish the following:

1. Extend the protections of legal planning to uncovered medical and long-term care costs. Safeguard your estate from Medicaid spend-down requirements by utilizing either a testamentary or Inter Vivos Special Needs Trust. The average attorney won't automatically suggest this option, so you will want to mention it.

2. If your *LifePlan* includes relying on VA or Medicaid benefits to pay for long-term care, you will also want your attorney to create a plan that will enable you to access those benefits without delays or wait times.

3. Consider including the protections of a Special Needs Trust (Safe Harbor Trust) in your planning. If you are single, your attorney will want to consider utilizing an "Inter Vivos" Special Needs Trust.

If your attorney…

- is unfamiliar with these planning techniques,
- doesn't believe in these planning techniques, or
- tries to talk you out of using them…

…find someone else who will help you with this type of planning.

Keep in mind that different attorneys often approach the same problems from different perspectives, and they may not agree on the same solution. Locate a competent estate planning and elder law attorney who will help you do the legal planning needed to achieve your goals. Visit the AgingOptions Resource Guide (https://agingoptions.com/) to find one near you.

Make Your Legal Documents Read Like Manuals of Instructions

As you learned in Chapter 4, your Powers of Attorney and other legal documents need to do more than assign authority and responsibility; they should read like manuals of instructions, so your agents know exactly what to do when the time comes. This is one of the most powerful tools in the *LifePlanning* process. Creating Powers of Attorney and other legal documents that read like manuals of instructions greatly minimizes the need for your agents to guess what you might have wanted, and then piece everything together. It's also a great way to minimize conflict.

Speaking of conflict, before I go into the details of each legal document, I want you to know that if you follow my guidance in the *LifePlanning* process to create your legal documents and then share them with your family, fiduciaries, and agents during a Family Meeting, there should be minimal disagreement when it's time for the fiduciaries to step into their roles. However, disagreements do happen and it's best to build instructions for handling conflict into each document.

Here's what I suggest:

1. Include a provision in each document that names a neutral third party who will be consulted in the event of disputes. This could be anyone—an attorney, a relative, a professional mediator, or someone else who can be trusted to be objective. For matters related to the Health Care Power of Attorney, the Living Will, the Mental Health Advance Directive, or the Handling of Remains, a geriatric care manager can serve as a neutral third party who can help you reach a consensus.

2. Include a provision in each document that explains what will happen if the neutral third party is unable to resolve the

dispute. I recommend that you include a provision for mandatory mediation.

3. Litigation should be your last resort, because it tends to turn into a war that fractures families forever.

Financial Power of Attorney

The Financial Power of Attorney allows your agent to manage your finances when you are unable to do so yourself. Your agent will need to do things like pay bills, file tax returns, manage investments, take care of home maintenance and repairs, attend to pets, service automobiles, manage rentals, run your business (or wind it down), and more.

Ask your attorney to work with you to catalog the tasks you can foresee your agents doing and then create detailed instructions for every task in order for them to manage your affairs with the least amount of effort needed. Detailed guidance will help your agents handle these tasks without being burdened by them. Not every lawyer will be interested in helping you do this. If you get pushback, find another attorney.

This detailed guidance will accomplish three things:

1. Minimize burdens
2. Bring predictability of outcome
3. Minimize conflict

Resolving Disputes

As I mentioned at the beginning of this section, it's important that your documents include detailed provisions for dispute resolution. In the Financial Power of Attorney, this protection is vital. Though it may be hard to imagine your named agents disagreeing about decisions made on your behalf, you should plan for that possibility. Make sure your Power of Attorney includes provisions for informal dispute resolution.

Ask your attorney to insert dispute resolution language that covers the following points:

1. A requirement that the agent keeps selected family members apprised of the financial dealings, health status, and decisions related to you and your care. This creates transparency that minimizes the risk of disputes.

2. Assurance that the agent's decisions regarding your health, housing, financial, and legal care shall be the final decision, not subject to court review, etc.

3. If there is disagreement, there is a mechanism that guides your agents to a resolution, preferably informal dispute resolution with a neutral third party. If the dispute can't be resolved informally, mandatory mediation is the next step.

Health Care Power of Attorney

The Health Care Power of Attorney allows your agent to direct your health care so that you can live where and how you want to, not where and how a social worker or hospital discharge planner thinks you should. Your Health Care Power of Attorney should be as detailed as your Financial Power of Attorney so that your agent knows exactly what you want, how to advocate for it, and what resources to use to make it happen.

Ask your attorney to insert language in the Health Care Power of Attorney that gives your health care agent the guidance needed to take actions consistent with your goals.

1. If you are hoping to access care in your own home, include directions for your agent so he or she can find, pay for, and manage your care without ending up as your unpaid caregiver.

2. Explain how the care you want will be paid for and where your agent can access those funds.

3. Explain your expectations for your health care agent to keep other family members informed and seek input before making a decision.

4. If you want your agent to work with outside professionals, such as geriatric care managers, include contact information and directions so your agent knows exactly what to do to find, pay for, and manage the help you need.

5. Include provisions for dispute resolution, including mandatory mediation if the disagreement cannot be resolved.

Living Wills

A Living Will details your preferences for medical intervention at the end of life, including artificial means of life support. If you're in this situation, it will be an emotional time for your children, and it's possible they won't agree on what to do. Being clear about your preferences will make things easier for everyone.

Ask your attorney to help you put together a Living Will that empowers your agent to make the decisions you prefer when you are unable to speak for yourself. Remember, the firmer you are about your dictates, the less flexibility the agent will have.

Most of us mean to say, "If there is no hope, pull the plug—but only when there's no hope." To that end, educate your agent, through language in the Living Will, that not only do you want there to be an inquiry, but in the end, the agent agrees with the medical determination that there is no hope before allowing the removal of life support.

1. If you want your agent to have the best and most objective information, consider inserting language that requires the

agent to consult with a geriatric care manager before making any decision about treatment.

2. Include language that requires agreement in the family about the decision to remove life support. Even if there is just one holdout, request a second opinion (see #3 below), which will buy more time to reach a family consensus, but state that the final decision is that of the agent, and should be beyond challenge.

3. Insert language that explains how decisions will be made if family members disagree about what should be done. Work with a geriatric care manager who will request a second (or additional) opinion from a doctor outside the hospital system where you are currently on life support.

Handling of Remains

I talked at length about this in Chapter 12. The handling of your remains is about more than choosing a method of disposition for your body after you die. It's about bringing closure to your life as quickly as possible with minimum drama. It's about creating a ritual that gives your family a dignified way to say goodbye to your last physical manifestation on this planet. If you want to avoid having your remains stuck in someone's garage, closet, or mantle because your kids couldn't agree on what to do with them, you must be absolutely clear about what your desires are.

Ask your attorney to include specific and detailed instructions about what should be done when you die.

1. Get clear about the type of funeral service you prefer, pre-plan the arrangements, and then insert the instructions (including contact details) in your legal documents.

2. Explain what your agent should do with your cremated remains. Be extremely specific.

Mental Health Advance Directives

A Mental Health Advance Directive describes what you want to happen if you are judged to be suffering from a mental disorder such as dementia or Alzheimer's disease that impairs your ability to make decisions for yourself or to communicate effectively.

As I explained in Chapter 12, people do not go from sane to insane overnight. It happens over time. During the twilight period, when a person has sufficient mental capacity to fool the world, but not the family, much mayhem can take place. Without a Mental Health Advance Directive, the only option available to your family will likely be a guardianship, which will take months to complete and destroy family harmony.

Ask your attorney to create a Mental Health Advance Directive as part of your estate plan.

1. Since many attorneys aren't familiar with this document, you may be told that you don't need it. Insist that your attorney create a Mental Health Advance Directive.

2. Cognitive decline in later life is the most common reason to create a Mental Health Advance Directive, but it's by no means the only one. Make sure that your attorney is aware of any mental health issues that may be part of your situation and ask that those be referenced in the language.

You Can Do This!

Creating a *LifePlan* empowers you to take control of your relationships with professionals and ask for exactly what you need. Much of what you'll be asking attorneys may be unfamiliar to them, so don't be surprised if you get some pushback. If you get more than a little, consider finding a different attorney. Visit the AgingOptions Resource Guide at https://agingoptions.com/ for a list of attorneys near you.

Managing Disputes

If you follow my guidance in the *LifePlanning* process to create your legal documents and then share them with your family, fiduciaries, and agents during a Family Meeting, there should be minimal disagreement when it's time for the fiduciaries to step into their roles. However, disagreements do happen, and when they do, here's what I suggest you do:

1. Include a provision in each document that names a neutral third party who will be consulted in the event of disputes. This could be anyone—an attorney, a relative, a professional mediator, or someone else who can be trusted to be objective. For matters related to the Health Care Power of Attorney, the Living Will, the Mental Health Advance Directive, or the Handling of Remains, a geriatric care manager can serve as a neutral third party who can help you reach a consensus.

2. Include a provision in each document that explains what will happen if the neutral third party is unable to resolve the dispute. I recommend that you include a provision for mandatory mediation. Litigation should be your last resort, because it tends to turn into a war that creates permanent damage.

Integrate Your Housing Plan

Choosing your Forever Home will be one of the most challenging parts of the *LifePlanning* process.

Step 1: Think Through Your Options

As I discussed in Chapter 10, your decisions about housing should start by understanding the options available, and then choosing the one that makes the most sense for you. You need to pick a path, either:

1. Live life in your own home, which makes you more dependent on your children, if you have them, and means they will likely inherit more when you die, or

2. Living in a retirement community so you won't be a burden, even though it means you will burn through your children's inheritance faster.

It comes down to deciding what's most important to you: leaving the biggest possible inheritance to your kids, or not being a burden.

Once you've made your housing decision, you're ready for the next step.

Step 2: Hold a Family Meeting

This is where you will discuss your goals for retirement, including your desire to avoid institutional care. Your ability to achieve this goal will be heavily dependent on your children's willingness to play an active role in your lives as you age. If you become physically or mentally compromised, your children will be the ones who make sure that you are not being taken advantage of or neglected at the hands of those who will be hired to care for your needs.

The Family Meeting will be revealing. During the conversation, you will learn much about your kids and whether the responsibilities of looking after you will fit into their lives. You'll discover whether they will be a good support system, and have more clarity about whether you want to place this level of responsibility on them. It's important that everyone is heard.

Step 3: Visit Continuing Care Retirement Communities (CCRCs)

It's a good idea to visit CCRCs in your area so you know what's out there. When you visit, don't limit your interactions to the person giving you the tour and the workers you encounter. After the tour has ended, ask to stroll around on your own so you can talk to more residents.

Ask residents questions about their experience living there:

1. What do you like about this community?
2. What do you dislike about this community?
3. If you had to do it all over again, would you choose to move here?

If you like what you see, your next step is to arrange for a weeklong trial stay in the community you like most so you can see what it would feel like to live there.

Step 4: Pick a Path

After the Family Meeting and CCRC visits, regroup and pick a path to take.

- Age in your home
- Move to a different, more age-appropriate home
- Move to a retirement community

Once you have chosen your path, there may be some follow-up work to do.

If you choose to age in your own home:

1. Find an occupational therapist and schedule a home safety evaluation so you know what hazards might exist in your home, and what changes, if any, might be needed to make the home safe for you as you grow older. If you find that your home is not age-friendly and you're not interested in making modifications, then work with a realtor to find a more suitable home.

2. Consider establishing a line of credit (possibly by taking out a reverse mortgage) so no payments will be due if the credit line is tapped. This will free up money for caregiving costs, making funds available for your children to use to pay for the care you need at home.

If you decide to move to a CCRC setting:

1. Contact the CCRC's sales office
2. Work with their housing specialist who will help negotiate a contract for you

You Can Do This!

Creating a *LifePlan* empowers you to take control of your housing and live exactly where you want.

Integrate Your Financial Plan

During the *LifePlanning* process, creating a financial plan typically happens after you have completed your plan for housing.

As you learned in Chapter 11, your financial plan will include things like detailed written instructions for your agents. This goes beyond the scope of service provided by some financial planners. That's why it's vital to give your financial planner clear guidance about what you expect. Whether you're already working with a financial planner or you're in the market for one, use this guide to make your preferences clear.

As stated earlier, your best bet is to work with a fee-only planner. If you need help finding one in your area, ask around.

Once you have a financial planner—ideally someone familiar with your current financial position—you will begin working on your Financial Dashboard.

Ask your financial planner the following questions:

- When should I retire? (If you are still working)

- How can I optimize my Social Security benefits? (If you have not started drawing Social Security benefits or are under 70)

- Should I convert my retirement accounts to Roth accounts?

- Should I purchase long-term care insurance? If the answer is yes, what percentage of my income or assets should I dedicate toward a long-term care insurance policy?

- How much money should I withdraw from savings to augment my Social Security and pension benefits so I can meet my monthly obligations without going broke, even if I live to be 105 years old?

- How can I gift money without running out?

- Is a reverse mortgage right for me?

- Are my retirement assets appropriately invested?

- What costs am I incurring in my investment portfolio, and can those costs be reduced?

Here's how to direct your financial planner to approach the creation of your Financial Dashboard.

Step One: Create the Financial Dashboard

This process involves several steps. Ask your financial planner to take these steps in order.

Establish Retirement Income Needs

Ask your financial planner to help you determine what level of income you will need to live comfortably.

- List your current "net" income amount, including all income sources.
- List each expense and its amount.
- Subtract all your expenses from your income.

The sum will need to be adjusted to account for expenses that are likely to increase, decrease, or go away over time. You will also need to adjust for inflation, along with the reality that your expenses will probably increase faster than your income.

Identify Income Sources

Ask your financial planner to determine the amount of liquid, invested assets required to make up the difference between your income needs and your Social Security and pension benefits. Your advisor will then test to see if the income generated by those invested assets is enough to bridge the gap, even if you live to be 105.

Your income sources in retirement will likely be one or more of the following:

1. Social Security
2. Pensions
3. Withdrawals from your investments

Determine a Safe Withdrawal Amount

Ask your financial planner to determine how much you can withdraw from your invested assets each year, while living the kind of life you want until you are age 105, without running out of money.

PRO TIP: Make it a point to repeat this exercise every two or three years with your financial planner.

Determine a Safe Gifting Amount

Work with your financial planner to determine how much of your nest egg you can withdraw now to give to your children or donate to your favorite charity, so you can witness them benefitting from your generosity while you are still alive.

Plan to Maximize Social Security Benefits

If you're counting on Social Security benefits for part of your income, ask your financial planner to help you determine the right time to start drawing those benefits. You might delay the benefits until you turn 70, or look for spousal benefits, or both.

If you delay taking your Social Security benefits, you may have to work longer or make withdrawals from your retirement or investment accounts. Withdrawing funds from those accounts will deplete your investments and reduce their future income-generating potential. Work with your financial planner to develop a plan that works for you. Remember, you want to see your investments last at least to age 105.

Step Two: Protect Assets from Long-Term Care Costs

Now, it's time to think about protecting your assets from long-term care costs. There are several ways to do this, and you'll want to work with your financial planner to choose the approach that's right for you.

Consider a Long-Term Care Insurance Policy

Work with your financial planner to determine whether you will be able to afford the purchase of either a traditional policy or an asset-based policy. Below is a summary of each type of policy and an overview of what your financial planner should consider during the analysis.

Option 1: Traditional Policy

When you're making a buying decision on a long-term care insurance policy, the question isn't whether you can afford the premiums today. The question is whether you'll be able to afford the premiums ten or fifteen years from now.

To make that assessment, you need to know what a good policy costs and whether your projected income is enough to cover it. A good policy is one that pays at least $11,000[110] in monthly benefits for at least five years in any setting of your choosing with an elimination period of six months or one year. It will have an inflation rider of five percent or more and include provisions to compensate family members.

This is where a financial planner can guide you. If you needed long-term care today, how much of the income would be available to cover the costs? Buy insurance that will cover whatever costs your income won't.

Option 2: Asset-based Policy

In this type of long-term care insurance, you give the insurance company a lump sum of money to be placed in a life insurance policy. The insurance amount should be no less than two times the amount of the original investment (ideally, it should be three to five times the original investment). Purchasing this type of policy will most likely mean taking money from your investable pool of funds.

Is this a good idea? It depends on whether you will need that pool of invested funds to be able to meet your monthly income needs later on.

If you can do without that amount, then it might be worth your time to invest in an asset-based long-term care insurance policy. If not, you may want to skip the long-term care insurance and depend on VA and/or Medicaid benefits.

Your Financial Planner's Role

Ask your financial planner to perform the following analyses to help you think through your options:

1. Ask your advisor to calculate how much disposable income you will have in retirement to cover premiums for a traditional long-term care insurance policy. Once you have that number, you can take it to an insurance agent and request a long-term care insurance quote.

2. Ask your advisor to tell you how much money you can free up to purchase an asset-based long-term care policy, and then go to an insurance agent and request a quote for that amount.

3. Regardless of the type of policy you choose, be aware of the possibility of a conflict of interest of your insurance agent earning a commission on the sale of a policy. Though it may not be a deal breaker, the conflict of interest is something you should be aware of.

In any case, if you go to an insurance agent with the open-ended question, "Which policy should I buy?" you risk being sold a policy that may not fit in your overall retirement plan. Arm yourself with the questions ahead of time so you can make sure your own interests are served.

Consider Converting Traditional Retirement Accounts to Roth Accounts

This is an important topic to raise with your financial planner. There are a variety of reasons to convert a traditional retirement account to a Roth account. We covered this in Chapter 11. Here's a recap of the most common:

1. Tax cost to your children
2. Gifts for estate tax reasons
3. Tax-free income
4. Long-term care costs

If you decide to forego long-term care insurance, Medicaid will be the most likely funding source for long-term care. Qualifying for Medicaid in the future requires planning today in order to navigate the five-year look-back period and tax consequences. Some of that planning, such as establishing a Safe Harbor Trust, will require legal work.

For the Safe Harbor Trust to work effectively, you will want to minimize the tax costs involved in the planning process. Traditional retirement assets can present an obstacle to Safe Harbor Trust planning, so you may want to convert those retirement assets to Roth accounts. Each conversion will create a tax bill. Ask your financial planner to assist you with this process. Make sure you can cover the tax bill from your income, not from the principal. Make sure that your advisor adjusts your Financial Dashboard to reflect any planned conversions. He or she will need to add conversion tax costs to income needs during the time period you plan to convert traditional accounts to Roth accounts.

Assess True Cost and True Risk

Finally, you will want to know the true cost of investing with your current financial planner. Will you pay a professional $10,000 every year to manage your investments? You are if you have a one percent cost on a $1 million portfolio.

This includes the fees the advisor charges along with the fees imposed by each investment product. Good financial advice is never free. The goal is to make sure you're not paying more than you should. What you want to do is to know that you are not paying above the average costs.

Assess Your Risk/Return Balance

You also want to understand the financial risk you are taking. In retirement, you want to minimize your risk, but not eliminate it completely. Taking no risk will mean placing assets in savings or money market accounts, which means you will lose money to inflation. Your income needs may, in part, dictate the amount of risk you have to take. Only take the level of risk you can tolerate.

Step 3: Get the Rest of Your Affairs in Order

Prepay Your Final Expenses

Find a local provider of your choosing and take care of this expense now.

Identify Professionals to Work with Your Agents

You are assembling the team that your agents will work with if something happens to you. You may already have some of these professional relationships in place. If not, start identifying providers today and list them in the appropriate legal documents.

Accounting

Locate an accountant who your agents can work with on financial matters like tax preparation. Continuity of service is an important consideration, so make sure that you will be able to continue receiving services should the accountant retire, become disabled, or pass away. Working with an accounting firm rather than a sole practitioner might be your best bet. Find a firm near you at https://cpadirectory.com/.

If you are choosing to allow your agents to file your taxes, you will want to sit with them and do the taxes together first to make sure that they understand your filing system and where to find the information they will need to complete the tax returns.

Bookkeeping

Given that your agents will have to pay your bills when you cannot do that task yourself, you might want to locate a bookkeeper to handle bill-paying responsibilities. Your chosen accountant could do this work if they offer bookkeeping services. Other options include:

- Hiring a professional money manager. Find one at https://secure.aadmm.com/find-a-dmm/.

- Hiring a concierge bill management service. Check out https://silverbills.com/.

If you are choosing to allow your agents to pay your bills, you will want to sit with them and pay bills for at least three to four months in the beginning, and then at least annually after that to make sure that they understand your filing system and where to find the necessary information. They might also be able to give you a hand in setting up an electronic system like Quicken (https://www.quicken.com/), QuickBooks (https://quickbooks.intuit.com/), or Mint (https://mint.intuit.com/) to make the process easier.

Financial Planner

If you don't already have a financial planner, you will want to identify one for your agent to work with. This website (http://www.letsmakeaplan.org/) has a Find a CFP Planner tool for names to start with. We suggest limiting your search to "fee-only" planners. Fee-only planners provide guidance without selling products, which means they will likely be a bit more objective than providers who earn commission from the products you buy, while offering free financial advice along the way.

Property Manager/Handyman

If you become incapacitated, your agents will need to maintain your home and any other properties you own, including rentals. If something needs repairs, your agents will find themselves spending time and energy to figure out who to turn to. Make this task easier for them by adding a local property management company to your team. Start your search here: https://www.narpm.org/find/property-managers.

Geriatric Care Manager

On the health care side, your Powers of Attorney most likely require your agents to work with a geriatric care management company. This will give your agents the guidance they need to keep you out of institutional care. It will also prevent them from being bogged down with the many tasks that will be required to organize your care. If you haven't already done so, start evaluating companies to see which one you would like to name in your Health Care Power of Attorney. Find a list of certified geriatric care managers at AgingLifeCare.org.

Look for a company that offers the following:

- 24-hour availability for emergency calls
- The ability to help your family select an independent caregiver rather than a caregiving agency, unless you can get the agency to bill by the job, not by the hour
- A demonstrated commitment to helping people find a way to access care at home
- No conflicts of interest in allied services they refer or offer
- A clear explanation of how they charge for their services (you should not have to pay anything at this time)

Account Credentials

Finally, you will want to provide a list of login credentials, passwords, and account information that your agents can use to manage your business electronically. Be careful here. In many cases, it is illegal for one to impersonate a real user, meaning that others should not log into your account using your ID and conduct business as if they were you. However, it's virtually impossible for your agents to manage your affairs without your credentials. For you to give them parallel authority on accounts is difficult at best and impossible in many instances. So, proceed with a healthy dose of caution. Make sure that your agents are also aware that they cannot access your accounts and impersonate you.

Once you have accomplished the above, you will have completed your financial portion of the *LifePlan*.

You Can Do This!

Creating a *LifePlan* empowers you to take control of your relationships with professionals and ask for exactly what you need. Some of the things you're asking your financial planner to do for you may be unfamiliar, so don't be surprised if you get some pushback. If you get more than a little pushback, you may want to consider finding a different financial planner.

Integrate Your Health Plan

After the financial aspects of the *LifePlanning* process have been addressed, it's time to focus on the health pillar.

Here's how to begin:

Eat Right

Consulting with a nutritionist to learn how you may be able to improve your eating habits is an important first step toward better health.

1. Visit your insurance company's website to locate a few nutritionists that accept your insurance plan.
2. Call to schedule an appointment.
3. Keep the appointment and follow the nutritionist's recommendations.

Exercise

Regular physical activity is essential if you want to create a nursing home-free future.

1. Work up to walking as many as 10,000 steps a day if you are sedentary.
2. Join a gym or work with a personal trainer.
3. Invest in a wearable fitness tracker such as a FitBit or an Apple Watch to track your activity.
4. If movement is difficult, consider using a sauna.

Socialize

Purposeful interactions will keep your mind sharp and help to prevent the most common reasons for institutionalized care: dementia and Alzheimer's disease.

1. Engage in a hobby that involves contact with others.
2. Join a club or social group.
3. Volunteer for service in a charitable or religious organization.

Find a Geriatric Care Physician Covered by Insurance

This will likely take some time. Here are a few tips on how to approach the search:

1. Create your provider list. Visit Healthgrades.com or Vitals. com and search the terms "geriatric clinics," "geriatricians," and "board-certified geriatric physicians." Create a list of all the results, including contact information.

2. Visit the geriatric clinics on your list to see if they will work for you. The ideal geriatric clinic will accept your insurance and coordinate their work with specialists and hospitals in your insurance network. If working with a geriatric clinic isn't possible or appealing, your next step is to evaluate geriatricians. Be careful here. Many of the names on your list will NOT be board-certified physicians; they will be internists and family practitioners who offer geriatric care services. Narrow your list to board-certified geriatricians, then make an appointment to visit their offices. You don't have to see a physician at this meeting; your goal is to visit the clinic, meet the office manager, see if they're accepting new patients, and then become a new patient if the office is right for you.

NOTE: If you go to your regular physician and ask whether you need to switch to a geriatrician, be prepared to hear this: "You don't need to switch. I see a lot of patients over age 70, and feel I have a good sense of geriatric medicine." Most people would simply accept this advice from their trusted doctor. However, I advise against it. There may be some internists or family practitioners who are familiar with geriatrics, but they are not specialists. As you read earlier, you wouldn't take your child to a family practice doctor if a pediatrician was available. The same applies to the other end of the age spectrum. Insist on a geriatrician.

Consider a Preventative Care Clinic

After you have chosen a geriatrician to serve as your primary care physician, I suggest working with a preventative care clinic. Make an appointment to see a physician, have them do a full blood panel, have the physician discuss the findings, and then take the findings to your regular physician to see what aspects of the work your insurance-covered physician might be able to complete. This will give you important insight into what actions you can take now to protect your good health.

Review Your Insurance

It's a good idea to review your current coverage on a regular basis. An insurance review will help you avoid paying more than necessary for coverage. It will also show you whether your coverage gives you access to the right professionals.

What to Look For in an Insurance Plan

As you've seen, nearly all insurance companies in America do a good job of allowing you access to world-class acute care. However, our system isn't so good at preventative care. I discuss the specific benefits you should look for in a health plan in Chapter 9. Here's the summary:

- Access to board-certified geriatric physicians or a similar alternative
- Access to a wide range of preventative care benefits, including gym memberships, nutritionists, and naturopaths
- The ability to see any doctor of your choice without having to get a primary care physician's referral
- A plan with no deductible (or a very small one) and no co-payments
- Access to a university-connected hospital

- No issue about in-network or out-of-network care; you should be covered nationwide the same as where you live

Tips for Choosing a Health Plan (Medicaid Advantage or Traditional Medicare/Medigap)

In Chapter 9, I walked you through your options and offered my recommendations. Here's the overview:

- You have two options: Traditional Medicare with a Medigap policy or a Medicare Advantage Plan

- Traditional Medicare is the government-sponsored program

- Medicare Advantage Plans are offered by private insurance companies

- Each type has its advantages and disadvantages; ask an insurance agent to help you evaluate your options

You Can Do This!

Creating a *LifePlan* empowers you to take control of your health so you can delay or avoid the need for long-term care.

CHAPTER 15

LIFEPLANNING SUCCESS

Foundational Insight

Traditional retirement planning gives you a 70 percent chance of going broke, becoming a burden, and ending up in institutional care.

LifePlanning gives you a better chance of living the kind of life you want—until the end.

Measuring the Success of *LifePlanning*

Since the mid-2000s, I have created *LifePlans* for more than 7,000 individuals and couples. After about a decade of working with clients, I started to get curious about the results.

In 2018, my team started measuring the success of *LifePlanning*. I wanted to know how many clients had managed to avoid the nursing home because of the work they'd done with us.

We had plenty of anecdotal evidence in the form of thank-you notes, five-star Google reviews, and glowing testimonials. But I wanted quantitative data, so we decided to survey the families of 200 clients who had created *LifePlans*. The survey asked three questions:

1. Where did the client die?

2. Did the family feel the work we had done on behalf of the client was of value to them?

3. Did the family access VA or Medicaid benefits and/or a long-term care insurance policy using our help?

More than 50 percent of those surveyed responded. The results were interesting. Just under 30 percent of the people responding reported that their elderly loved one achieved exactly what they were hoping for: they died at home. The families were grateful because they knew exactly what to do to make that happen. They knew to call a geriatric care manager. They knew how to advocate to bring their elderly loved one home. And in most cases, they knew where the money was going to come from to pay for care.

That was the good news.

The bad news was that the rest of those surveyed, just over 70 percent of the people, did not die at home. The family didn't feel well prepared, and money issues were not addressed.

How could that be? As I began looking back at the records from those clients, one important theme emerged. Nearly all of the clients who had died at home had held a facilitated Family Meeting. At this meeting, the parents talked to their children about their *LifePlan*. The parents were humble enough to say, "I will grow old, and this doesn't only involve me. It will impact all of you." They then shared their plans and preferences. Instead of making pronouncements, they listened to everyone's feedback, and then adjusted their plans based on that feedback. This underscores the importance of family involvement in the ways I've described throughout this book.

In 2019, my company partnered with Dr. Carol Redfield at Seattle Pacific University to conduct a study of families who hadn't responded to our initial survey. Our sample was small—just 14 clients—but those results confirmed our earlier findings. When a client created a *LifePlan* for retirement and held a Family Meeting, that client was able to die without being forced into institutional care, without losing assets to uncovered care costs, and without burdening family members.

They Did It

In 2021, a woman came to me for a *LifePlan*. Judith was in her 80s and lived in Seattle in an older home. Her daughter, Rosalind, was concerned that Judith's home was no longer safe. Judith was digging in her heels, determined to stay put.

"We need to meet so we can talk about where you're going to live," I told Judith during one of our phone calls. "Bring your daughter. If you really want to live out your life at home, we have to pull everything together."

On meeting day, Judith and Rosalind sat across the table from me.

"Rosalind, where do you live?" I asked the daughter.

"Maple Valley," she replied. Maple Valley was about a 40-minute drive from Seattle. It often takes much longer.

"How often do you go see your mom?" I asked.

Rosalind looked uncomfortable. "Well, I try and see her every week at the very least," she said.

"If your mom falls ill, you know you'll have to go there every day, not every week," I said. "You can hire people to provide care, but someone's got to be there to make sure that the hired hands do their jobs and don't take advantage of her."

"I get it," Rosalind said. "I'll do what I can."

I turned to Judith. "Mom, if you're serious about not burdening your daughter, who lives 27 miles away from you, either move in with her or buy a house close to her."

As the meeting ended, Judith and Rosalind promised to think about what I said.

Four months later, Rosalind called me. "Rajiv, you will never guess what happened," she said, the excitement evident in her voice. "Our next-door neighbor's house just went up for sale and I'm buying it for Mom!"

I knew right then that Judith had the family involvement it would take to die at home in her own bed.

What does it take to make this happen? It has nothing to do with legal planning. It has nothing to do with financial planning. It has everything to do with opening your eyes to the gaps in the plan, and then deciding to bridge them with meaningful action.

I have hundreds of stories of clients who have decided to amend their original retirement housing plans after creating a *LifePlan* and learning about the concept of a Forever Home. I've had clients who originally moved to Florida move again to other parts of the country so they could be in a Forever Home close to their children. Other couples moved to Florida because that's where their children were. There's another case that I'm working on right now where the daughter has been living with Dad for the last two years. Dad is healthy now, but the time will come when he won't be. This daughter has a care management service lined up so that when Dad falls ill, she will supervise the people providing his hands-on care instead of being recruited into service as his unpaid caregiver. More than a few clients, dead set against retirement communities, chose private residences of some kind for their Forever Homes, only to change their minds and move to a Continuing Care Retirement Community (CCRC).

Aging at home without going broke and without being a burden on your family is possible for you. It is done routinely. I can promise you that if you follow my advice, you will be able to live out your life in your own home, if that is what you want, so long as you follow my plan to the tee.

My next example of *LifePlanning* success is the story of Louise Smith. Louise's story is featured in *The Path to Happily Ever After,* a program that made its debut on public television stations across America in early 2023.

Louise called my office and told me that she listened to me on the radio every week. "I want to do my planning with you, but you'll have to come to my home," she said. I told her that house calls were no problem, so we set an appointment.

She lived in a nice home on Mercer Island, in the community where Bill Gates lives. Louise was a widow with no children, and no family in the picture. She had a $3 million estate.

"I like what you say on the radio," she told me. "I want you to be my agent."

I had been in law practice for about eight years by then, and I had the care management services in place.

"Sure, I'll do it, but we have to talk about housing," I said. "If I get a call in the middle of the night, you're too far away. It's about an hour from my house to Mercer Island on a good day. If you want me to be your agent, you need to be in a place where they have several levels of care."

I helped Louise find housing in a Continuing Care Retirement Community. She didn't like the first one she chose, so I helped her find another one. A few years later, her health started getting worse. If she didn't have full-time care in her apartment, she would end up in the nursing home wing of her retirement community. That's not what she wanted, so I arranged for caregivers to provide 24/7 care in her home at about half of what the same care would have cost in a nursing home. I stopped in about once a month to make sure things were going okay.

One day, as I was driving home after doing my radio show, I realized that it had been a while since I had looked in on Louise. Something told me I needed to see her, so I drove to her apartment. The caregiver let me in. "She's about to pass," the caregiver whispered.

After making sure Louise was comfortable, I sat on the edge of her bed. "It's okay, Louise," I said, gently squeezing her hand. "It's okay to go, honey. It's time for you to be with your mom and dad again. It's time for you to see your husband again. I know you love them."

She gave me a feeble smile. I went to get some crushed ice, then put a few pieces in her mouth.

After about 90 minutes, I had to leave. As I got into my vehicle, my phone rang. It was the caregiver telling me that Louise had died. She died at home, just like she wanted to.

CHAPTER 16

CREATING YOUR LIFEPLAN

LifePlanning Resources

I f you're interested in creating a *LifePlan*, you can do it on your own using the guidance in this book. The following resources, all available at https://agingoptions.com/, can make the journey even easier.

Buy *LifePlanning* workbooks.

Join the Portal and get access to the online retirement planning course via the AgingOptions Academy.

Enroll in a live online *LifePlanning* workshop.

Use the AgingOptions Resource Guide to find professionals to help implement your *LifePlan*.

Schedule a Peace of Mind Consultation with a *LifePlanner* to check over your self-created *LifePlan*.

Work with a *LifePlanner* who coaches you through the planning process.

Learn more at https://agingoptions.com/.

Storing, Managing, and Sharing Your LifePlan

There are many services that allow you to upload and store your legal documents in a secure digital vault, such as LegalVault and Trustworthy. However, after years of working with clients and helping them develop *LifePlans*, I realized that those services were missing something. They didn't make the process into a family affair.

So, I decided to invent a system that did.

Once you have created your *LifePlan* and held your Family Meeting, it is vital that your fiduciaries and agents have access to your plan and all your legal documents. To make this easy for you, I have created an online system called the *LifePlan* Organizer.

Here's what the *LifePlan* Organizer can do:

- **Store every document related to your retirement plan in the *LifePlan* Organizer's secure digital archive.** Upload everything—Wills, Trusts, Powers of Attorney, Living Wills, Deeds, and much more to eliminate paper clutter and keep everything in one place, accessible 24/7.

- **Document and store detailed instructions for your agents in the event of a health emergency.** This includes the names and contact information of the professionals who will assist your agents when the time comes. This increases the odds that your agents will know what to do to bring you back home after a health crisis, and how to manage your life in the way you prefer during an extended period of incapacity.

- **Make it easy for your agents to manage your life during any period of incapacity.** The *LifePlan* Organizer simplifies the management of any situation your agents might face by allowing them exclusive access to the documents and directions you choose. As a health crisis unfolds, your agents log into the *LifePlan* Organizer, which provides step-by-step guidance that will enable them to help you avoid the nursing home, avoid going broke, and avoid being a burden. Agents can view documents, read instructions, notify other agents and family members about changes in your condition, and contact the professionals you have chosen to assist when the time comes—all from within the *LifePlan* Organizer.

Learn more about the *LifePlan* Organizer and other *LifePlanning* resources at https://agingoptions.com/.

If You're Concerned

I'm often approached by people who are worried about elderly loved ones—usually their parents—who have prepared for retirement in the usual way but have not shared their plans with the family.

"What should I do?" one woman asked me after attending one of my workshops, her concern clearly evident. "My parents are in their 80s and still relatively healthy, but my sisters and I have no idea what plans they've made, where any of their documents or passwords are, or even what they want," she said. "Whenever I try to bring up the subject, they tell me to mind my own business. I'm worried because if something happens to them, it will be a disaster."

Unfortunately, this situation is far more common than you might think. If the people you care about (most often parents) won't talk about their plans, and you will be the one left to pick up the pieces after a health crisis, there are some things you can do to prepare.

1. Identify geriatric care managers who serve your parents' locale. Meet with a few and choose one you like. Tell the

geriatric care manager about your situation and ask him or her to be available to help in a health crisis.

2. If your parents haven't drafted Power of Attorney documents and they still have the mental capacity to do so, offer to help them work with an attorney to draft those documents, plus any others they may need. If you are a named agent, ask them questions that will help you understand their preferences and directions.

3. Discreetly inquire about what resources might be available to pay for long-term care if they need it.

It won't be easy. Your parents may refuse to discuss it. If that's the case, locating a geriatric care manager may be all you're able to accomplish, but you'll have the help you need during the health crisis that is coming.

CHAPTER 17

AFTERWORD

As you've seen, I've been with families in key moments of stress, confusion, grief, and relief. It's part of the job when you're an elder law attorney.

These experiences often show up in my dreams. Some dreams are simple replays of meetings and conversations. Others are like scenes from a Tim Burton movie. Holding a Family Meeting in a treehouse. Signing documents in a submarine. Medicaid planning for a family of newts. I've seen it all in my dreams. I wake in the morning with fragments in my head, the details just out of reach.

Not long ago, I started having a recurring dream about a couple whose identities I couldn't see. They were in their late 50s and they came to my office for a consultation. They wanted to make sure they didn't end up in a nursing home, and they had heard I could help them do that. As I helped them create their *LifePlan*, we met several times. Each dream captured disconnected bits of those meetings.

When it was time for the Family Meeting, we held it in my office. The couple walked into the room, and their five daughters filed in behind them. I couldn't see faces, but I noticed that the youngest daughter, a girl who appeared to be in her later teens, looked just like my daughter, Abby.

And then it hit me. The youngest daughter was my wife, Jamie, as a teenager. I looked at my documents, and the date was 1982. My clients were Bill and Vivian Wallace, and this was their Family Meeting—conducted by the 2022 version of me in a dream-induced miracle of time travel.

This was the Bill Wallace I never got to meet. He was handsome and magnetic, a larger-than-life man with a crooked smile. He was smart and witty, and he adored his wife and daughters. You could see it in his eyes.

I had spent my entire life trying to help people avoid Bill's fate, yet I hadn't been able to save Bill.

Now, here we were.

The rest of this Family Meeting disappeared into a dreamlike haze, but I remember how it ended. Everyone left the room, but Bill hung back. "You did it, kid," he said as he reached out to shake my hand. Bill was a man of few words, but I knew what he meant. He was grateful. The look in his eyes said it all.

A portrait of Bill and Vivian Wallace taken in 1944.

Vivian Wallace holding her firstborn daughter, Pam.
This shot was taken in Alaska in 1944.

In the 1940s, Bill Wallace worked the fishing boats in Alaska.
In this photo, taken in Petersburg, Alaska, you can get
a glimpse of the vibrant person Bill was.

Bill, Vivian, and Jamie Wallace pause for a photo-op with their dogs.
A big dog lover, Bill bred Brittany Spaniels. In this shot,
he's holding Buck, his main pup, while Jamie holds
Beau, the family poodle.

Nani (grandma) Vivian in one of her favorite places: relaxing on the couch with two napping children on her lap. This photo was taken when Vivian was living with Rajiv and Jamie.

Rajiv often says that "aging is a family affair." Back in the day, Rajiv's weekly radio show was often a family affair, too. Here's a shot of Rajiv's son, Sam, sitting in on an early AgingOptions radio broadcast that Rajiv did from home in 2009.

Bill and Vivian Wallace in the 1970s.

Rajiv and Jamie pose for a photo with Rajiv's parents,
Dr. B. B. and Sharda Nagaich.

Vivian often visited Bill in the nursing home with baby Abby and
Sid in tow. When Bill lived in the nursing home, Vivian, Rajiv,
Jamie, the kids, and the entire Wallace family visited regularly
to shower him with love.

SELECTED BIBLIOGRAPHY

Banerjee, Sudipto. "Utilization Patterns and Out-of-Pocket Expenses for Different Health Care Services Among American Retirees." *EBRI Issue Brief*, no. 411 (February 2015): 4–20. https://papers.ssrn.com/sol3/papers.cfm?abstract_id=2570582.

Bodenheimer, Thomas. "Primary Care: Will it Survive?" *New England Journal of Medicine* 355, no. 9 (August 2006): 861–864. https://www.nejm.org/doi/full/10.1056/nejmp068155.

Boult, Chad, Lisa B. Boult, Lynne Morishita, Bryan Dowd, Robert L. Kane, and Cristina Urdangarin. "A Randomized Clinical Trial of Outpatient Geriatric Evaluation and Management." *Journal of the American Geriatrics Society* 49, no. 4 (April 2001): 351–359. https://doi.org/10.1046/j.1532-5415.2001.49076.x.

Bredesen, Dale E. "Reversal of cognitive decline: A novel therapeutic program." *AGING* 6, no. 9 (September 2014): 707–717. https://www.aging-us.com/article/100690/pdf.

Brickell, Kiri L., James B. Leverenz, Ellen J. Steinbart, Malia Rumbaugh, Gerard D. Schellenberg, David Nochlin, Thomas H. Lampe, Ida E. Holm, Vivianna Van Deerlin, Wuxing Yuan, Thomas D. Bird. "Clinopathological concordance and discordance in three monozygotic twin pairs with familial Alzheimer's disease." *Journal of Neurology, Neurosurgery & Psychiatry* 78, no. 10 (October 2007): 1050–1055. https://jnnp.bmj.com/content/78/10/1050.long.

Clark, Philip G., Bryan J. Blissmer, Geoffrey W. Greene, Faith D. Lees, Deborah A. Riebe, Karen E. Stamm. "Maintaining exercise and healthful eating in older adults: The SENIOR project II: Study design and methodology." *Contemporary Clinical Trials* 32, no. 1 (January 2011): 129–139. https://doi.org/10.1016/j.cct.2010.10.002.

Campbell, Jean Y., Samuel C Durso, Lynsey E. Brandt, Thomas E. Finucane, and Peter M. Abadir. "The Unknown Profession: A Geriatrician." *Journal of the American Geriatrics Society* 61, no. 3 (March 2013): 447–449. https://doi.org/10.1111/jgs.12115.

Dunlop, Dorothy, Jing Song, Emily K. Arntson, Pamela A. Semanik, Jungwha Lee, Rowland W. Chang and Jennifer Hootman. "Sedentary Time in US Older Adults Associated with Disability in Activities of Daily Living Independent of Physical Activity." *Journal of Physical Activity and Health* 12, no. 1 (January 2015), 93–101. https://doi.org/10.1123/jpah.2013-0311.

Fleming, Kevin C., Jonathan M. Evans, and Darryl S. Chutka. "A Cultural and Economic History of Aging in America." *Mayo Clinic Proceedings* 78, no. 7 (August 2003): 914–921. https://www.researchgate.net/publication/10679992_A_Cultural_and_Economic_History_of_Old_Age_in_America.

Gawande, Atul. *Being Mortal*. New York: Metropolitan Books, 2014.

Hing, Esther, Donald K. Cherry, and David A. Woodwell. "National Ambulatory Medical Care Survey: 2003 Summary." *Advance Data from Vital and Health Statistics*, no. 365 (October 2005): 1–48. https://www.cdc.gov/nchs/data/ad/ad365.pdf.

Hollis, Jack, Christina M. Gullion, Victor J. Stevens, Phillip J. Brantley, Lawrence J. Appel, Jamy D. Ard, Catherine M. Champagne, Arlene Dalcin, Thomas P. Erlinger, Kristine Funk, Daniel Laferriere, Pao-Hwa Lin, Catherine M. Loria, Carmen Samuel-Hodge, William M.

Vollmer, Laura P. Svetkey. "Weight Loss During the Intensive Intervention Phase of the Weight-Loss Maintenance Trial." *American Journal of Preventive Medicine* 35, no. 2 (August 2008): 118–126. https://doi.org/10.1016/j.amepre.2008.04.013.

Jack, Clifford R., Jr., Terry M. Therneau, Stephen D. Weigand, Heather J. Wiste, David S. Knopman, Prashanthi Vemuri, Val J. Lowe, Michelle M. Mielke, Rosebud O. Roberts, Mary M. Machulda, Jonathan Graff-Radford, David T. Jones, Christopher G. Schwarz, Jeffrey L. Gunter, Matthew L. Senjem, Walter A. Rocca, Ronald C. Petersen. "Prevalence of Biologically vs Clinically Defined Alzheimer Spectrum Entities Using the National Institute on Aging-Alzheimer's Association Research Framework." *JAMA Neurology* 76, no. 10 (October 2019): 1174–1183. https://jamanetwork.com/journals/jamaneurology/fullarticle/2737282.

Jaul, Efraim and Jeremy Barron. "Age-Related Diseases and Clinical and Public Health Implications for the 85 and Over Population." *Frontiers in Public Health*, no. 5 (2017): 335. https://www.ncbi.nlm.nih.gov/pmc/articles/PMC5732407/pdf/fpubh-05-00335.pdf.

Johnson, Richard W. "What is the Lifetime Risk of Needing and Receiving Long-Term Services and Supports?" *ASPE Research Brief* (April 2019). https://aspe.hhs.gov/reports/what-lifetime-risk-needing-receiving-long-term-services-supports-0.

Johnson, Richard W., Desmond Toohey, and Joshua M. Wiener. *Meeting the Long-Term Care Needs of Baby Boomers: How Changing Families Will Affect Paid Helpers and Institutions.* The Retirement Project Discussion Paper Series, vol. 7, no. 14. Washington, DC: The Urban Institute, 2007.

Lester, Paula E., T.S. Dharmarajan, and Eleanor Weinstein. "The Looming Geriatrician Shortage: Ramifications and Solutions." *Journal of Aging and Health* 32, no. 9 (2020): 1052–1062. https://doi.org/10.1177%2F0898264319879325.

Qato, Danya M. and Amal N. Trivedi. "Receipt of High Risk Medications among Elderly Enrollees in Medicare Advantage Plans." *Journal of General Internal Medicine* 28, no. 4 (April 2013): 546–553. https://www.ncbi.nlm.nih.gov/pmc/articles/PMC3599014/pdf/11606_2012_Article_2244.pdf.

Rovner, Joshua and Austin Long. "Theories of Failure and Intelligence Reform: Evaluating the 9/11 Commission Report." *Breakthroughs* 14, no. 1 (Spring 2005): 10–21.

Scheckler, Samara, Jennifer Molinsky, and Whitney Airgood-Obrycki. *How Well Does the Housing Stock Meet Accessibility Needs? An Analysis of the 2019 American Housing Survey.* [Cambridge, MA]: Joint Center for Housing Studies of Harvard University, 2022. https://www.jchs.harvard.edu/sites/default/files/research/files/harvard_jchs_housing_stock_accessibility_scheckler_2022_0.pdf.

Snowden, David A. "Healthy Aging and Dementia: Findings from the Nun Study." *Annals of Internal Medicine* 139, no. 5, part 2 (September 2003): 450–454. https://doi.org/10.7326/0003-4819-139-5_Part_2-200309021-00014.

Stamatkis, Emmanuel, Joanne Gale, Adrian Bauman, Ulf Ekelund, Mark Hamer and Ding. "Sitting Time, Physical Activity, and Risk of Mortality in Adults." *Journal of the American College of Cardiology* 73, no. 16 (April 2019): 2062–2072. https://doi.org/10.1016/j.jacc.2019.02.031.

Stephenson, Aoife, Suzanne M. McDonough, Marie H. Murphy, Chris D. Nugent and Jacqueline L. Mair. "Using computer, mobile and wearable technology enhanced interventions to reduce sedentary behavior: a systematic review and meta-analysis." *International Journal of Behavioral Nutrition and Physical Activity*, no. 14 (2017): 105. https://doi.org/10.1186%2Fs12966-017-0561-4.

Sullivan, Amy D., Katrina Hedberg, and David Hopkins. "Legalized Physician-Assisted Suicide in Oregon, 1998–2000." *New England Journal of Medicine* 344, no. 8 (February 22, 2001): 605–607. https://www.nejm.org/doi/full/10.1056/NEJM200102223440811.

ABOUT THE AUTHOR

Rajiv Nagaich, J.D. L.L.M.

Rajiv Nagaich is an elder law attorney and a nationally known retirement planning visionary who has electrified the nation with his new approach to retirement planning—called *LifePlanning*. Rajiv is one of the country's most influential retirement planning thought leaders. He is the host of two public television specials (*Master Your Future and The Path to Happily Ever After*) and the *AgingOptions Radio Show*, which has been dispensing retirement planning advice to people in the Seattle area for more than twenty years.

Rajiv is an unlikely hero. Inspired by his father-in-law's senseless suffering nearly two decades ago, he became a fearless lone wolf on a mission to fix what's wrong with retirement planning in America. Taking on a fractured system that has 70 percent of us sleepwalking into our worst nightmares about old age, Rajiv found a way to beat that system. Now, he's telling the world.

Nationally recognized by his peers for his cutting-edge work with retirees and his contributions to the practice of Elder Law, Rajiv has received wide praise for his efforts. He was inducted as Fellow by the National Academy of Elder Law Attorneys (NAELA) in 2014. He is also a three-time winner of the NAELA Pacesetter Award, and a commissioner at the Law and Aging Commission at the American Bar Association.

Rajiv is founding partner of the Life Point Law firm in the Seattle area and Chief Executive Officer of AgingOptions. He holds a Masters in Tax Law (L.L.M.) from the University of Washington and J.D. from Seattle University School of Law.

LEARN MORE

Get started on your *LifePlan* for retirement with these resources:

- Buy the Master Your Future *LifePlanning* Workbook at https://booksale.agingoptions.com/work-book.

- Access free resources, take online courses, register for live workshops, watch videos, buy DVDs, locate professionals, get help from a *LifePlanner,* and more at https://agingoptions.com.

- Watch *The Path to Happily Ever After,* Rajiv Nagaich's latest public television special. Learn more at https://agingoptions.com.

- Buy additional copies of *Your Retirement: Dream or Disaster?* at Amazon.com. Visit https://yourretirementdreamordisaster.com/ for more information.

Follow Rajiv Nagaich and AgingOptions on Social Media

Rajiv Nagaich
Facebook: https://www.facebook.com/TheRajivNagaich
LinkedIn: https://www.linkedin.com/in/rajivnagaich/
Twitter: https://twitter.com/rajivnagaich

AgingOptions
Facebook: https://www.facebook.com/AgingOptions
LinkedIn: https://www.linkedin.com/company/aging-options
Twitter: https://twitter.com/AgingOptions

Learn more about Rajiv Nagaich at http://rajivnagaich.com/ and https://agingoptions.com.

Questions? Comments? Email info@rajivnagaich.com.

ENDNOTES

[1] Amos Bailey and VJ Periyakoil, "Where do Americans die?", Multi-cultural Palliative Care, Stanford School of Medicine, quoted in Michael Long, "Do the math: The chances of a swift, easy death are slim," Matters of Life and Death, LancasterOnline, August 2, 2020, https://lancasteronline.com/features/do-the-math-the-chances-of-a-swift-easy-death-are-slim-column/article_1f518d60-033e-11eb-949e-03b07ed13985.html.

[2] Amy D. Sullivan, Katrina Hedberg, and David Hopkins, "Legalized Physician-Assisted Suicide in Oregon, 1998–2000," *New England Journal of Medicine* 344, no. 8 (February 22, 2001): 605, https://www.nejm.org/doi/full/10.1056/NEJM200102223440811.

[3] Sudipto Banerjee, "Utilization Patterns and Out-of-Pocket Expenses for Different Health Care Services Among American Retirees," *EBRI Issue Brief*, no. 411 (February 2015): 1, https://papers.ssrn.com/sol3/papers.cfm?abstract_id=2570582.

[4] Joanne Binette, "2021 Home and Community Preference Survey: A National Survey of Adults 18–Plus," Livable Communities, AARP Research, November 2021, https://doi.org/10.26419/res.00479.001.

[5] *2022 Alzheimer's Disease Facts and Figures* (Chicago: Alzheimer's Association, 2022), 29, https://www.alz.org/media/Documents/alzheimers-facts-and-figures.pdf.

[6] "Older Adults' Health and Age-Related Changes," American Psychological Association, updated September 2021, https://www.apa.org/pi/aging/resources/guides/older.

[7] "Stroke Facts," Centers for Disease Control and Prevention, updated October 14, 2022, https://www.cdc.gov/stroke/facts.htm.

[8] One study performed six months after a stroke found that in people 65 and over: 30 percent needed assistance to walk, 26 percent needed help with activities of daily living (such as bathing, toileting, etc.), 19 percent had trouble speaking, 35 percent had feelings of depression, and 50 percent had some degree of paralysis. Here's the most important statistic though: 26 percent became nursing home

residents. Jose Vega, "Facts and Statistics About Strokes," verywellhealth.com, updated April 6, 2022, https://www.verywellhealth.com/facts-and-statistics-about-stroke-3146382.

[9] Harris Poll, *The Nationwide Retirement Institute® 2021 Long-Term Care Consumer Survey*, November 2021, 11, https://nationwide financial.com/media/pdf/NFM-21387AO.pdf.

[10] Centers for Medicare & Medicaid Services, *Medicare Coverage of Skilled Nursing Facility Care* (Baltimore: U.S. Department of Health & Human Services), 14, https://www.medicare.gov/Pubs/pdf/10153-Medicare-Skilled-Nursing-Facility-Care.pdf.

[11] "*Jimmo v. Sebelius* Settlement Agreement," Centers for Medicare & Medicaid Services, April 4, 2013, https://www.cms.gov/medicare/medicare-fee-for-service-payment/snfpps/downloads/jimmo-factsheet.pdf.

[12] Joshua Rovner and Austin Long, "Theories of Failure and Intelligence Reform: Evaluating the 9/11 Commission Report," *Breakthroughs* 14, no. 1 (Spring 2005): 10–21.

[13] "Aging | HHS.gov," U.S. Department of Health & Human Services, updated April 27, 2022, https://www.hhs.gov/aging/index.html.

[14] Ari Houser, Wendy Fox-Grage, and Kathleen Ujvari, *Across the States: Profiles of Long-Term Services and Supports: Executive Summary, State Data, and Rankings*, 10th Edition (Washington, DC: AARP, 2018), A-6, https://www.aarp.org/content/dam/aarp/ppi/2018/08/across-the-states-profiles-of-long-term-services-and-supports-full-report.pdf.

[15] Houser, *Across the States*, 10th edition, A-6.

[16] *Projections and Implications for Housing a Growing Population: Older Households 2015-2035* (Cambridge, MA: Joint Center for Housing Studies of Harvard University, 2016), https://www.jchs.harvard.edu/sites/default/files/harvard_jchs_housing_growing_population_2016.pdf.

[17] Amos Bailey and VJ Periyakoil, "Where do Americans die?" Multi-cultural Palliative Care, Stanford School of Medicine, quoted in Michael Long, "Do the math: The chances of a swift, easy death are slim," Matters of Life and Death, LancasterOnline, August 2, 2020, https://lancasteronline.com/features/do-the-math-the-chances-of-a-swift-easy-death-are-slim-column/article_1f518d60-033e-11eb-949e-03b07ed13985.html.

[18] Administration for Community Living, "How Much Care Will You Need?" U.S. Department of Health & Human Services, last modified February 18, 2020, https://acl.gov/ltc/basic-needs/how-much-care-will-you-need.

[19] Administration for Community Living, *2020 Profile of Older Americans*, May 2021, 3, https://acl.gov/sites/default/files/Profile%20of%20OA/2020Profile OlderAmericans_RevisedFinal.pdf.

[20] Administration for Community Living, *2020 Profile*, 13.

[21] Ari Houser, Wendy Fox-Grage, and Kathleen Ujvari, *Across the States: Profiles of Long-Term Services and Supports: Executive Summary, State Data, and Rankings*, 9th Edition (Washington, DC: AARP, 2012), 22, http://www.aarp.org/content/dam/aarp/research/public_policy_institute/ltc/2012/across-the-states-2012-executive-summary-AARP-ppi-ltc.pdf.

[22] Houser, *Across the States*, 10th edition, 8.

[23] Houser, *Across the States*, 10th edition, 11.

[24] Jane Gross, "How Medicare Fails the Elderly," *New York Times*, October 15, 2011, Opinion, http://www.nytimes.com/2011/10/16/opinion/sunday/how-medicare-fails-the-elderly.html.

[25] Richard W. Johnson, Desmond Toohey, and Joshua M. Wiener, *Meeting the Long-Term Care Needs of Baby Boomers: How Changing Families Will Affect Paid Helpers and Institutions*, The Retirement Project Discussion Paper Series (Washington, DC: The Urban Institute, 2007).

[26] Sudipto Banerjee, "Utilization Patterns and Out-of-Pocket Expenses for Different Health Care Services Among American Retirees," *EBRI Issue Brief*, no. 411 (February 2015): 16, https://papers.ssrn.com/sol3/papers.cfm?abstract_id=2570582.

[27] Amy D. Sullivan, Katrina Hedberg, and David Hopkins, "Legalized Physician-Assisted Suicide in Oregon, 1998–2000," *New England Journal of Medicine* 344, no. 8 (February 22, 2001): 605, https://www.nejm.org/doi/full/10.1056/NEJM200102223440811.

[28] Joanne Binette, "2021 Home and Community Preference Survey: A National Survey of Adults 18–Plus," Livable Communities, AARP Research, November 2021, https://doi.org/10.26419/res.00479.001.

[29] Amos Bailey and VJ Periyakoil, "Where do Americans die?" Multi-cultural Palliative Care, Stanford School of Medicine, quoted in Michael Long, "Do the math: The chances of a swift, easy death are slim," Matters of Life and Death, LancasterOnline, August 2, 2020, https://lancasteronline.com/features/do-the-math-the-chances-of-a-swift-easy-death-are-slim-column/article_1f518d60-033e-11eb-949e-03b07ed13985.html.

[30] "Reagan's Letter Announcing his Alzheimer's Diagnosis," Ronald Reagan Presidential Library & Museum, accessed August 17, 2022, https://www.reaganlibrary.gov/reagans/ronald-reagan/reagans-letter-announcing-his-alzheimers-diagnosis.

[31] Lawrence K. Altman, "THE DOCTOR'S WORLD; A Recollection of Early Questions About Reagan's Health," New York Times, June 15, 2004, https://www.nytimes.com/2004/06/15/health/the-doctor-s-world-a-recollection-of-early-questions-about-reagan-s-health.html.

[32] Richard Harris, "Sandra Day O'Connor and Alzheimer's: A Personal Story," Forbes, March 19, 2019, Retirement, https://www.forbes.com/sites/nextavenue/2019/03/19/sandra-day-oconnor-and-alzheimers-a-personal-story/?sh=920c05609152.

[33] Lawrence K. Altman, "REAGAN'S TWILIGHT—A special report.; A President Fades Into a World Apart," New York Times, October 5, 1997, http://www.nytimes.com/1997/10/05/us/reagan-s-twilight-a-special-report-a-president-fades-into-a-world-apart.html.

[34] Harris, "Sandra Day O'Connor."

[35] Efraim Jaul and Jeremy Barron, "Age-Related Diseases and Clinical and Public Health Implications for the 85 and Over Population," Frontiers in Public Health, no. 5 (2017): 1–7, 335, https://www.ncbi.nlm.nih.gov/pmc/articles/PMC5732407/pdf/fpubh-05-00335.pdf.

[36] This restriction varies by state.

[37] Matthew Frankel, "Retirement Planning: How to Map Out Your Financial Success," Motley Fool, updated September 20, 2022, https://www.fool.com/retirement/.

[38] Julia Kagan, "Retirement Planning," Personal Finance, Investopedia, updated November 21, 2021, https://www.investopedia.com/terms/r/retirement-planning.asp.

[39] *Merriam-Webster*, s.v. "retirement plan (*n.*)," accessed November 15, 2022, https://www.merriam-webster.com/dictionary/retirement%20plan.

[40] Richard W. Johnson, "What is the Lifetime Risk of Needing and Receiving Long-Term Services and Supports?" *ASPE Research Brief*, April 2019, 4, https://aspe.hhs.gov/reports/what-lifetime-risk-needing-receiving-long-term-services-supports-0.

[41] Associated Press, "Court filing claims Brooke Astor lives in squalor," World, NBC News, July 26, 2006, https://www.nbcnews.com/id/wbna14046911.

[42] "Long-Term Care Insurance Facts – Data – Statistics – 2020 Reports," American Association for Long-Term Care Insurance, accessed November 15, 2022, https://www.aaltci.org/long-term-care-insurance/learning-center/ltcfacts-2020.php.

[43] U.S. Department of Health & Human Services, "Long-Term Services and Supports for Older Americans: Risks and Financing, 2020," *ASPE Research Brief*, January 2021, https://aspe.hhs.gov/sites/default/files/private/pdf/265126/LTSSOlAmRB.pdf.

[44] "Long-Term Care."

[45] Medicaid in Washington State. Every state has different asset and income limits, and these limits are updated annually. In 2022, Medicaid's Washington asset limit was between $59,380 and $130,380. Consult with an elder law attorney in your state.

[46] Medicaid in Washington State. Every state has different limits, and these limits are updated annually. Consult with an elder law attorney in your state.

[47] Erica York, "2022 Tax Brackets," Tax Foundation, November 10, 2021, https://taxfoundation.org/2022-tax-brackets/.

[48] Kevin C. Fleming, Jonathan M. Evans, and Darryl S. Chutka, "A Cultural and Economic History of Aging in America," *Mayo Clinic Proceedings* 78, no. 7 (August 2003): 915, https://www.researchgate.net/publication/10679992_A_Cultural_and_Economic_History_of_Old_Age_in_America.

[49] Amos Bailey and VJ Periyakoil, "Where do Americans die?" Multi-cultural Palliative Care, Stanford School of Medicine, quoted in Michael Long, "Do the math: The chances of a swift, easy death are slim," Matters of Life and Death, LancasterOnline, August 2, 2020, https://lancasteronline.com/features/do-the-math-the-chances-of-a-swift-easy-death-are-slim-column/article_1f518d60-033e-11eb-949e-03b07ed13985.html.

[50] "Americans Nearing Retirement 'Terrified' of Future Health Care Costs, Nationwide Study Finds," Nationwide, December 7, 2016, https://news.nationwide.com/americans-nearing-retirement-terrified-of-future-health-care-costs-nationwide-study-finds/.

[51] "Specialists in Aging: Do You Need a Geriatrician?" Health, Johns Hopkins Medicine, accessed November 15, 2022, https://www.hopkinsmedicine.org/health/wellness-and-prevention/specialists-in-aging-do-you-need-a-geriatrician.

[52] Amy Jamieson, "'Medication Fog': What It Is and How It Can Cause Dementia-Like Symptoms," Health News, Healthline, March 14, 2020, https://www.healthline.com/health-news/medication-fog-can-produce-dementia-like-symptoms-in-seniors.

[53] Chad Boult et al., "A Randomized Clinical Trial of Outpatient Geriatric Evaluation and Management," *Journal of the American Geriatrics Society* 49, no. 4 (April 2001): 351–359, https://doi.org/10.1046/j.1532-5415.2001.49076.x.

[54] Jane Caffrey, "Casey Kasem and a lesson about end-of-life care," CNN, updated April 18, 2016, https://www.cnn.com/2014/06/20/health/casey-kasem-end-of-life-care/index.html.

[55] Alan Duke, "Casey Kasem's kids take stepmom to court," CNN, updated October 8, 2013, https://www.cnn.com/2013/10/08/showbiz/casey-kasem-family-battle/.

[56] "Judge Rejects Children's Request For Conservatorship of Casey Kasem," CBS News Los Angeles, November 19, 2013, https://www.cbsnews.com/losangeles/news/judge-rejects-childrens-request-for-conservatorship-of-casey-kasem/.

[57] Tony Maglio, "Casey Kasem's Final Days: How the Family's Bitter Battle Got to This Point," The Wrap, June 12, 2014, https://www.thewrap.com/casey-kasem-kerri-jean-kerri-julie-lewy-body-disease-elder-abuse/.

[58] Rachel Wells, Jane Caffrey, and Holly Yan, "Radio icon Casey Kasem spotted in Washington state," CNN, May 15, 2014, https://www.cnn.com/2014/05/15/showbiz/casey-kasem-whereabouts/.

[59] Steve Almasy, "Casey Kasem alert but in critical condition," CNN, updated June 6, 2014, https://www.cnn.com/2014/06/05/showbiz/casey-kasem-hospitalized/index.html.

[60] Associated Press, "Casey Kasem's Condition Declining, Daughter says He 'Won't Be With Us Much Longer,'" Music News, Billboard, June 6, 2014, https://

www.billboard.com/music/music-news/casey-kasems-condition-declining-daughter-says-he-wont-be-with-us-much-longer-6113884/.

[61] Alan Duke, "Casey Kasem's family feud: Judge allows water, food infusions stopped," CNN, updated June 11, 2014, https://www.cnn.com/2014/06/10/showbiz/casey-kasem-timeline/.

[62] Associated Press, "Casey Kasem's daughter can stop food, medication, judge rules," Illness, Fox News, April 5, 2016, https://www.foxnews.com/entertainment/casey-kasems-daughter-can-stop-food-medication-judge-rules.

[63] "US DJ Casey Kasem's children sue stepmother for wrongful death - BBC News," News, BBC, November 26, 2015, https://www.bbc.com/news/entertainment-arts-34930866.

[64] "Table 26. Normal weight, overweight, and obesity among adults aged 20 and over, by selected characteristics: United States, selected years 1988–1994 through 2015–2018," CDC, 2019, https://www.cdc.gov/nchs/data/hus/2019/026-508.pdf.

[65] "Older Adults | MyPlate," MyPlate, U.S. Department of Agriculture, accessed November 15, 2022, https://www.myplate.gov/life-stages/older-adults.

[66] "Grapefruit Juice and Some Drugs Don't Mix," U.S. Food & Drug Administration, updated July 1, 2021, https://www.fda.gov/consumers/consumer-updates/grapefruit-juice-and-some-drugs-dont-mix.

[67] Jack F. Hollis et al., "Weight Loss During the Intensive Intervention Phase of the Weight-Loss Maintenance Trial," *American Journal of Preventive Medicine* 35, no. 2 (August 2008): 124, https://doi.org/10.1016/j.amepre.2008.04.013.

[68] Salynn Boyles, "Food journal: Write it down, shed more pounds," *Atlanta Journal-Constitution*, July 16, 2012, Life, https://www.ajc.com/lifestyles/health/food-journal-write-down-shed-more-pounds/Ho3zprCK8QlNHDlvQrjzeN/.

[69] Philip G. Clark et al., "Maintaining exercise and healthful eating in older adults: The SENIOR project II: Study design and methodology," *Contemporary Clinical Trials* 32, no. 1 (January 2011): 129–139, https://doi.org/10.1016/j.cct.2010.10.002.

[70] "Exercise and Arthritis," American College of Rheumatology, updated December 2020, https://www.rheumatology.org/I-Am-A/Patient-Caregiver/Diseases-Conditions/Living-Well-with-Rheumatic-Disease/Exercise-and-Arthritis.

[71] "Strength training can help protect the brain from degeneration," University of Sydney, February 11, 2020, https://www.sydney.edu.au/news-opinion/news/2020/02/11/strength-training-can-help-protect-the-brain-from-degeneration.html.

[72] Fabian Herold et al., "Functional and/or structural brain changes in response to resistance exercises and resistance training lead to cognitive improvements – a systematic review," *European Review of Aging and Physical Activity*, no. 16 (2019): 1–33, https://eurapa.biomedcentral.com/track/pdf/10.1186/s11556-019-0217-2.pdf.

[73] U.S. Department of Health & Human Services, *Executive Summary: Physical Activity Guidelines for Americans*, 2nd edition, 2018, 4, https://health.gov/sites/default/files/2019-10/PAG_ExecutiveSummary.pdf.

[74] "You're Never Too Old: Keep Active as You Age," NIH News in Health, December 2011, https://newsinhealth.nih.gov/2011/12/youre-never-too-old.

[75] Emmanuel Stamatkis et al., "Sitting Time, Physical Activity, and Risk of Mortality in Adults," *Journal of the American College of Cardiology* 73, no. 16 (April 2019): 1, https://doi.org/10.1016/j.jacc.2019.02.031.

[76] Dorothy Dunlop et al., "Sedentary Time in US Older Adults Associated with Disability in Activities of Daily Living Independent of Physical Activity," *Journal of Physical Activity and Health* 12, no. 1 (January 2015), 93–101, https://doi.org/10.1123/jpah.2013-0311.

[77] Edward R. Laskowski, "What are the risks of sitting too much?" Adult health, Healthy Lifestyle, Mayo Clinic, July 13, 2022, https://www.mayoclinic.org/healthy-lifestyle/adult-health/expert-answers/sitting/faq-20058005.

[78] Aoife Stephenson et al., "Using computer, mobile and wearable technology enhanced interventions to reduce sedentary behavior: a systematic review and meta-analysis," *International Journal of Behavioral Nutrition and Physical Activity*, no. 14 (2017): 1–17, 105, https://doi.org/10.1186%2Fs12966-017-0561-4.

[79] Beverly Merz, "Sauna use linked to longer life, fewer fatal health problems," Heart Health, Harvard Health Publishing, Harvard Medical School, February 25, 2015, https://www.health.harvard.edu/blog/sauna-use-linked-longer-life-fewer-fatal-heart-problems-201502257755.

[80] Michelle Diament, "Socializing Key to Memory, Fighting Alzheimer's and Dementia," Health, AARP Bulletin, November 21, 2008, https://www.aarp.org/health/brain-health/info-11-2008/friends-are-good-for-your-brain.html.

[81] David A. Snowden, "Healthy Aging and Dementia: Findings from the Nun Study," *Annals of Internal Medicine* 139, no. 5, part 2 (September 2003): 450–454, https://doi.org/10.7326/0003-4819-139-5_Part_2-200309021-00014.

[82] Dale E. Bredesen, "Reversal of cognitive decline: A novel therapeutic program," *AGING* 6, no. 9 (September 2014): 707–717, https://www.aging-us.com/article/100690/pdf.

[83] Gayatri Devi, "A new way to think about Alzheimer's disease," Opinion, CNN, January 3, 2020, https://www.cnn.com/2020/01/03/opinions/diagnosing-treating-alzheimers-opinion-devi/index.html.

[84] Clifford R. Jack, Jr. et al., "Prevalence of Biologically vs Clinically Defined Alzheimer Spectrum Entities Using the National Institute on Aging-Alzheimer's Association Research Framework," *JAMA Neurology* 76, no. 10 (October 2019): 1174–1183, https://jamanetwork.com/journals/jamaneurology/fullarticle/2737282.

[85] Kiri L. Brickell et al., "Clinopathological concordance and discordance in three monozygotic twin pairs with familial Alzheimer's disease," *Journal of Neurology, Neurosurgery & Psychiatry* 78, no. 10 (October 2007): 1050–1055, https://jnnp.bmj.com/content/78/10/1050.long.

[86] Atul Gawande, *Being Mortal*, (New York: Metropolitan Books, 2014), 44.

[87] Jean Y. Campbell et al., "The Unknown Profession: A Geriatrician," *Journal of the American Geriatrics Society* 61, no. 3 (March 2013): 447–449, https://doi.org/10.1111/jgs.12115.

[88] "Geriatrics Workforce by the Numbers," American Geriatrics Society, accessed November 15, 2022, https://www.americangeriatrics.org/geriatrics-profession/about-geriatrics/geriatrics-workforce-numbers.

[89] Paula E. Lester, T.S. Dharmarajan, and Eleanor Weinstein, "The Looming Geriatrician Shortage: Ramifications and Solutions," *Journal of Aging and Health* 32, no. 9 (2020): 1052–1062, https://doi.org/10.1177%2F0898264319879325.

[90] Campbell, "Unknown Profession."

[91] Mark Lachs, *What Your Doctor Won't Tell You About Getting Older: An Insider's Survival Manual for Outsmarting the Healthcare System* (New York: Penguin, 2011), chap. 1, loc. 184 of 6245, Kindle.

[92] Danya M. Qato and Amal N. Trivedi, "Receipt of High Risk Medications among Elderly Enrollees in Medicare Advantage Plans," *Journal of General Internal Medicine* 28, no. 4 (April 2013): 546–553, https://www.ncbi.nlm.nih.gov/pmc/articles/PMC3599014/pdf/11606_2012_Article_2244.pdf.

[93] Rajiv Nagaich, *The AgingOptions Radio Show*, 770 KTTH, Seattle, WA: KTTH, August 4 2012.

[94] Paula Span, "Older People Need Geriatricians. Where Will They Come From?" *New York Times*, January 3, 2020, The New Old Age, https://www.nytimes.com/2020/01/03/health/geriatricians-shortage.html.

[95] Esther Hing, Donald K. Cherry, and David A. Woodwell, "National Ambulatory Medical Care Survey: 2003 Summary," *Advance Data from Vital and Health Statistics*, no. 365 (October 2005): 38, https://www.cdc.gov/nchs/data/ad/ad365.pdf.

[96] Thomas Bodenheimer, "Primary Care—Will It Survive?" *New England Journal of Medicine* 355, no. 9 (August 2006): 861–862, https://www.nejm.org/doi/full/10.1056/nejmp068155.

[97] Sheryl Burgstahler, "Universal Design: Process, Principles, and Applications," DO-IT, University of Washington, 2021, https://www.washington.edu/doit/universal-design-process-principles-and-applications.

[98] Samara Scheckler, Jennifer Molinsky, and Whitney Airgood-Obrycki, *How Well Does the Housing Stock Meet Accessibility Needs? An Analysis of the 2019 American Housing Survey* ([Cambridge, MA]: Joint Center for Housing Studies of Harvard University, March 2022), https://www.jchs.harvard.edu/sites/default/files/research/files/harvard_jchs_housing_stock_accessibility_scheckler_2022_0.pdf. This resource refers to rental units only.

[99] Gillian B. White, "Nowhere to Go: The Housing Crisis Facing Americans with Disabilities," *Atlantic*, December 15, 2015, https://www.theatlantic.com/business/archive/2015/12/renting-with-a-disability/420555/.

[100] School of Health Professions, "Patients Want to Age in Place, and Occupational Therapists are Helping," Daily Dose, Texas Tech University Health Sciences Center, May 28, 2020, https://dailydose.ttuhsc.edu/2020/may/shp-patients-want-to-age-in-place-occupational-therapists-are-helping.aspx.

[101] Federal Bureau of Investigation, *2021 Elder Fraud Report*, 2021, https://www.ic3.gov/Media/PDF/AnnualReport/2021_IC3ElderFraudReport.pdf.

[102] "Have Americans Reached a New Era of Optimism about Aging?" Pfizer, June 17, 2012, https://www.pfizer.com/news/press-release/press-release-detail/have_americans_reached_a_new_era_of_optimism_about_aging.

[103] Patricia Mertz Esswein and Eileen Ambrose, "How to Shop for a Continuing Care Retirement Community," Retirement, Kiplinger, January 9, 2018, https://www.kiplinger.com/article/retirement/t010-c000-s002-how-to-shop-continuing-care-retirement-community.html.

[104] "Housing Choice Vouchers Fact Sheet," U.S. Department of Housing and Urban Development, accessed August 18, 2022, https://www.hud.gov/topics/housing_choice_voucher_program_section_8.

[105] "Section 202 Supportive Housing for the Elderly Program," U.S. Department of Housing and Urban Development, accessed August 18, 2022, https://www.hud.gov/program_offices/housing/mfh/progdesc/eld202.

[106] Mexican Border period (May 9, 1916, to April 5, 1917, for Veterans who served in Mexico, on its borders, or in adjacent waters); World War I (April 6, 1917, to November 11, 1918); World War II (December 7, 1941, to December 31, 1946); Korean conflict (June 27, 1950, to January 31, 1955); Vietnam War era (November 1, 1955, to May 7, 1975, for Veterans who served in the Republic of Vietnam during that period. August 5, 1964, to May 7, 1975, for Veterans who served outside the Republic of Vietnam.); Gulf War (August 2, 1990, through a future date to be set by law or presidential proclamation). "Eligibility for Veterans Pension," U.S. Department of Veterans Affairs, updated October 12, 2022, https://www.va.gov/pension/eligibility/.

[107] Washington, Oregon, District of Columbia, Nebraska, Iowa, Minnesota, Illinois, Kentucky, Pennsylvania, Maine, Vermont, New York, Massachusetts, Rhode Island, Connecticut, New Jersey, Maryland, Hawaii. Janelle Fritts, "Does Your State Have an Estate or Inheritance Tax?" Tax Foundation, June 21, 2022, https://taxfoundation.org/state-estate-tax-inheritance-tax-2022/.

[108] Medicaid eligibility rules vary by state. Check with a qualified elder law attorney to find out the rules that apply to you.

[109] Relias Media, "Study: Emergency providers often lack consensus on what patients intend when end-of-life forms come into play," ED Management, June 1, 2015, https://www.reliasmedia.com/articles/135432-study-emergency-providers-often-lack-consensus-on-what-patients-intend-when-end-of-life-forms-come-into-play.

[110] Current as of 2022.

HEARTS to be HEARD

Giving a Voice to Creativity!

From: Circe'
To: Kids who love to write stories!

How would you like to have your story in a book? A real book!
Hearts to be Heard will make that happen.

Get started now at
HeartstobeHeard.com

Also visit HH Kid's Corner for creative writing activities!
HeartstobeHeard.com/kids-corner/

PARENTS:
Explore the
possibilities for your
child & others. Visit:
HeartstobeHeard.com/parents

Printed in the USA
CPSIA information can be obtained
at www.ICGtesting.com
LVHW011242261123
764801LV00010B/7

9 781774 822517